TAKING BACK OUR SPIRITS

TAKING BACK OUR SPIRITS

Indigenous literature, public policy, and healing

JO-ANN EPISKENEW

University of Manitoba Press

University of Manitoba Press
Winnipeg, Manitoba
Canada R3T 2M5
www.umanitoba.ca/uofmpress

Printed in Canada on acid-free paper.

Cover design: Doowah Design
Interior design: Karen Armstrong Graphic Design

Cover image: Helen Madeleine, *Dancers* (detail). Reproduced by permission of the artist.

Library and Archives Canada Cataloguing in Publication

Episkenew, Jo-Ann
    Taking back our spirits : Indigenous literature, public policy, and healing / Jo-Ann Episkenew.

Includes bibliographical references and index.
ISBN 978-0-88755-710-1

    1. Canadian literature (English)—Indian authors—History and criticism. 2. Native peoples—Canada—Government relations. 3. Native peoples—Canada—Social conditions. 4. Healing in literature. I. Title.

PS8089.5.I6 E65 2009   C810.9'897   C2008-907933-7

The University of Manitoba Press gratefully acknowledges the financial support for its publication program provided by the Government of Canada through the Book Publishing Industry Development Program (BPIDP), the Canada Council for the Arts, the Manitoba Arts Council, and the Manitoba Department of Culture, Heritage, Tourism and Sport.

CONTENTS

For *nôsisimak* Keenan, Randall, Mia, Asher, Ella, Ethan, Paulina, Michaela, Dakota, Bradford, Baby Amelia and the boy, Candace, Brandon, Bradley, Mathew, Kyle, Tony's family, Jayden, Luscious, Jessie, Junior, Raquel and Khylin, Landyss and Kaidin, Dion's boys. You are our future.

Acknowledgements

Danke schön, mein Doktorvater Prof. Dr. Hartmut Lutz for your unfailing support and respectful and thought-provoking feedback. *Danke schön* to Ruth Lutz for your hospitality and encouragement. *Danke schön* to the rest of the staff at the Institute for English and American Studies at Ernst-Moritz-Arndt Universität for supporting me throughout my long-distance educational journey.

Thanks to the Indigenous Peoples' Health Research Centre of Saskatchewan for the financial support, which enabled me to devote a substantial block of time to my research and, therefore, finish this book in a timely, and significantly less stressful, manner. I would also like to acknowledge Gabriel Housing. The affordable housing that they provided me enabled me to pursue higher education with one less stressor.

Kinanâskomitin to elders Ken Goodwill, Isador Pelletier, Danny Musqua, Maria Campbell, and Velma Goodfeather for your stories, direction, and encouragement. Also *kinanâskomitin* to my colleagues Dr. Eber Hampton and Willie Ermine for inspiring me to think about stories in different ways. *Kinanâskomitin* to my colleagues in the Association for Bibliotherapy and Applied Literatures (Hoi, Michelle, and Allison) and the Canadian

Association for Commonwealth Literatures and Language Studies (Renate, Deanna, and Kristina) for motivating me to reflect and reconsider every time that I slipped into complacency. *Kinanâskomitin* to David Carr of the University of Manitoba Press for help constructing the title, since mine are, indeed, boring. *Kinanâskomitin* to Heidi Harms and Glenn Bergen whose eagle eyes found all those nasty, little mistakes that I long ago ceased to see. And, *kinanâskomitin* to my colleagues in the Department of Indian Languages, Literatures, and Linguistics for their expertise on languages, grammar, and spelling.

Thanks to my friends, mentors, and role models, Dr. Sherry Farrell Racette and Dr. Linda Goulet, for many inspiring conversations over tea and cappuccino. Thanks, also, to the rest of "The Crows" for always reminding me to situate my research in the context of the community. And thanks to Deb and Laureen for helping me stay sane (relatively, of course).

Thanks to my late mother and father, Wilma and Jim Thom, who instilled in me a love for reading and an appreciation for higher education. Thanks to Rayne, Sable, Eagle, and Bianca for motivating me to return to school to pursue a university degree (and another one and another one). And, thanks to my husband, Clayton Episkenew. Together we walk a path of healing. You believed in me, listened to every word of this book many times, and reminded me that I must never give up.

*   *   *

Sections of this book have appeared previously in revised form in the following publications: "Contemporary Indigenous Literature in Canada: Healing from Historical Trauma," in *Indigeneity: Culture and Interpretation*, eds. G.N. Devy, Geoffrey V. Davis, and K.K. Chakravarty (Andhra Pradesh, India: Orient Blackswan, 2008), and "Living and Dying with the Madness of Colonial Policies: The Aesthetics of Resistance in Daniel David Moses' *Almighty Voice and His Wife*," in *What is Your Place? Indigeneity and Immigration in Canada*, ed. Hartmut Lutz, with Thomas Rafico Ruiz, Beiträge zur Kanadistik, Band 14, Shriftenreihe der Gesselschaft für Kanada-Studien (Augsburg: Weßner-Verlag, 2007).

chapter 1

Myth, policy, and health

In my second year as an undergraduate student, I had an epiphany.[1] I realized that all knowledge worth knowing—or, more specifically, knowledge that my university considered worth teaching—was created by the Greeks, appropriated by the Romans, disseminated throughout western Europe, and through colonialism eventually made its way to the rest of the people of the world, who apparently were sitting on their thumbs waiting for enlightenment. This was the subtext of the curriculum in all classes with the exception of Indigenous Studies. Given that my experience does not differ substantially from that of students at other universities in the West, I consider myself lucky to have attended a university that offered Indigenous Studies.

What an assault! As an Métis woman, I knew that Indigenous communities had created a body of knowledge that enabled our ancestors to survive for millennia before the Johnny-come-lately new nation-state of Canada established itself on top of Indigenous peoples' lands. Because I was painfully aware of the injuries that colonialism and racism had inflicted on Indigenous communities, I was hell-bent to discover where these arrogant attitudes originated and establish who was to blame. (Although I was not young, I was still naive at the time.) The best way, I thought, to accomplish this monumental task was to study stories.

Several years later, having learned that racism and oppression had been a part of the world for much longer than I could research, I was forced to abandon my quest. I did, however, begin to learn something that I believe is more important and certainly more productive than finding out who is to blame. I began to understand the healing power of stories in general and of Indigenous literature in particular.

Not only does Indigenous literature respond to and critique the policies of the Government of Canada; it also functions as "medicine" to help cure the colonial contagion by healing the communities that these policies have injured. It accomplishes this by challenging the "master narrative," that is, a summary of the stories that embody the settlers' "socially shared under-standing."[2] This master narrative is, in fact, the myth of the new Canadian nation-state, which valorizes the settlers but which sometimes misrepresents and more often excludes Indigenous peoples. Indigenous literature acknowl-edges and validates Indigenous peoples' experiences by filling in the gaps and correcting the falsehoods in this master narrative. Indeed, Indigenous litera-ture comprises a "counterstory" that resists the "oppressive identity [that the settler myth has assigned Indigenous people] and attempts to replace it with one that commands respect."[3]

Myth as Menace

For many years, anthropologists traversed the Americas collecting Indigenous creation myths. Their goal was to understand better the diverse peoples indigenous to the new land. Believing that Indigenous cultures, and indeed Indigenous peoples, were well on their way to extinction, anthropolo-gists sought to preserve these stories for posterity, often mourning the loss of such noble peoples. It is not surprising that anthropologists would look to creation myths to gain a better understanding of Indigenous peoples. To understand any people, one must necessarily understand their creation story, which "recounts how the world was formed, how things came to be, for contained within creation stories are relationships that help to define the nature of the universe and how cultures understand the world in which they exist."[4] It is ironic that, although anthropologists continue to be fascinated with Indigenous peoples' stories, they rarely examine the myths that their own people hold dear, especially those myths that tell the story of the estab-lishment of the new nation-states that occupy North America and dominate the world. Do these stories lack the cachet of Indigenous peoples' stories, or could there be a more complex reason for their absence in anthropological studies?

In his 2003 Massey lecture, Thomas King tells his audience that "stories are wondrous things," but then adds the caveat "they are dangerous."[5] Indigenous people would certainly agree. The myth of the colonization of the Americas is truly a dangerous story, which continues to have disastrous effects on the health and well-being of Indigenous people. For millennia, attitudes of superiority were based on nation or class or religion. Only with the rise of imperialism and the establishment of European colonies in Africa, Asia, Australia, and America was the concept of "racial" identity added to the list of markers of superiority. The colonial myth is a story of imagined White superiority.

The White settler population looked at the evidence at hand—the superiority of their technology, the might of their military, their ever-increasing numbers, and the truth of their god—and judged themselves the superior race. As a consequence of this belief in the myth of White superiority, the dominant White colonial society began to confer upon its own, almost automatically, a set of privileges that they had not earned. It was not until the second half of the twentieth century that scholars revealed that the logical thought process proving White superiority had been based on a faulty premise:

> The environmental historians Alfred Crosbey and William McNeill showed in the 1970s that the New World's true conquerors were germs: mass killers such as smallpox, bubonic plague, influenza and measles. These arrived for the first time with the Europeans (who had resistance to them) and acted like biological weapons, killing the rulers and half the population of Mexico and Peru in the first wave…. Despite their guns and horses, the Spaniards did not achieve any major conquests on the mainland until *after* a smallpox pandemic swept through. The Maya, Aztecs, Incas, and Floridians all repelled the first efforts to invade them.[6]

Although the evidence proves that the White invaders would have found it difficult, if not impossible, to overcome the Indigenous armies without their invisible biological allies first eliminating more than half of the population, the popular myths of the North American nation-states remain unchanged. The myth of White superiority has become entrenched in the psyche of the North American settler population and has resulted in their consistently positioning their darker-skinned neighbours on the bottom of the social strata. It is clear, then, that myths continue to wield enormous power, even "in a predominantly scientific, capitalistic, Judeo-Christian world governed by physical laws, economic imperatives, and spiritual precepts."[7]

Literacy—the ability to read and write—has become another marker of superiority. Indigenous peoples were literate in their ability to "read" the land, a skill upon which the colonizers depended in their early days on this continent. Indigenous people were not, however, literate in the way that Europeans privilege.[8] Indigenous cultures were oral ones until well into the twentieth century, exhibiting great diversity but still sharing certain characteristics as oral cultures. Indigenous peoples understood that language has the power to change the course of events in both the material and the spiritual worlds. Furthermore, because Indigenous societies shared and transmitted their collective truths by way of oral narratives, Indigenous peoples placed high value on memory and honesty. Women or men were only as true as their words. Passed down through the generations, oral narratives explained the history of the peoples, reinforced cultural practices and norms, and articulated the peoples' relationship with the world. And, oral narratives were adaptable because they could be revised to meet the changing needs of their societies and, therefore, could evolve as their contexts changed.[9] Thus, stories were central to the functioning of Indigenous societies.

What happens, then, to people of oral cultures if invaders wrest control of the education of their children? And, what happens if the invaders remain and take control of the land and of every aspect of the people's lives, systematically de-educating the children so that they lose their ability to communicate in their native languages and, therefore, lose access to those foundational narratives of their people? What happens if these invading powers supplant the myths of the people with new myths in which the people are either maligned or ignored? By way of public policy and bureaucratic action, the colonial regime that is the legacy of British and, to a lesser extent, French imperialism, executed these very actions against the people of the Indigenous nations of Canada.

Bringing "Progress" to the Natives

Both the colonizers and Indigenous peoples witnessed the settlers' numbers increasing while the Indigenous population waned, and both groups understood that an increase in population meant an increase in military might. They also observed that technological advances gave the settlers more sophisticated weaponry than that of the Indigenous peoples. European settlers believed that it was their right to take control of Indigenous peoples' land. However, if the imperial powers were to seize control of Indigenous lands they must first disempower the Indigenous population. As Joseph Gold writes, disempowerment began with disease, moved forward with increased immigration and settlement, and culminated in the creation of the

Dominion of Canada in 1867. Not coincidentally, Canadian government officials began to develop policies to control the proliferation of Indigenous languages and stories shortly after the establishment of the Dominion. These policies made it "possible to falsify history in order to undermine group and individual identity and so in a sense invalidate the life experience of those [they wished] to disempower."[10] That is not to say that the colonizers falsified history in a concerted and self-conscious manner. Rather, the colonizers believed so fervently in the veracity of their own mythology that they did not consider that there might be another perspective on history. Furthermore, the colonizers believed so zealously in their superiority to their fellow human beings that they considered it their responsibility to eradicate pagan superstition and replace it with "truth."

Believing that Indigenous epistemologies were merely pagan superstition, the colonizers sought to eradicate those epistemologies by imposing "modern" education and Christian evangelism. Their goal was to eliminate Indigenous cultures and bring modernity and progress to Indigenous peoples. This was what Rudyard Kipling termed the "White man's burden."[11] However, as Ronald Wright contends, the word "progress" is a loaded term: "Our practical faith in progress has ramified and hardened into an ideology—a secular religion which, like the religions that progress has challenged, is blind to certain flaws in its credentials. Progress, therefore, has become 'myth' in the anthropological sense. By this I do not mean a belief that is flimsy or untrue. Successful myths are powerful and often partly true."[12] What the settlers could not foresee were the consequences of the myth of progress, especially the social and environmental consequences. Today, the very ideas that formed the foundation of the myth of White superiority now threaten the survival of humanity. Nevertheless, most settlers still choose to believe in the myth of the establishment of the Canadian nation-state because it buttresses their feelings of superiority and confers upon them privileges that have become normalized.[13] It also rationalizes the settlers' seizure and occupation of Indigenous lands.

Despite a growing body of evidence to the contrary, the Canadian myth does not acknowledge that the nation was founded on a practice of psychological terrorism and theft. "When government policies and practices that systematically discriminate are juxtaposed with the Canadian state's formal commitment to democratic equality, hypocrisy is revealed," argues Dara Culhane. "In these ways, Aboriginal peoples strike repeated blows to the heart of Canada's liberal self-image and international personality."[14] Still, the

Canadian myth persists, ignoring or negating all evidence that calls its veracity into question and continuing to proclaim Canada a liberal, inclusive, and multicultural nation founded on peaceful negotiation. Stephanie McKenzie contends that "contemporary attempts to justify this nation's beginnings are often arrested in the traumatic recall of the holocaust that happened here."[15] Indeed, few settlers are willing to admit that there is "a darker aspect of Canadian history, one rarely highlighted in a country that fancies itself an angel in an imperfect world.... The Canadian self-image is that we have a bland history that is exemplified by the perception that the American West was violent and colorful, while in Canada it was peaceful and bland."[16] Culhane argues that "it is within this space between the ideal and the real that ideologies of justification are constructed in law, government, imagination, and popular culture. This is the space wherein lies are legitimized and truths silenced. In the histories of colonial laws we can see both the mendacity and the crudeness of the original lie of European supremacy."[17]

This distorted collective vision mollifies the guilt that settlers experience when faced with evidence that their prosperity is built on the suffering of others. Ward Churchill observes that "holding Indians in a state of perpetual subordination/destitution is a prerequisite to maintaining the relatively lavish level of comfort enjoyed by the settlers and collectively announced as their own entitlement. The implications of this cause/effect relationship are ready-made to instil a sense of guilt among beneficiaries, especially those so prideful of their self-proclaimed 'humanitarian enlightenment' as the settlers. Since guilty feelings are at best an uncomfortable sensation, the implications—or the nature of the relationship itself—must be denied."[18] Legal scholar Brian Slattery adds that belief in the myth has permeated the Canadian judicial system: "All national myths involve a certain amount of distortion...but some at least have the virtue of broad historical accuracy, roughly depicting the major forces at work. The myth that underlies much legal thinking about the history of Canada lacks that redeeming feature."[19] Thus, to assuage settler guilt and to maintain settler control of the land, Indigenous stories still reside in the margins of history and literature.

The Genesis of "White Privilege"

Admitting that their prosperity and privilege is built on Indigenous peoples' suffering would injure the collective self-esteem of the majority White settler population. In Canada, this is unacceptable. One of the unearned privileges that White-skinned people enjoy is that of denying any evidence that calls into question their right to a guilt-free existence.

Following the awakening of social consciousness in the 1960s and 1970s and supported by subsequent human rights legislation, racism in its overt forms has become a cultural faux pas among White people who consider themselves educated and enlightened. That is not to say that blatant racism does not exist in Canada. It does, and to remedy blatant racism, "cultural awareness training" proliferates. The basic premise of cultural awareness training is that if White people could only learn to understand Indigenous peoples' strange and exotic ways, they would come to appreciate us and put an end to their racist behaviours. However, cultural awareness training does not acknowledge the more subtle forms of racism—the racism of structures and systems—that are founded on and support "White privilege."[20]

Most White people do not recognize and acknowledge the benefits that accompany their skin colour. Feminist scholar Peggy McIntosh explains how she came to understand the privileges that she enjoys as a White woman: "Thinking through unacknowledged male privilege as a phenomenon, I realized that, since hierarchies in our society are interlocking, there is most likely a phenomenon of white privilege that was similarly denied and protected. As a white person, I realized I had been taught about racism as something that puts others at a disadvantage, but had been taught not to see one of its corollary aspects, white privilege, which puts me at an advantage."[21] McIntosh argues that "White privilege" is a more useful term than "racism" for discussing the distinctions between the Indigenous and White populations. White privilege and its foundational myth of White supremacy continue to have a profound effect on Indigenous peoples' health, both individually and collectively.

Since White privilege is a socio-cultural health determinant for the Indigenous population, its foundational myths must be debunked if Indigenous people are to improve the state of their health. Okanagan writer and activist Jeannette Armstrong asserts that "lies need clarification, truth needs to be stated, and resistance to oppression needs to be stated, without furthering division and participation in the same racist measures."[22] Without truth, there can be no reconciliation; without truth, there can be no healing; and without a shared narrative of our collective reality (past and present), there is no truth.

You Call it Policy—We Call it Tyranny!

Canada's "Indian" policies constitute a form of "psychological terrorism," which has had a profound effect on the health of its Indigenous victims.

Many Indigenous people have turned the violence inherent in these policies inward, where it has become "toxic and effective self-loathing, culturally and individually."[23] That the policy-makers fought to eradicate Indigenous knowledges and beliefs by eliminating Indigenous languages and stories suggests that they understood their power.

The health problems that Indigenous people experience today began with the occupation of their lands. At that time, Indigenous people suffered what Eduardo Duran and Bonnie Duran have termed a "soul wound," arguing that the "core of Native American awareness was the place where the soul wound occurred": "The core essence is the fabric of the soul and it is from this essence that mythology, dreams, and culture emerge. Once the core from which the soul emerges is wounded, then all the emerging mythology and dreams of a people reflect the wound. The manifestations of such a wound are then embodied by the tremendous suffering that people have undergone since the collective soul wound was inflicted half a millennium ago. Some of the diseases and problems that Native Americans suffer today are a direct result of the soul wound."[24] This soul wounding has become the legacy of colonialism for the generations of Indigenous people who face the continual pressure to acculturate into settler society—the same society that created the genocidal policies and practices that continue to affect them today.

The "Indian" policies of the settler government have taken many forms, yet all have been promoted as means of helping Indigenous people. In his 10 March 1925 radio address, Cayuga Chief Deskaheh expressed his contempt for the policies of the settler governments of Canada and the United States: "Over in Ottawa they call that policy 'Indian Advancement.' Over in Washington they call it 'Assimilation.' We, who would be the helpless victims, say it is tyranny."[25] Regardless of what the bureaucrats label their policies—assimilation, acculturation, advancement—their goal has been to make Indigenous cultures disappear. One cannot overemphasize the damage that these policies have had on the mental, physical, emotional, spiritual, and social health of Indigenous people.

Postcolonial Traumatic Stress Response and Other Health Concerns

"Acculturation stress," write Duran and Duran, "is a continuing factor in the perpetuation of anxiety, depression, and other symptomatology that is associated with PTSD [post-traumatic stress disorder]."[26] What Duran and Duran label "other symptomatology" includes violence, rarely against the settlers but rather against oneself, one's family, or one's community, and addiction as a form of self-medicating to temporarily ease the despair of personal and political powerlessness. Addiction and violence are not the only consequences of postcolonial trauma, however. In her address to researchers at the Community-Based Research and Aboriginal Women's Health and Healing Colloquium, Métis writer, playwright, and community activist Maria Campbell argued that Indigenous women suffer from chronic low-level depression that is a direct result of living with colonial policies and historical trauma. James Pennebaker adds that physical harm typically accompanies the psychological stress of discrimination: "The dangers of being discriminated against go far beyond psychological stress, higher than average rates of heart disease and other health problems. Infant mortality, alcohol and drug problems, and even death due to suicide and murder are much higher than average."[27] Duran and Duran list a host of scholarly articles that hypothesize why Indigenous people suffer disproportionate rates of alcoholism. The list includes "poverty, poor housing, relative ill-health, academic failures, cultural conflict with majority society, and racism."[28] They also note that it is significant that "these articles usually do not make mention that these problems are the direct result of the policies of the…government toward Native American people."[29]

Today, multiple generations of Indigenous people live with intergenerational post-traumatic stress disorder, which is the direct result of multiple generations of colonial policies all focussed on dealing with the "Indian problem." Gerald Vizenor notes that when historical trauma is not publicly acknowledged and honoured in story, subsequent generations inherit and display the effects of that trauma: "Wounded Knee has had post-traumatic effects on several generations [of Indigenous people] because the stories of the survivors were seldom honoured in the literature and histories of dominance."[30] Terry Mitchell and Dawn Maracle argue that the term PTSD is not suitable for describing the Indigenous peoples' response to historical trauma and suggest another term, "post-traumatic stress response"[31] (PTSR). They explain that the term PTSD "individualizes social problems and pathologizes traumatized people"; whereas PTSR as a "diagnostic profile provides a useful tool in confirming the long-term impact of colonialization, which may increase access to appropriate healing resources."[32] Kuna/Rappahannock playwright Monique Mojica highlights colonialism as the root cause of present-day trauma by using the terms "postcolonial traumatic stress disorder" and "ethno stress."[33] Perhaps the most accurate term to describe Indigenous people's responses to long-term historical trauma would be "postcolonial traumatic stress response."

Revelations that Rock the Nation

Prompted by the public outcry that followed the Winnipeg police shooting death of Indigenous political leader J.J. Harper in 1988, the Government of Manitoba established the province's Aboriginal Justice Inquiry:[34] "for two years, a panel criss-crossed the province, hearing heart-breaking stories from aboriginal people struggling to fit into the justice system. When it was over, the panel had heard from more than 1,000 people, amassing 27,000 pages of transcripts."[35] The inquiry panel made public its report in 1991, just one year after the armed standoff at Oka between the Mohawks of Kanasatake and the Canadian Armed Forces, and once again brought Indigenous issues to the public eye. Then, in 1992, the Grand Chief of the Assembly of First Nations, Phil Fontaine, made public another shocking revelation—that he had been sexually abused as a young child while attending a residential school. "Indian" residential schools had been created by a Government of Canada policy and were operated by churches, ostensibly to "civilize the Indians" to enable them to function in a modern society.[36] Although his was not the first revelation of abuse at residential schools—the first legal suit had been filed in the courts in 1990—Fontaine's disclosure was headline news because of his stature as a public figure.[37] By breaking the code of silence, it seemed as if Grand Chief Fontaine had implicitly granted other former students permission to make public the narratives of their own experiences. A torrent of similar revelations followed Fontaine's.

Although the story of Indigenous people suffering abuse at the hands of colonial officials well into the twentieth century might have been news to mainstream Canadians, it was certainly not news to Indigenous people, who were well aware that abuse took place in far more settings than the justice system and the residential schools. Helping their people heal from the effects of historical trauma has been a priority for Indigenous governments and organizations for decades. Nevertheless, when these narratives made their way into the mainstream media, they rocked the nation and forever altered the national discourse by and about Indigenous peoples.

Even more importantly, these stories challenged the mythology of the Canadian nation-state, thereby embarrassing the settlers and their government. Because the collective esteem of the settlers was threatened, the settler government began to take action to address the concerns that Indigenous people were expressing in their stories, concerns that focussed on healing individuals, families, and communities traumatized by colonial policies and practices. It was only when stories of abuse became public and the rest of the country became aware of experiences that were all too familiar to the

Writing in English is simultaneously a political act and an act of healing that provides the foundation for the process of decolonization. Jace Weaver uses the term "communitism" to describe Indigenous literature in English, a term that he creates by combining the words "community" and "activism": "[Indigenous] Literature is communitist to the extent that it has a proactive commitment to Native community, including what I term the 'wider community' of Creation itself. In communities that have too often been fractured and rendered dysfunctional by the effects of more than 500 years of colonialism, to promote communitist values means to participate in the healing of the grief and sense of exile felt by Native communities and the pained individuals in them."[42] In other words, Indigenous literature is intrinsically communal in that it seeks to heal the dislocation caused by the breaches in psychosocial integration inherent in the process of colonialism. The goal of communitism is to heal Indigenous communities by reconnecting Indigenous individuals to the larger whole.

Gloria Bird and Joy Harjo draw our attention to the subversive nature of the practice of writing in English to recover Indigenous communities. They term this subversive practice "reinventing the enemy's language": "'Reinventing' in the colonizer's tongue and turning those images around to mirror an image of the colonized to the colonizers as a process of decolonization indicates that something is happening, something is emerging and coming into focus that will politicize as well as transform literary expression.... It is at this site where 'reinventing' can occur to undo some of the damage that colonization has wrought."[43] Clearly, there is an irony in this.[44] The language and literary traditions that the colonial educational systems forced on Indigenous peoples caused enormous damage to individuals and communities. Yet, the very language and literary traditions forced upon us are the tools of contemporary Indigenous literature in English. Contemporary Indigenous writers manipulate the English language and its literary traditions to narrate Indigenous experiences under colonialism in an effort to heal themselves and their audiences from the colonial trauma.

Although the English language cannot communicate accurately the practices and norms of Indigenous cultures, it does provide Indigenous writers with some advantages regarding the distribution of their literary works. It is ironic that since the colonizers began to classify the many diverse peoples indigenous to this land using generic terms, such as "Indian," "Aboriginal," "Native," and "Indigenous," we have come to acquire more commonalities than we had in the past. We share a history of similar experiences as a result of colonial policies, and our communities suffer from similar wounds. With

Indigenous people that the term "healing" became central to any discourse relating to the Indigenous peoples of this country.

"Healing" does not imply that Indigenous people are sick, however. Ward Churchill argues that "to be sick is one thing, wounded another; the latter requires healing, the former a cure."[38] Colonialism is sick; under its auspices and supported by its mythology, the colonizers have inflicted heinous wounds on the Indigenous population that they set out to civilize. Although Indigenous people understand their need to heal from colonial trauma, most settlers deny that their society is built on a sick foundation and, therefore, deny that it requires a cure. White people are typically horrified to learn about the damage that their governments have caused Indigenous people. McIntosh explains that White people have been "taught to think of their lives as morally neutral, normative, and average, and also ideal, so that when we work to benefit others, this is seen as work that will allow 'them' to be more like 'us.'"[39]

Not surprisingly, few Indigenous people are able to trust today's politicians and their bureaucrats, who purport to be willing and able to help Indigenous people deal with the trauma that their predecessors and their policies have caused. Instead, Indigenous people look to their own communities to find resources with which to heal traumatized spirits. Over the last three decades, Indigenous people have witnessed the healing power of stories as they have begun to reassert their individual and collective narratives.

Linguistic Subversion and Its Applications

Indigenous peoples have believed in the healing power of language and stories since time immemorial, and today's Indigenous writers continue to apply this belief to the creation of works of literature and theatre in English. Although most writers would prefer to tell their stories in their Indigenous languages, many do not speak those languages. Forced upon them by the policies of the colonial regime, English has become the lingua franca for the many diverse Indigenous peoples of this land, diverse peoples who share similar experiences under colonialism and who desire to heal from those experiences. Although English is not always their language of choice, today's writers use it to create literary works that aspire to accomplish many of the same aims as the oral stories did: to explain the history of the people, to buttress cultural practices and norms, and to articulate their relationship with the world.[40] Armstrong explains that, "although severe and sometimes irreparable damage has been wrought, healing can take place through cultural affirmation."[41]

the exception of some Indigenous people living in Quebec, almost all speak English, even those who are still able to speak their Indigenous language. Thus, by writing in English, contemporary Indigenous writers are able to reach a large and diverse audience, which Louis Owens has termed "a het eroglot gathering" that includes not only "tribal relations" but also "Indian readers from the same or other tribal cultures who may not be familiar with the traditional elements essential to the work but who may recognize the coercive power of language to 'bring into being'; and non-Indian readers who approach the novel with a completely alien set of assumptions and values."[45] Because Indigenous writers are cognizant of their diverse audience, they have embedded a multiplicity of implied readers within the text of their narratives, so that each category of implied reader will understand the narrative somewhat differently, depending on their societal positionality.

Transformational Stories, Healing Stories

In his study of reading fiction as a means of improving mental and emotional health, Joseph Gold explains that human beings can be distinguished from other sentient beings in how we construct and understand our lives by creating narratives. Gold observes how we craft and re-craft our autobiographies every day, even in our dreams. We *are* our stories.[46] This is true for all people, regardless of race or culture, not only individually but also collectively. Humans in every society construct and articulate their shared reality in the form of narrative.

Terry Tafoya, an Indigenous psychologist from the Warm Springs and Taos Pueblo nations, explains that from an Indigenous perspective "stories are a type of medicine and, like medicine, can be healing or poisonous depending on the dosage or type. Indigenous people have heard poisonous stories in the colonial discourse. To heal, people must write or create a new story or script of their lives."[47] Anishinaubae writer Basil Johnston agrees that "words are medicine that can heal or injure and possess an element of the Manitou that enabled them to conjure images and ideas out of nothing."[48] As a Métis person, I am intimately aware of the destructive power of stories. I grew up in Winnipeg, once the centre of the Métis homeland, in the 1950s and '60s, when Indigenous people faced overt personal and systemic racism. Through their stories of the "rebellions," our teachers taught us that the Métis were traitorous and prone to insanity. Stories taught us that not only our environment but also our very identities made our lives perilous. As a result, those who could hide their identities did so to protect themselves and their children, and hoped for a better future. But living a false story—a lie—has negative consequences on children's development and identity formation.

Many Indigenous writers echo Johnston and Tafoya's sentiments referencing their traditional Indigenous knowledges regarding the healing aspects of language and story. Muskogee poet Joy Harjo writes that "to speak, at whatever the cost, is to become empowered rather than victimized by destruction. In our tribal cultures the power of language to heal, to regenerate, and to create is understood."[49] Anishinaubae poet and scholar Armand Ruffo writes that elder Art Solomon taught him that "the need for healing, the need for expression go hand-in-hand." Ruffo goes on to say that Art Solomon challenged Indigenous writers to write for the betterment of their people, especially the young: "To bring hope to young Native people so that they too can express themselves and heal is a communal task."[50]

Cree playwright Oskiniko Larry Loyie writes "there is more to native writing than just our traditional stories. Writing is healing, one way for us to deal with the anger that is present amongst us."[51] Inuvialuit writer Alice Masak French agrees and describes how writing helped her to let go of the repressed emotions associated with her residential school experience:

> As you write, everything that you've kept down and held down for so many years comes out and you have so many problems because of it, mainly because you weren't able to and weren't willing to deal with them. But, now you suddenly have to deal with them, because you are writing this book. And that's where the healing comes in. You let it out, you cry about it, you get mad about it, you get angry, frustrated, and then you look at it in pieces until it all comes out. Sometimes there is someone to blame and sometimes there isn't. You get an understanding. So, that's why it was a healing process.[52]

Shushwap Kootenai playwright Vera Manuel reminds us that "a tremendous responsibility is attached to telling the unresolved grief stories of First Nations' people. Words have power; they cause us to feel the emotions of the story they are telling."[53]

In her review of Beatrice Culleton's novel *In Search of April Raintree*, Maria Campbell used its effectiveness as an instrument of healing as a benchmark for evaluation. In a letter to Culleton, Campbell writes that the novel "is a powerful story because, with gentleness, it deals with the sickness in our society and our people. It is the kind of writing that will begin the healing of our people, *and* help a dominant society understand and feel the lives of a people it almost destroyed."[54] Indigenous writing is not merely "what Suzette Henke has called 'scriptotherary.'"[55] Campbell acknowledges the power of literature both to heal Indigenous people from postcolonial traumatic stress response and to cure the settlers from the delusions learned from their mythology. In this way Indigenous literature is able to construct a common truth about our shared past.

Implicating the Audience

Contemporary Indigenous literature serves two transformative functions—healing Indigenous people and advancing social justice in settler society—both components in the process of decolonization. Charlotte Linde contends that "telling a story is a 'relational act' that necessarily implicates the audience,"[56] or the reader, in the case of written stories. Willie Ermine, *Oskapêwis* (helper) to the Nêhiyêwak (Cree) elders of Sturgeon Lake, Saskatchewan, explains that the elders teach that *âtayôhkêwin* (sacred stories) are not only spiritual stories but are themselves spirit. He explains that they enter into the listener and transform that person.[57] I believe that everyday stories, *âcimowina*, the stories that are the foundation of contemporary Indigenous literature, although not spiritual, are nevertheless spirit. Everyday stories, too, have transformative powers, but they must first implicate the audience before transformation can occur.

For Indigenous readers, "implicating the audience" means talking about the historical trauma and the postcolonial trauma that abounds in our communities. Current treatments of post-traumatic stress response are based on the conversion of the emotions relating to the traumatic events into story and then the sharing of that story with others: "in order for a patient to recover, the traumatic memory must be recalled and told to others."[58] In that way, Indigenous people are able to reconstruct and repair our "personal myths." [59]

"Personal myths" are the narratives "that each of us naturally constructs to bring together the different parts of ourselves and our lives into a purposeful and convincing whole."[60] We come to understand the text of our lives during the process of constructing our personal myths. Personal myths play a central role in the construction of identity. Without a complete and coherent personal myth, a person is prone to suffer from emotional and mental illness. By reconstructing a complete and coherent personal myth and then sharing that myth with others, one can heal from the effects of postcolonial traumatic stress response. At one level, this is a function of Indigenous literature.

It is not only writing Indigenous literature but also reading it that has a healing function.[61] Joseph Gold's theories shed light on reading as a "life support system" and can be used to argue that reading contemporary

Indigenous literature enables Indigenous readers, and audience members of theatrical productions, "to make sense of the text" of their lives. Reading Indigenous literature helps Indigenous people understand how colonial public policies have affected our relatives in the past and continue to affect us in the present. In the process of "reading for our lives," we reassemble our individual and collective memories to gain a sense of both personal and community control, thereby reclaiming the Indigenous knowledges that colonial policies attempted to eradicate, clarifying feelings about self and community, and validating Indigenous ideas, values, and beliefs.[62] Gold explains: "What novelists do is to order and organize these [traumatic] experiences and thoughts so that they can get control over them. They do this by, and while, writing them into a story, a novel. Then other people can join the experience of their reading the novel to the experience of their lives.... *it makes you feel less alone and more 'normal.'* When you see that someone else can have known about how you feel, you are being recognized, understood and known."[63] By enabling readers to see their lives and their experiences reflected back to them in the form of narrative, Indigenous literature transforms its readers from individuals often living in isolation to members of a larger community of shared stories.

Silence leads to isolation, causing many Indigenous people to suppress their feelings, believing that they are alone in their experiences and responses. The effects of emotional repression on emotional and spiritual health are long lasting. Reading literature by other Indigenous people who share the same experiences and who are able to articulate their feelings about those experiences can be a healing experience for both writers and readers. Whether the stories are told in the form of narrative, poetry, or performance, they "implicate" Indigenous readers/audiences, by giving voice and validation to their collective experience. Stories show us that we are not alone and that our life experiences are worthy of mention. A story can help dislocated "tribal relations" reconnect with their communities and make those all-important psychosocial connections necessary to support emotional health. The same story might help other Indigenous readers who are not tribal relations but who have suffered the effects of postcolonial trauma. The concrete world of story helps readers examine their experiences and their emotional responses to them.

The colonial experience has instilled in many Indigenous people feelings of shame; however, given the colonizers' brutal attack on both Indigenous languages and families, many people have neither the models nor the language to articulate their feelings. Tafoya explains that story, ritual, and ceremony operate on a concrete level, rather than operating in abstractions, and are, therefore, easily understood. Stories provide vocabulary for readers to discuss trauma for which they might not have vocabulary in their lives. As well, stories bypass self-defence mechanisms and make it safe for readers to examine sensitive issues.[64] In other words, the "literature speaks for us, says back to us truths too painful for us to utter in our own words."[65] In this way, Indigenous readers are, therefore, transformed.

Contemporary Indigenous literature does not only "implicate" its Indigenous readers, however. Although healing from the trauma of colonialism is a prime function of contemporary Indigenous literature, healing without changing the social and political conditions that first caused the injuries would be ineffectual. Susanna Egan writes that "for trauma on a major scale, testimony is a powerful political tool."[66] When their testimony reaches a large and diverse audience, it is possible for Indigenous writers to effect healing by advancing social justice. Indigenous narratives serve a socio-pedagogical function in that their objective is to change society by educating the settler readers about the Indigenous perspective of Canadian society. The narratives implicate settler readers by exposing the structures that sustain White privilege and by compelling them to examine their position of privilege and their complicity in the continued oppression of Indigenous people.

The Chapters that Follow

The chapters that follow make the link between Canadian public policies, the injuries they have inflicted on Indigenous people, and Indigenous literature's ability to heal individuals and communities. To that end, I examine works of contemporary Indigenous literature with two goals in mind: to reveal how they critique the policies of the settler government of Canada and to determine how they effect individual and communal healing from those policies. This topic is more than just an area of scholarly interest to me; it is personal. I recently attended a national meeting of Indigenous scholars and observed that our common preoccupation was our need to dedicate ourselves to helping our communities heal from historical injustice and the trauma it has caused. Although our approaches varied according to discipline, our goals were the same.

It is difficult to explain how inextricably connected Indigenous people are to family and community. The joys and the sadness that our families and communities experience are our joys and sadness, too. When I turn on the news and hear of a tragic accident or terrible crime in the Indigenous community, I wonder whose family has been affected. It could be the family of one or more of my students. It could be the family of a friend. Or, it could very well be my family. Although I work in "the ivory tower," I do not live there. The topics I address in this book were first the topics of endless conversations with friends at kitchen tables and in coffee shops. But coffee-table chats don't make scholarly books, and scholarly conventions require me to footnote what I know. In the following chapters I will try to provide both "insider" and scholarly knowledge in a way that is true to my community.

Chapter 2 is designed to provide readers, especially literary scholars, with an overview of both colonial policies and the subsequent policies of the settler government of Canada, which affect the characters in the works of Indigenous literature and the Indigenous people who write and read them. I am neither a historian nor a policy analyst. My goal is not to provide an exhaustive analysis of the Government of Canada's "Indian" policies—clearly a monumental task—but rather to supply readers with the context needed to understand the literature under discussion. Spatial limitations prevent me from analyzing works of literature that address every policy I summarize, but I will attempt to mention literary works that refer to the policies I describe.

Although this book is not specifically a study of genre in Indigenous literature, I have chosen, for convenience if nothing else, to organize the chapters and the literary works into autobiography, fiction, and drama. Chapter 3 focuses on autobiography, and the works I examine are Maria Campbell's *Halfbreed* and Basil Johnston's *Indian School Days*. I argue that, in the early days of Indigenous literature, Indigenous people seeking to tell their stories found autobiography accessible both to them as writers and to their communities. However, as subsequent would-be writers came to recognize autobiography's strengths and weaknesses, they began to experiment with other literary forms, such as fiction and theatre. Chapter 4 examines fictional works, namely Beatrice Culleton Mosionier's *In Search of April Raintree*, Shirley Sterling's *My Name Is Seepeetza*, and Richard Wagamese's *Keeper 'n Me*. All can be described as "life writing" that straddles the boundaries of autobiography and fiction and that uses the imagination as a healing implement. Chapter 5 explains how Indigenous communities have applied theatre as a vehicle for community self-examination and healing. To illustrate, I examine Vera Manuel's "Strength of Indian Women," a play that has been staged at an array of healing conferences. Indigenous people have also made great advances in professional theatre, so I also examine two exemplary works, Daniel David Moses's *Almighty Voice and His Wife* and Ian Ross's Governor General's Award-winning *fareWel*.

My choice of texts could be described as idiosyncratic. I write about the literature that speaks to me and to my students. Some of the texts I discuss— Maria Campbell's *Halfbreed* and Beatrice Culleton Mosionier's *In Search of April Raintree*—have been the subject of copious literary criticism. Others, such as Basil Johnston's *Indian School Days*, Ian Ross's *fareWel*, and Daniel David Moses's *Almighty Voice and His Wife* should, I think, receive more scholarly attention than they have had to date. The remainder of the texts have generated little to no scholarly attention, yet Richard Wagamese's *Keeper 'n Me*, Shirley Sterling's *My Name Is Seepeetza*, and Vera Manuel's "Strength of Indian Women" are incredibly popular with students, both Indigenous and non-Indigenous.

By "reinventing" both "the enemy's language" and literary traditions, Indigenous writers contribute to the construction of what Frantz Fanon has termed a "national culture"—albeit under Fourth World conditions—thereby furthering the process of decolonization. With individual and communal decolonization as my goal, I choose to follow Jace Weaver's lead and resist "the temptation to discuss what is worth reading, what is worthy of being in the canon…this Eurocentric trap in non-Native criticism has led, albeit perhaps by inadvertence and with honourable intentions, to a denial of Native personhood and damage to Native subjectivity."[67]

chapter 2

Policies of devastation

In response to the report of the Royal Commission on Aboriginal Peoples (1996), the Government of Canada, in 1998, released a new policy document called *Gathering Strength: Canada's Aboriginal Action Plan*, which it describes as "a long-term, broad-based policy approach designed to increase the quality of life of Aboriginal people and to promote self-sufficiency."[1] Within this document is a "Statement of Reconciliation: Learning from the Past," which acknowledges the destruction that the policies of the colonial regime caused:

> Sadly, our history with respect to the treatment of Aboriginal people is not something in which we can take pride. Attitudes of racial and cultural superiority led to a suppression of Aboriginal culture and values. As a country, we are burdened by past actions that resulted in weakening the identity of Aboriginal peoples, suppressing their languages and cultures, and outlawing spiritual practices. We must recognize the impact of these actions on the once self-sustaining nations that were disaggregated, disrupted, limited or even destroyed by the dispossession of traditional territory, by the relocation of Aboriginal people, and by some provisions of the Indian Act. We must acknowledge that the result of these actions was the erosion of the political, economic and social systems of Aboriginal people and nations.... The Government of Canada recognizes that

policies that sought to assimilate Aboriginal people, women and men, were not the way to build a strong country.[2]

Indeed, Canada's policies have affected us so profoundly that many Indigenous people have adopted a policy number as identity marker! Only in Indigenous Canada might someone identify herself as "a Bill C-31," and only in Indigenous Canada would people instantly know the meaning and significance of that label. It would be difficult for readers to develop a thorough understanding of contemporary Indigenous literatures without some foundational knowledge of Indigenous peoples' historical and political relationship with the settler Government of Canada. In this chapter, I will explain how government policy has insinuated itself into every aspect of life for Indigenous people and then summarize briefly the many policies that appear in works of Indigenous literature.

Indigenous People Post-Confederation: A Challenge for the New Nation

In the early days of contact, the newcomers valued Indigenous people as military allies and business partners, albeit by necessity rather than by affection. The role that Indigenous people once fulfilled had been critical to the survival of the newcomers; however, by 1867, colonial officials determined that they had outgrown their usefulness.[3] As the power relationships shifted so did colonial attitudes. Colonial officials who had once valued their former associates now deemed them to be obstacles to progress. In his short story "The Wampum Belt Tells Us…," Basil Johnston describes this shift in power relationships from the time of Jacques Cartier to the War of 1812.

By 1867, the colonial government had established the Dominion of Canada. It had a presence in a significant portion of the country and was working diligently to settle the remainder. Progress, for the settler government, meant expanding the Dominion from Atlantic to Pacific. Immigrants were needed to make the dream a reality, and, indeed, the settler government believed that "Canadian immigrants were harbingers of the future."[4] To that end, it advertised extensively throughout Europe and the United States offering free, unoccupied land to those willing to make the necessary "improvements."[5] Having defeated and subjugated the citizens of the French colonies, the regime preferred that its new colonists be English-speakers. Nevertheless, the regime accepted European immigrants who did not speak English, albeit reluctantly, because cultural differences were minimal. The regime was intolerant of racial differences, however, and "deemed unsuitable" those people who were not White.[6] Thus, officials turned away Black settlers from Oklahoma and taxed Chinese immigrants excessively. The Indigenous population posed a particular problem. The settler government had accepted responsibility for the welfare of the Indigenous populations but would not accept the original inhabitants of the land into its society. Torn between their conflicting beliefs in social progressivism and social Darwinism,[7] the Government of Canada, albeit unofficially, also "deemed unsuitable" the original inhabitants of the country. The problem, however, was that, unlike African Americans and Chinese, Indigenous people had nowhere else to go.

The Indigenous population was also problematic for the colonial government because they still comprised the majority population in the Northwest and were the de facto owners of that land by way of their continuous occupancy. To address this issue, colonial officials devised strategies for addressing "the Indian problem" that differed radically from those of the Americans. In comparison to the American regime, which controlled the Indigenous population by employing horrendous physical violence, the strategies of the colonial regime in Canada seem relatively benign on the surface. By employing much subtler methods, not the least of which made use of the Indigenous peoples' own oral communication networks, officials were able to seize control of the Indigenous peoples' lands with relatively little bloodshed.[8] Many nations' territories straddled the border between Canada and the United States, and therefore Indigenous people were well aware of the violence that their relatives were suffering at the hands of both the military and settlers to the south. Colonial officials were able to use that knowledge to wield power and control over the Indigenous population with the ever-present "threat of warfare and its attendant starvation."[9] The Indigenous population had already been drastically reduced by disease and was already convinced that resistance against the colonial oppressors was futile, rendering the tactics of the settler-invader government more than a little heavy-handed. Knowledge of the power of the colonizers and of their propensity for violence worked in tandem to engender fear in the Indigenous population, and the colonial government exploited that fear to subjugate the people. "Psychological terrorism" became an accepted practice of the Dominion government.[10]

Constructing "Docile Bodies"

The colonial regime was oppressive in its relationship with Indigenous people, which was defined by the regime's goal of eradicating Indigenous differences and forcibly assimilating the Indigenous population into the colonizer's capitalist, free-market society. Granted, the Indigenous population had participated in capitalism since the beginnings of the fur trade and many of the Métis were resolute free traders.[11] However, there was little place for Indigenous competitors in the free-market economy of post-Confederation Canada, and those who did participate paid a price: "In order for 'free markets' to be 'free,' the exchange of labour, land, currency, and consumer goods must not be encumbered by elements of psychosocial integration such as clan loyalties, village responsibilities, guild or union rights, charity, family obligations, social roles, or religious values. Cultural traditions 'distort' the free play of the laws of supply and demand, and thus must be suppressed."[12] Officials understood that, to maintain power, the regime must have control over all imperial subjects, including Indigenous people; however, controlling the Indigenous people posed a greater challenge than did controlling the settlers. In the minds of the colonial officials, Indigenous people were unpredictable and potentially dangerous because they were unaware of many of the "truths" that constituted the knowledge that comprised the narrative that was the foundation of the empire. Officials recognized that, unlike those born to the empire, Indigenous people had not been indoctrinated into the colonial ideology from birth, and an intrinsic part of that ideology was the unquestioning comprehension that the will of the empire would prevail.

Many of Michel Foucault's theories about the relationship between knowledge and power apply to the colonization of this land and the creation of the Canadian nation in the late nineteenth century. Foucault argues that any power can maintain authority only when its subjects willingly take an active role in their own subjugation: "When conditions are established for persons to experience ongoing evaluation according to particular institutionalized 'norms,' when these conditions cannot be escaped, and when persons can be isolated in their experience of such conditions, then they will become the guardians of themselves. In these circumstances, persons will perpetually evaluate their own behavior and engage in operations on themselves to forge themselves as 'docile bodies.' According to Foucault, we live in a society where evaluation or normalizing judgment has replaced the judiciary and torture as primary mechanism of social control: This is a society of the everpresent 'gaze.'"[13] People living in Indigenous societies were not accustomed to life under the same "everpresent gaze" as were the European settlers. And, unlike the citizens of the empire, who had intimate knowledge of the power of the judiciary and their own rulers' history of employing torture, Indigenous people, even though they had become resigned to coexisting peacefully with the newcomers, were not at the same stage of willingness to take an active role in their own subjugation under the power and authority of the colonial regime. In "The Wampum Belt Tells Us...," Johnston describes the Anishinaubae's shock when Jacques Cartier's men Lebrun and Parisé explain the feudal system and describe how their families occupied the bottom rung of the ladder of European society. The Anishinaubae cannot conceive of a world in which leaders are masters of the people rather than their servants. Changing this mindset was a challenge for colonial officials, who were charged with ensuring that the Indigenous population learn that the empire was always and already dominant and that they must become its subjects or perish.

Cognizant that they were living in the path of the colonial juggernaut, the Indigenous people understood the futility of resistance and were eager to live peacefully with the colonizers. Thus, Indigenous people were on their way to becoming "docile bodies" ripe for subjugation. It is ironic that the colonial officials still feared the Indigenous nations even though they were clearly in a weakened state and, rather than resisting settlement, were attempting to negotiate agreements to share the land with the newcomers.[14] However, because Indigenous people were not constituted in the ideology of the empire, colonial officials reasoned that they must take extraordinary measures to ensure their docility as imperial subjects. If we define ideology as those things that we take so for granted that we do not hold them up for critical examination, then it becomes clear that ideologies must necessarily be intolerant for their very survival. Ideologies are, by implication, competitive because each differing ideology calls into question the veracity of the others by its very existence. Colonial officials were aware that they had to take action to minimize Indigenous differences before they would be able to control the Indigenous population. Before Indigenous people could be constituted as imperial subjects, they had to replace their ideologies with that of the empire.

At the time of Confederation, the prevailing truth of the empire was the belief in progress. Progress constituted a line, an inclining plane, if you will, of continual improvement from primitive to civilized, pagan to Christian, oral to written, and so forth. Even today, "the annihilation of Indigenous peoples is often considered an inevitable by-product of civilization, a process by which backward cultures are naturally eliminated through progress which can't be stopped. Cultural elimination is often, by default, accepted government policy."[15] Since the empire's way was the way of "progress," and by implication the superior way, colonial officials believed that Indigenous knowledges had no value in modern society. This position was steeped in colonial ideology, and, accordingly, colonial officials set out to purge Indigenous peoples of their traditional knowledges and replace them with the "truths" of the empire.[16] Their means was directed cultural replacement. To that end, colonial officials created policies to re-educate—although most Indigenous people would argue that a better term would be "de-educate"—the Indigenous population. De-education consisted of purging the knowledges from Indigenous societies, knowledges that were housed in the collective oral narratives, and replacing them with imperial knowledge. This was not simply a battle of ideologies, however. There was something much more concrete at stake: "The fusion of Indigenous cultures with their land is so complete that the only way to take the land is to destroy the Indigenous culture."[17]

Namoya Tawâw (There is no room)

In contemporary Canada, where multiculturalism is enshrined in law, difference is tolerated only in approved venues like the plethora of multicultural festivals that take place in Canada each year.[18] The settlers believe in the inevitability of their culture's dominance and the corresponding demise of Indigenous cultures (with the exception of those aspects that can be displayed at multicultural festivals as quaint reminders of the past): "The iconography of settler triumphalism is everywhere and always apparent…from the exalted statuary littering public spaces to the names bestowed upon the places themselves. And then, to be sure, there is the haughty supremacist aura with which the settlers have imbued their culture—and by extension themselves—in the canons of their literature, their cinema and the academic (mis)representations which continue to be imposed upon native youth with more force and sophistication today than ever before."[19] Although the contemporary ideology of the neo-colonizers professes to embrace difference, the evidence suggests that in contemporary Canada difference is embraced only when convenient, entertaining, and colourful. Some believe that cultural synthesis is only truly embraced in the restaurants of contemporary Canada.[20]

Ironically, the very goal that was the foundation of colonial "Indian" policy, the assimilation of the Indigenous peoples into colonial society, was incompatible with the ideology of the colonizers. Because those steeped in imperial ideology believed without question in their superiority over the Indigenous people, neither the regime nor colonial society in general was willing to welcome the Indigenous peoples into its midst. To do so would have required tolerance of difference, and the colonizers interpreted difference as evidence of inferiority. Their real, unarticulated agenda, then, became the eradication of Indigenous population by eradicating Indigenous differences, and public policy became the weapon of choice. The colonial bureaucrats designed policies that would bring to fruition the imperial agenda. The consequences for Indigenous people were devastating: "Although assimilation policy very nearly succeeded in eliminating native languages and spiritual practices, it failed to integrate the natives into free market society, thus leaving them utterly dislocated."[21] Canadian government policies traumatized Indigenous people and shattered the social fabric of Indigenous societies.

Peter Hudson and Brad McKenzie describe the process of colonization and demonstrate its deleterious effects on the colonized. In the first stage of this process, the colonizers seize power and assume the right to make decisions over the lives of the colonized. Then, the colonizers devalue the traditions, customs, and ways of the colonized. Finally—and it is here that Foucault's concept of "docile bodies" comes into play—the colonized and colonizers become conditioned to think of themselves and each other in a prescribed, and hierarchical, set of ways and behave accordingly. As a consequence, the colonized often become conditioned to behave in such a way as to support the negative opinions of themselves that the colonizers maintain.[22] The colonizers classify these behaviours as "social problems," and these problems, needless to say, belong to the colonized. However, because Indigenous communities, as a result of the colonial process, are now rife with social problems, having neither assimilated nor disappeared, the colonial officials find themselves in a situation—as those who hold the power—in which they must develop more policies to address these social problems. In Canada, almost all of the policies of the colonial regime have failed in their attempts to assimilate the Indigenous population or to address the social problems that early policies have caused. Thus, colonial trauma begat social problems that begat more policies and that begat more social problems, ad nauseam, ad infinitum.[23] It is only today, after well over a century of oppressive policies, that the colonial regime has thought to ask for Indigenous peoples' input into the development of even more colonial policies, as if we are in possession of some magic solution to heal all the trauma and injuries that the settler-invader government policies have inflicted.

The imperial powers believed that the juggernaut of their modern civilization would doom the Indigenous peoples' way of life to extinction. This belief provided, and some would argue continues to provide, the philosophical foundation of all of Canada's policies that address Indigenous peoples. Deeming their society to be unquestionably superior, the colonial officials considered it their moral duty to take action to ensure that the remaining Indigenous people would have the tools necessary to fit into, and hopefully disappear into, modern society. Certainly, this belief was at odds with the reality. Because of the racism that underpinned its ideology, settler-invader society would not accept Indigenous people into its midst, rendering false their rhetoric of a benevolent, inclusive society—a delusion. This delusion, nevertheless, prevailed, and the colonial officials sought to develop policies that would transform it into fact, clearly an impossible task.

Policies Governing Identity: Indians/Not-Indians

"A threat to social organization is always preceded by an acknowledged perception of differentness—an order set apart from the main social order—and there is a political need for this apartness to be defined," argue Dean Neu and Richard Therrien.[24] Thus, one of the first actions that the colonial officials undertook was the assignment of identity, which entailed determining whom they would deem to be an Indian and whom they would not. This proved to be exceedingly complex. The colonial regime rigidly defines and dictates Indian identity rather than allowing identity to be negotiated and naturally shifting as required by Indigenous people themselves.[25] However, the issue was never one of determining who was Indigenous and who was White. To the colonial officials, that was easy to differentiate. What the agents of the colonial regime found difficult was determining who was Indian enough to be considered "pure" (or perhaps "pure-ish" would be a better term) from those who were merely "mixed" and, therefore, impure. In some cases, officials attempted to assign a suitable quantum of Indian blood as the determining factor.[26] In other cases, they examined lifestyle. Often it was impossible to tell "pure" Indians from "mixed," especially in those communities where members of both groups lived virtually the same lifestyle, spoke the same languages, and were often blood relatives.

Furthermore, to their dismay, colonial officials observed that some Indigenous people had become "contaminated" by contact with Europeans by having converted to Christianity or engaging in agriculture or commerce or any practice that the colonial officials deemed to be "inauthentic."[27] Bonita Lawrence argues that "in the context of over two centuries of colonial contact, so-called authentic Indianness was a rare commodity. And yet authenticity was a commodity that Europeans craved and which colonial governments clearly demanded in order to acknowledge Indianness."[28] Even more problematic were those Indigenous people who were visibly mixed but lived what colonial officials judged to be an "authentic" Indian lifestyle. In the end, many colonial officials arbitrarily assigned identity so that "ethnic differentiation was not a matter of blood, but a social process reinforced by government policy."[29]

In their frustration, some of the more flexible, or perhaps more frustrated, colonial officials gave Indigenous men the choice of signing on to the treaties, thereby being identified as Indians with Indian "status," or of being granted halfbreed scrip, thereby being identified as "halfbreeds," that is to say "not-Indians." Little did they know that, by accepting halfbreed scrip, and thus being identified as "not-Indians," these Indigenous men would inadvertently assist the colonial powers in speeding their people on a journey into a legal oblivion where they would have no rights. Some more inflexible authorities allocated identities, in effect, by whim in the same way as they might allocate food rations or trade goods. Their actions forever divided families and communities.

Furthermore, in their decisions, colonial officials applied European patriarchal principles to their designations so that, regardless of the traditional beliefs and practices of their nations, Indigenous men became the "heads of households" and Indigenous women, as their daughters and spouses, became mere legal appendages, indeed property, and their identities became inextricably linked to those of their fathers or husbands.[30] The process of identifying who was Indian and who was not-Indian began a series of oppressive practices which, to use Lawrence's terminology, have become "naturalized," and today only a few scholars and artists hold them up for critical examination to reveal that they are not natural at all.

The process of developing policies that would effectively appropriate Indigenous peoples' right to identify themselves became one of the first orders of business for the colonial regime. In 1876, during the negotiations of the numbered treaties, the newly formed Government of the Dominion of Canada passed the *Indian Act*, which amalgamated and expanded several pre-Confederation acts that pertained to the Indigenous peoples. In the 1876 Act, Indian "status" was narrowly and exclusively defined.[31] Although the Act makes no mention of the mixed-blood/métis/Métis/halfbreed/country-born people, the very act of defining who are "Indians" implies the presence of their opposite, "not-Indians." A reasonable person would think that, as the opposite of Indians, not-Indians would naturally be White; however, this was not the case. Since the colonizers were White and this legislation is a colonial instrument designed to subjugate the Indigenous population, it does not deal with White people, either explicitly or implicitly, except in reference to their obligation to care for and control the Indigenous population. Inequality has become "naturalized" in contemporary Canada. With few exceptions, White people do not question the existence of the paternalistic *Indian Act*, which controls every aspect of the lives of Status Indians. Likewise, most White people accept that, unlike Status Indians, they are not subject to special legislation because they constitute "normal" in Canada today.

The relationship between the colonial policy-makers and the Indigenous (Indian/not-Indian) populations is not simply a binary of two poles. Instead of a binary, the relationship is, in effect, a triangle. The colonizers occupy the apex of this triangle and from that implicitly superior position they dole out legislation and dubious "privileges" to the Indians, who are positioned at one corner/pole of the base of the triangle. Not-Indians are also positioned at the base of this triangle at its opposite corner/pole, having no legislation, no privileges, but some dubious freedoms, at least in the early years when Indians were subject to the "pass laws" described later. In 1954, V.F. Valentine, an anthropologist employed by the Government of Saskatchewan, observed how this relational positioning created a caste system, with the colonizers occupying the position of the "ruling" caste and the Indians the ruled. Valentine observed that, in this caste system, those Indigenous people whom the colonizers deemed to be "not-Indians" were, in effect, "'outcasts,' with little mobility possible out of their group."[32]

The ideology of imperialism is dependent upon binary oppositions: light/dark, civilized/savage, modern/primitive, good/evil, male/female, Christian/pagan, to name but a few. If we accept Jacques Derrida's analysis of binaries wherein one pole is naturally privileged over the other, the colonial authorities, as people steeped in the ideology of imperialism, situated the Indigenous peoples, both Indian and not-Indian, on the undesirable pole of each of these binaries, that is, dark, savage, primitive, feminine, pagan, and therefore evil. However, within this binary they created yet another binary comprised of Indian/not-Indian. In this binary, the colonial officials chose to privilege Indian, not because they valued them in any way—in their minds Indians were clearly primitive savages—but because of pragmatic reasons.

The colonial officials wanted to open up the land for settlement and, learning from their experiences in the East and observing the American experience, they were cognizant that Indians were capable of disrupting this process. The colonial bureaucrats needed to minimize this possibility by putting the Indians somewhere that they could be kept minimally comfortable. The bureaucrats considered this a stop-gap solution that would hold until the Indigenous peoples vanished into oblivion, as any primitive peoples were wont to do in the face of the advancement of a superior civilization. Thus, the colonizers agreed to grant the Indians small tracts of land (that is to say, grant them the land that had always belonged to them), miniscule financial aid, and farming implements, predicting that in a short time period there would be no Indian problem because there would be no Indians.

The process of designating Indigenous people as "not-Indians" that began in the midst of the negotiations of the numbered treaties was critical to the imperial regime's Indian/not-Indian policy, the goal of which was to disappear the Indian by eliminating her or his legal status as Indian. To accomplish this end, officials classified Indians who were not present when the treaties were signed as "not-Indians." Along with this group of Indigenous people were the halfbreeds, mixed-bloods, country-born, métis, and Métis whom colonial officials deemed to be "not-Indian-enough"; they, too, became "not-Indians." Likewise, Indian women who married Whites or not-Indians became "not-Indians." And, as the colonial officials assigned identity, the number of "Indians" rapidly diminished.

This is not to say that those persons classified "Indian" would remain Indian. Because they fell under the jurisdiction of the *Indian Act*, the policy that colonial officials developed to coordinate and control their orderly assimilation of Indians into the colonial society—in other words, turn them into "not-Indians"—their Indian "status" was tenuous at best. Under the implementation of the policy, an Indian who became educated, or was absent from the reserves for a long period of time, or joined a profession, could apply to become enfranchised. Any Indian who applied for and was granted enfranchisement would no longer be an Indian in the eyes of the law but ideally would become a member of civilized (read White) society: "the method by which they could join the state was patently bureaucratic—and economic: enfranchisement, by which they would give up their 'Indianness' and 'hand-outs.'"[33] This process of voluntary enfranchisement failed for many reasons, not the least of which were the racist attitudes of the colonizer culture, which did not accept former Indians into White society. Instead, those enfranchised lost the little land and privileges afforded them as Indians and joined the ranks of the landless not-Indians. As a result, few Indians enfranchised voluntarily.[34]

Most Indians had no desire to leave their communities, and in any case the White communities were adamant that they did not want Indians to join theirs. Yet, the official objective of the colonial officials was to fully assimilate Indians into White society, as evidenced by the words of director of the Department of Indian Affairs Duncan Campbell Scott, who wrote: "the happiest future for the Indian race is absorption into the general population…. [T]his is the object of the policy of our government."[35] To that end, the colonial regime adopted a policy of coercing assimilation by forcing enfranchisement, which remained in practice for several decades.[36] This assimilationist policy succeeded in decreasing the numbers of Status Indians; however, as the number of Status Indians decreased, the number of "not-Indians" increased proportionately. Even worse for the former Indians, neither the policy nor the regime that created it took any action to integrate the newly created "not-Indians" into the mainstream society as equal members with equal opportunities. The policy merely transformed Indians with legal status as Indians into Indians without status, thereby creating a racialized underclass of "not-Indians" who occupied the margins of society both White and Indian.

In the Northwest Resistance of 1885, Indians and not-Indians united to fight against colonial oppression. As a result of the normalization of the Indian/not-Indian division, it is unlikely that this will ever happen again. Indians in the areas covered by the numbered treaties have come to believe that any political union with their not-Indian relatives would put at risk their rights and privileges. By giving some Indigenous people advantages, albeit paltry ones, and others none, the colonial regime created a rigid new division between Indigenous peoples solely based on its own policies. With something to lose, many "Indians" turned their back on their "not-Indian" relatives.

Although acting as a unified body and thus gaining strength in numbers would appear to be a logical strategy for mutual gain, Status Indian political organizations today steer clear of any association with Métis political organizations for fear of "weakening" their status with the federal government. Colonial officials continue to perpetuate this division by advancing a belief that any "Indians" who align themselves with "not-Indians" will threaten the treaty rights of their communities. For example, in 1976, I was the secretary-treasurer of the West-Central Native Women's Association of Saskatchewan, which was one of the small regional groups that comprised the Native Women's Association of Saskatchewan, a formidable political body at the time. Our board of directors consisted of twelve women, six Status/treaty and six non-Status or Métis. At one meeting, the representative of the Province of Saskatchewan Department of Social Services, which funded the organization's transition house for women in crisis, told us that if we persisted in working together our funding would be in jeopardy and advised us to split into two organizations, one for Indians and one for "not-Indians."

Later, the group did divide and has since ceased to have any political presence in the province. Even today the colonial regime's policies of divide and conquer continue to work as planned. When the Federation of Saskatchewan Indian Nations responded to the Aboriginal Justice Report, then Vice-chief Lawrence Joseph, rather than working collaboratively with other Aboriginal groups, complained that First Nations had been "lumped in" with other Aboriginal people—Métis and Inuit—who he referred to as "the Métis, the Inuits, the coulda-beens, the shoulda-beens, the wanna-bes."[37] This division has intensified with the passing of time, so that today one could hardly recognize that we were once related. Thus, as a consequence of colonial policies, "status" under the *Indian Act* became status in society and produced a class system that continues to divide Indigenous peoples to this day.

Indian identity as marked by Indian status was, and still is, unstable, as Government of Canada demographer Eric Guimond points out in his studies, aptly titled "Fuzzy Definitions and Population Explosion: Changing Identity of Aboriginal Groups in Canada"[38] and "Changing Ethnicity: The Concept of Ethnic Drifters."[39] This instability was primarily caused by the gendered natures of the policies of identity, which privileged men over women. While Indian women could lose their status by marrying not-Indian or White men, not-Indian women and White women and their subsequent children could acquire Indian status by marrying Indian men. As a result, some families drifted in and out of Indian status over the generations until Bill C-31 amended the *Indian Act* in 1985, ostensibly, but not successfully, eliminating the inherent sexism it contained.[40]

Based on a complex formula, "not-Indian" individuals who had lost their status could apply to have it reinstated as could two generations of their descendants. Not only did this amendment to policy attempt to eliminate current and future removals of Indian status based on its sexist philosophical underpinnings, it attempted to retroactively correct the policy. However, although this amendment reinstated individuals to the colonial regime's list of Status Indians, it did not guarantee that their home communities would allow them to become band members. The bands were inundated with new members but were given no additional funding to support them. Consequently, many people who are legally Status Indians are not allowed to participate in band elections or live on-reserve. When seen through the eyes of the ten-year-old narrator of Lee Maracle's "Dear Daddy," the lunacy of Canada's "Indian" policies becomes clear. One morning the narrator's mother asks her daughter, "Do I look any browner?" She goes on to explain, "I am an Indian now": "She said it as though it were something you could become, and I began to think she was really losing it. She went through a whole bunch of explaining about Bill C-31. I hear that line a lot since she got her 'status back.' Bill C-31. You know when you are ten, Bill C-31 sounds like the name of some kind old man who runs about fixing things for Native women."[11] Like the narrator's mother, the people, mostly women, who regained their "status" through the provisions of Bill C-31, saw benefits when they left the ranks of the "outcasts," the not-Indians. They had the right to post-secondary education and subsidized health care, and if they regained band membership, they could live on the reserve, if housing were available, and be buried with their ancestors.

Despite the professed improvements that Bill C-31 offered, the colonial regime still controls Indian identity, and that policy still aims to disappear the Indian. The new, improved *Indian Act* sets out to do this through the designation of Indians as 6(1) and 6(2), depending on the status of their parents. Children of those people whom the colonial regime classifies as 6(1) can marry not-Indians and their subsequent children will still be Indian; children of those people classified as 6(2) will lose their status if they marry not-Indians.[42] The *Indian Act* has failed miserably as an instrument of assimilation but has succeeded as a weapon of national and cultural destruction.

Policies that Governed Indians

The missionaries who operated in tandem with the fur trade were not the dominant colonial force in the early years of colonization, but missionary influence grew in strength by the time of Confederation. Most of the early missionaries were French and Catholic and, thus, had little to no influence with the Anglo-Protestant-dominated government of the new Dominion of Canada. However, the Protestant missionaries who became increasingly active in the nineteenth century had an enormous influence on the content of the policies that the colonial regime developed. As they travelled the country searching for souls to save, the missionaries collected a massive amount of data about the customs, habits, and languages of the Indigenous peoples. The material that the missionaries gathered and compiled in ethnographies, lexicographies, and anthropological handbooks became foundational documents for public policies relating to Indigenous people.[43] Unfortunately, the missionaries viewed Indigenous people through a lens of intolerance and evangelical fervour that resulted in biased reporting. That the Indigenous population were savage heathens was a given both for missionaries and colonial officials. The only question was whether or not they could be civilized.

Although "policy makers and administrators tended to see [Indigenous people] as primitive and inferior, undeserving of respect, and probably incapable of attaining the higher culture of the white man,"[44] the missionaries were more optimistic. The missionaries considered the Indigenous peoples, as the title of C.L. Higham's study suggests, "noble, wretched, and redeemable." The missionaries' influence resulted in the colonial regime's programmatic approach to the colonization of North America that would irrevocably and fundamentally alter the lives of those who were designated Indians.

This colonial program took the form of a three-pronged line of attack: convert the Indigenous population to Christianity, transform them into farmers, and compel them to adopt the European dress and lifestyle. It is important to note that an agrarian lifestyle was also a requisite component of Christian civilization. In particular, "Anglican missionaries coupled migrancy to sin, and argued that to convert the heathen one had to curb their itinerance."[45] Although hunting had been tolerated as an acceptable pastime for the nobility, the missionaries considered it to be savagely unreliable as a mainstay for it was dependent on the whims of nature, over which Christians had been divinely charged to take dominion. The missionaries believed that the Indians had to change and petitioned the colonial officials to establish policies to induce that change.

Even though the policies that followed the signing of the numbered treaties, in time, affected all those people designated Indians, the colonial regime was more stringent in the way that it imposed its policies on some Indian nations while imposing them less stringently on others. Helen Buckley argues that the treaty Indians,[46] especially those on the Prairies, encountered a level of oppression that other Indians did not: "the treaty nations and their member bands share a particular history in association with the Canadian government, including a degree of control that was not imposed in the eastern provinces or in British Columbia."[47] Two policies in particular had a major effect on treaty Indians in the latter half of the nineteenth century and the first half of the twentieth, policies that are the subject of a number of works of Indigenous literature that are set in the area covered by treaties One, Two, Four, Six, and Seven.[48] The first of these policies governed Indian agriculture by establishing the permit system, which controlled the sale of farming stock and grain that Indians had acquired when they negotiated the treaties. It also created the position of farm instructor, which would become a position of enormous power on Indian reserves, second only to that of the Indian agent. The second policy established the pass system, which restricted treaty Indians' right to move freely from place to place. These policies served to place treaty Indians on the margins of the new Canadian society by treating them as if they were dependent children or mentally incompetent. The evidence suggests that this was no accident. Indeed, this was the belief to which the government policy makers and most of Canadian society adhered.[49]

Policies that Controlled Indian Agriculture

At the time that they negotiated the treaties, most of the leaders of the Indian nations had resigned themselves to the harsh reality that their communities must abandon their hunting and gathering lifestyles if they were to prevent their people from starving. They believed that farming was the way of the future. That is not to say that the Indigenous peoples of the Canadian Plains were strangers to agriculture. Many communities in what is now southern Manitoba and Saskatchewan had engaged in agriculture for years, albeit in a limited fashion, having acquired corn and squash from the Mandan people from the region now called North Dakota.[50] As other crops became available, these communities did not hesitate to expand their agricultural repertoire. As early as 1804, Indians from the northwestern shores of the Great Lakes, throughout southern Manitoba, and to forts Carleton and Vermillion and Edmonton House were gardening extensively, growing potatoes, barley, onions, carrots, peas, pumpkins, melons, cucumber, and thyme. They had acquired some of the produce from the Métis, some from eastern First Nations, and some from the Whites.[51]

Although the yields of hunting and gathering activities formed the greater part of their diets, Indigenous people of the Plains were highly dependent on the buffalo herds, whose numbers were decreasing at an alarming rate. Throughout the treaty-making process, the leaders of these nations adamantly insisted that the colonial regime help them to establish themselves as farmers so that their people would be able to maintain their self-sufficiency. In her study of the effects of colonial policy on Indian farming in the areas of the numbered treaties, Sarah Carter writes: "The 1870s are generally described as a time during which prairie Indians, clinging desperately and stubbornly to the 'old ways,' preferred to roam the plains aimlessly in search of buffalo and only reluctantly settled on reserves after much cajoling by the government. Once on their reserves, according to this interpretation, Indians proved indifferent, apathetic, even hostile toward government efforts to teach them to farm. But from the beginning it was the Indians that showed the greater willingness and inclination to farm and the government that displayed little serious intent to see agriculture established on the reserves."[52] The Indian leaders who negotiated the early numbered treaties (One, Two, and Four) demanded that the colonial regime supply them with seed, stock, and farming implements. The leaders who negotiated Treaty Six, having observed the deficiencies of the early treaties, also exacted an agreement from the colonial official that the regime would provide them with training in farming practices.[53]

After signing the treaties, colonial officials had to devise ways to implement the terms of those treaties and fulfill the promises they had made on behalf of the imperial power. To that end, colonial officials went to work developing policies. Carter points out that "Indian policy for the North-West was never the result of long-term planning, of adopting and deliberatly [sic] carrying out a predetermined, settled course…. Only with hindsight might these [policy] responses take on the appearance of a settled course purposefully carried out."[54] Under the terms of the treaties, the colonial officials, on behalf of the imperial power, agreed to provide Indians with stock and seed in exchange for the right to settle on their land. Indians did not, and still do not, hold title to the land that their communities occupy. Rather, the Crown possesses legal title and merely reserves the land for the Indians.

Since the treaties enabled the Crown to become holder of the title to the land, it would follow that the Indians should, at least, have become legal owners of the stock and seed promised them in the treaties. This was not the case. Following a series of policy decisions and inadvertent actions, colonial officials came to believe that title to the Indians' stock, agricultural produce, and farming implements were the property of the Crown. Accordingly, they ordered that all farming implements and stock be branded "ID" for "Indian Department."[55] Daniel David Moses's historical drama *Almighty Voice and His Wife*, which will be discussed in detail in Chapter 5, illustrates the extreme consequences to Indigenous communities of this policy.

The colonial regime required each "Indian band" to select land that would be reserved for them and then officials would order that the land be surveyed. Hence, the name "Indian Reserves." Often this process was lengthy since, despite its promise that the bands would be able to pick their land, colonial officials frequently rejected the bands' selection and forced them to make alternate selections.[56] Given the vast size of the land and the fact that the Indians had to travel hundreds of kilometres on foot or, if lucky, by horse, this process took time. Occasionally, the colonial officials refused to supply rations to Indians until they selected land that met with official approval. Given their state of near-starvation, the Indians were forced to capitulate and move to land that the colonial officials preferred, albeit under duress.[57] Bands found themselves in an impossible situation when colonial officials—adhering to what they interpreted as the letter of the treaties rather than what the Indians considered to be their spirit—would refuse to supply bands with agricultural supplies, stock, and seed unless the surveys were complete and the bands were actively engaged in farming on their new reserves. However, without these supplies, stock, and seed, it was difficult, if not impossible, for the Indians to begin to farm on their new lands.[58] At a minimum, they would have required axes to cut trees, oxen to pull roots, and ploughs to break the land.

Once Indians and colonial officials agreed upon the land to be designated as reserves, the surveys completed, and the Indians having taken residence, colonial officials were still reluctant to fulfill the regime's obligations under the treaties. Even though game was becoming increasingly scarce, colonial officials were painstakingly slow to deliver farming implements, stock, and seed. Often, by the time the colonial officials deigned to fulfill the colonial regime's obligations, the seed arrived too late to plant in the short growing season of the Canadian Prairies.[59] Often the prospect of starvation forced Indians to go hunting rather than to plant even though they were sincere in their desire to become farmers. Indeed, the situation became so desperate that they often found themselves with nothing to eat but the little seed that they had. Sometimes, the Indians ate their dogs and horses to stay alive.[60]

Having served as Minister of the Interior until 1876, David Laird became both lieutenant-governor and Indian superintendent for the Northwest. After observing the reluctance of his superiors in Ottawa to fulfill their obligation to supply the Indians with farming stock and implements, "he warned that the government had to chose [sic] one of three policies: 'to help the Indians to farm and raise stock, to feed them, or to fight them.'"[61] His words fell upon deaf ears. In the early days of the numbered treaties, although anxious to begin farming and stay self-sufficient, Indians were essentially dependent upon the colonial regime not only for food rations, but also for clothing, shelter, and every form of household goods, which they had formerly obtained from the buffalo.

In the early days of the treaties, colonial officials expected the Indian superintendent not only to fulfill his own role but also to fulfill the role of farm instructor. This proved to be an impossible situation. Consequently, the Indian Branch of the Department of the Interior, which became the Department of Indian Affairs in 1880, began the process of hiring farm instructors. Most farm instructors came from eastern Canada and, regardless of their qualifications, were hired as political patronage appointments. Indeed, Prime Minister John A. MacDonald himself selected many farm instructors from a list of his loyal supporters.[62]

The first farm instructors began their travel to the Northwest in 1879, several years after the first of the numbered treaties was signed.[63] Few of the instructors were familiar with farming and environmental conditions on the Prairies, which differed significantly from those in the East. In most cases, the Indians knew more about growing conditions on the Prairies than the men sent to instruct them in farming did, although few Indians were familiar with the technology of farming. In later years, the farm instructors often came from the ranks of the many White men whose own farms had failed, which galled the Indians.[64] Farm instructors were also responsible for distributing rations from the colonial regime's storehouses. Under the government's "work for rations" program, all Indians, with the exception of the very elderly and the infirm, had to work for the superintendent or farm instructor to obtain the food needed to keep them from starving.[65] This work often took the form of building the farm instructor's home, barn, and sheds. Clearly, these men's time would have been better spent building their own homes and establishing their own farming operations. Having control over the regime's storehouses made the position of farm instructor a powerful one, indeed, for in times of famine, which were not infrequent, he held the power of life and death over the Indians. The Indian agent and farm instructor were the most powerful men on Indian reserves.

Over time, however, many Indians excelled in their agricultural pursuits. Rather than being pleased at the apparent success of the policies of their government, the White settlers who had become the Indians' neighbours reacted with jealousy and resentment. When Indians succeeded at farming, the White settlers attributed their success to the government assistance they received. When Indians failed, they blamed them for being lazy, incompetent savages. Hardly the attitude of people willing to welcome Indians who had enfranchised into their midst! The Indians were in an impossible situation, which they had no power to change or even influence. The settlers were potential voters, unlike the Indians who did not get the right to vote until the latter half of the twentieth century. When farmers protested vociferously to the government about the Indians becoming competitors in the agriculture business, the politicians listened and instructed the policy-makers to take action.

To placate the settlers, the colonial regime created a new policy based on pseudo-scientific thought. That policy would effectively curb the growth of

Indian farming operations rather than allow the Indians to become success-ful farmers who could compete in the free-market economy with the White settlers. Designed to transform the Indians into peasant farmers, the policy's stated intent was to enable them to develop "naturally" using only the most primitive of tools to farm small plots of land for their own subsistence, not for profit. Hayter Reed, deputy superintendent general of the Department of Indian Affairs, was the mastermind of this scheme. Justifying his posi-tion using the pseudo-scientific thought that was popular in the nineteenth century, Reed abruptly changed colonial policy. It was his position—the official position—that "Indians should not make an 'unnatural' leap from barbarism to a nineteenth-century environment, including all its appli-ances. The Indian was 'prone to desire to imitate the white man's nineteenth century civilization somewhat too hastily and too early.... The fact is often overlooked that these Indians who, a few years ago, were roaming savages, have been suddenly brought into contact with a civilization which has been the growth of centuries. An ambition has thus been created to emulate in a day that white men have become fitted for through the slow progress of gen-erations.'"[66] It appears that, in Reed's opinion, the Indians who had become very successful and competitive farmers were "unnatural" because they had earned their success in only a few years instead of through "the slow progress of generations." Clearly, there is an irony in Reed's argument. Although Reed came from a culture that valued artifice over nature and believed that the role of civilization was to tame nature, in this instance, he argued in favour of natural change rather than man-made social change. Reed set about, through the development of his peasant farmer policy, to thwart the Indians' "unnatural" advancement. Colonial officials instructed the farming instruc-tors to discourage the Indians from engaging in potentially lucrative grain farming and encourage, instead, their cultivation of small gardens comprised of root crops.[67] The results were disastrous for the Indians. The evidence clearly reveals that colonial officials, under Reed's direction, deliberately set Indians up to fail as farmers and used the agricultural and other policies to accomplish their efforts.

Policies that Controlled Freedom of Movement

Indians' ability to succeed at agriculture was also hampered by the poli-cies that created the pass system, one of the many negative outcomes of the second resistance in 1885. The resistance supplied the colonial regime with the justification to implement a draconian policy intentionally designed to monitor and control the Indians, whom White society had come to consider a threat to its safety.[68] In 1885, at the urging of the military, the policy-makers created the pass system to inhibit the Indians' ability to travel freely off their reserves. Reserves were posted with signs prohibiting trespassing, which prevented not only Whites but also the Indians' not-Indian relatives from entering. In the following years, at the request of the missionaries, colonial officials used the pass system to prevent Indians from visiting neighbouring reserves to take part in religious ceremonies, particularly the sun dance.

The pass system also impeded Indians' abilities to engage in agriculture because the Indian agent or farm instructor could refuse to issue passes when the Indians wanted to sell grain, for which they needed a permit, or to purchase supplies. The Indian agent and farm instructor controlled the people's movements and did not always have their best interests in mind. Carter explains: "The most notorious of the post-1885 measures was the pass system, first initiated on a large scale during the crisis of 1885. Those who wished to leave their reserves were required to obtain passes from the agent or farm instructor declaring the purpose of their absence, the length of absence, and whether or not they had permission to carry arms. The pass system was never a law; it was never codified in the *Indian Act*, and it can only be described as a 'policy.'"[69] The pass system made the Indians even more vulnerable to starvation than they were previously because it confined them to small pieces of land that were not always suitable for agriculture. When White settlers failed at farming, they could move on and try their hand at farming in other locations or work in the towns or cities. However, according to the *Indian Act* of 1876, no Indian was eligible to apply for a homestead.[70] The colonial regime, through its employees and law enforcement agencies as repressive state apparatus, would not allow Indians to leave their reserves without official permission, no matter how desperate their circumstances became, unless they applied for enfranchisement, the colonial tool for disappearing the Indians. To do so meant that they would be allowed to leave the reserves, but they could never return to family and community, because under the law they would no longer be Indians.

It is interesting to note that, because the pass system had no foundation in law, some police were reluctant to enforce it. Nevertheless, although the police would not always arrest Indians caught off reserve without a pass, the threat of punishment was always there. Ken Goodwill, an elder from the Standing Buffalo Reserve near Fort Qu'Appelle in southern Saskatchewan, remembers that when the police would not charge Indians for violating the pass policy, the Indian agent would. Then he would force them to appear in his own court on the reserve where he was judge, prosecutor, and jury. The

Indians charged had no one to act in their defence. Not surprisingly, the Indian agent would uphold his own arrest and judge the Indians as being guilty as charged. Goodwill recalls that the Indian agent would decide on their punishment and then mete it out.[71]

Clearly, the colonial officials used this policy that created the pass system as both a physical and psychological weapon, a blunt instrument with which they assaulted Indian people's sense of security. By doing so, they worked to break the spirits of Indian people. The government did not abolish the pass system until 1941.[72]

Policies that Controlled Indians' Consumption of Alcohol

In comparison to the agricultural policies and the permit system, the policy that prohibited the sale and consumption of liquor seems rather benign. However, Indigenous people agree that alcohol has caused enormous problems since Europeans introduced it in the early years of the fur trade, and the alcoholism that plagues Indigenous communities is always present in literary works. The Indigenous people of the territory that became the settler state of Canada did not produce alcohol, and, as a result, had no experience with alcohol until contact with the Europeans. Liquor, nevertheless, became an important trade item as early as the seventeenth century, and for over two hundred years was a staple trade good. Some fur traders used alcohol to control the Indians; however, it did not take long for the fur company executives to conclude that supplying Indians with liquor proved to be counterproductive. Drunken trappers did not harvest many furs. As the Indians became more sophisticated in the business of the fur trade, they began to use alcohol to control the fur trade company representatives by forcing them to compete with each other by offering stronger liquor in larger quantities.[73] All the while, the consumption of alcohol began to tear at the social fabric of Indigenous communities.

The European employees of the fur trade companies were the Indians' first models for alcohol consumption. In their study of alcohol and Indigenous peoples of the North, John Hamer and Jack Steinberg look a variety of scholarly arguments that try to explain why alcohol has had such a deleterious effect on the Indigenous peoples. They point out that some scholars argue that since the fur traders were often hard-drinking, violent men, theirs was the behaviour that Indians came to consider the norm when consuming alcohol. Drinking to excess, then, was the model.[74] Others, they note, claim that cultural differences between the Indians and the Europeans also caused Indians to drink because the culture of the Indigenous nations was based on binary oppositions such as "feast/famine, success/failure, power/powerless." These scholars suggest that it would then follow that, when consuming alcohol, Indians would be either sober or drunk with no middle ground.[75] Still other scholars contend that in cultures in which the prophetic nature of dreams and visions are valued as fundamental to spiritual life an alcohol-induced stupor became a way to fast-track visions.[76] Arthur J. Ray has a different explanation. He points out that because the success of the Indigenous societies depended on each individual working collaboratively for the betterment of the group, many individuals had no alternative but to suppress negative feelings about others. When they consumed alcohol, their inhibitions loosened, resentments came to the surface, and violence ensued.[77] For whatever reason, from early on Indians drank to get drunk, and drinking caused problems in their communities.

A popular explanation for the widespread alcoholism among Indigenous people argues that we have a genetic inability to control alcohol. However, since alcoholism was not a ruinous problem among Indigenous people until assimilation subjected them to extreme dislocation, this argument lacks credence. If Indigenous people were handicapped by the "gene for alcoholism," the same must be said of the Europeans, since those subjected to conditions of extreme dislocation also fell into it, almost universally.[78] Bruce K. Alexander points out that as a result of extreme dislocation among the Orkney men employed by the Hudson's Bay Company, "alcoholism became rampant" even though the Orkney men had been selected "because of their characteristic sobriety and obedience."[79] It is important to note that the alcoholism that has become rampant among Indigenous people in Canada can be found in every former imperial colony around the world where the colonized experience disempowerment and extreme dislocation.[80]

At the request of the missionaries, who considered alcohol to be an impediment to their evangelical mission, and the traders, who had witnessed how alcohol could be harmful to business, the fur companies attempted to control or even ban its use in trade by developing policies intended to control their employees. Enforcement, however, was impossible and only became minimally effective much later when the fur trade had virtually disappeared. As time passed, Indigenous people also witnessed the damage that alcohol was doing to their communities and petitioned colonial officials to take action against the sellers. In his 1874 meetings with Reverend John McDougall, a representative of the Canadian government, Chief Crow-that-Makes-the-Large-Footprint, who spoke on behalf of the Siksika people, described the effect of alcohol on the Siksika, including the American whiskey traders' relentless pursuit of their business and the community's inability to come to terms with this problem: "If left to ourselves we are gone. The whiskey brought among us by our traders is fast killing us off and we are powerless before the evil—totally unable to resist the temptation to drink when brought in contact with the Whiteman's water. We are also unable to pitch anywhere that the trader cannot follow us. Our horses, buffalo robes and other articles of trade go for whiskey. A large number of our people have killed one another and perished in various ways under the influence and now that we hear of our great mother sending her soldiers into our country for our good we are glad."[81] It is clear that although Chief Crow-that-Makes-the-Large-Footprint beseeched the colonial regime to use the law to stop the American whiskey trade, he did not ask that the colonial regime develop laws to criminalize his people for consuming alcohol. Yet, that is exactly how the regime chose to solve the problem. Clearly, colonial bureaucrats believed that the Indians were more easily controlled than the American whiskey traders.

The colonial regime passed a law whereby any Indian caught consuming alcohol would be guilty of criminal offence. (Although the provincial governments have jurisdiction over the sale of alcohol, the federal government controls the Criminal Code and the Indians.) This law became part of the *Indian Act* of 1876 and remained in effect until the *Indian Act* underwent major revisions in 1951. One of the revisions permitted Indians to possess small amounts of alcohol, but they could still face criminal charges if they were drunk. No other Canadians lived under such scrutiny, nor were they subject to such severe punishment for a relatively minor offence. In 1960, the Supreme Court of Canada finally struck down this law finding it to be contrary to Canada's fledgling Bill of Rights.[82]

Although alcohol has been present in Indigenous communities for more than three hundred years and has caused untold suffering, some Indian people have come to equate the right to consume alcohol with social and legal equality. To these people, any laws designed to restrict their consumption of alcohol are symbols of the patronizing attitudes of the imperial lawmakers. In a distorted leap of logic, the freedom to consume alcohol, for some Indigenous people, has become synonymous with freedom from colonial rule. In his humorous short story "Don't Call Me No Name!" Basil Johnston describes the lengths two World War II veterans go in order to be served alcohol. The protagonists, Meegis and Konauss, like many Indigenous people, consider the consumption of alcohol a symbolic activity. Unfortunately,

people whose psychosocial connections have been breached are suscep-
tible to addictions, and alcohol addiction is one that has plagued fractured
Indigenous communities. Thus, every work of literature studied in the chapters that follow references alcoholism and its devastating consequences.

Policies that Controlled Indian Education

Alcohol consumption is not the only area of jurisdictional conflict for Status
Indians. Because they fall under the jurisdiction of the federal government,
Status Indians often fall into a jurisdictional quagmire when dealing with areas designated as provincial responsibility under the Canadian Constitution.
Even though education in Canada falls under provincial jurisdiction, the
education of Status Indians became the responsibility of the federal government. Thus, it was the federal government that was responsible for the policy
that created residential schools for Indian children.

Of all the policies that the colonial regime initiated, the policy that established and regulated the residential school system had, and continues to have,
the most far-reaching destructive effects on both Indians and not-Indians in
this country. Over the last twenty years, many former students have publicly
revealed that school officials abused them in every way possible: culturally,
physically, emotionally, sexually, and spiritually. Government and church records not only confirm these reports, they also provide evidence that school
officials neglected the students by failing often to adequately provide the
necessities of life: food, clothing, health care, and, ironically, education.
Currently former students have filed more than 10,000 civil suits against the
Government of Canada and the churches that operated the schools for their
abuse of Indigenous children.[83] The Anglican Church of Canada teeters on
the brink of bankruptcy because of these suits. John S. Milloy writes that
"in thought and deed the establishment of this school system was an act of
profound cruelty rooted in non-Aboriginal pride and intolerance and in the
certitude and insularity of purported cultural superiority."[84] Former students
agree.

Colonial officials reasoned that, by controlling the education of Indian
children, they could bring about the complete assimilation of the remnants of
the Indian tribes into civilized society. To that end, they looked for an appropriate model after which to design an educational system for Indian children.
Indian leaders agreed that their children needed to learn "the cunning of
the Whiteman"[85] and favoured the day schools that had been operating on a
number of reserves for many years. The colonial officials disagreed. Because
the children spent the greater part of their days at home, their families

exerted a stronger influence than did schools. The children who attended day school were not being assimilated into colonial society. They still thought and behaved as Indians. Even worse, the colonial officials discovered that these children could become formidable political adversaries when they merged the European-style schooling with their traditional Indigenous education. This had already happened with some of the highly educated Métis of Red River and was beginning to happen with some of the graduates of Indian day schools. Day-school education had armed these children with the skills they needed to negotiate and argue with colonial officials and had made their graduates skilled advocates on behalf of their people. This was not the end that the colonial regime desired.[86] Another alternative, then, one that the regime could control, was necessary. Turning their gaze to the few church-run residential schools that were already in operation and to the American industrial schools for Indians, colonial officials found the model that would become the cornerstone of their assimilationist policies.[87]

The colonial officials and the churches considered adult Indians lost causes but believed that there could be hope for the children if all things Indian were eradicated from their thinking. They reasoned that, by removing Indian children from their families and communities and placing them in an environment where they would be taught to think, act, and believe as civilized Christians, Indian children could be completely resocialized. In his 1887 memorandum to Prime Minister John A. MacDonald, then Deputy Superintendent of Indian Affairs Lawrence Vankoughnet quotes a clergyman whose words formed the principles for the residential school policy; he writes:

> Give me the children and you may have the parents, or words to that effect, were uttered by a zealous divine in his anxiety to add to the number of whom his Church called her children. And the principle laid down by that astute reasoner is an excellent one on which to act in working out that most difficult problem—the intellectual emancipation of the Indian, and its natural sequel, his elevation to a status equal to that of his white brother. This can only be done through education…. Only by a persistent continuance in a thoroughly systematic course of educating (using the word in its fullest and most practical sense) the children, will the final hoped and long striven for result be attained.[88]

Since Christianization was a component of the "long striven for result[s]," Indians could not be assimilated into civilized society if they were not

Christianized. Consequently, the colonial bureaucrats assigned the churches a central role in the implementation of the policy. The residential schools would become a concrete representation of the colonial regime's "ideological commitment to suppress the native culture as rapidly as possible and fashion a new generation of Indian children raised in isolation from their parents, in the image of the white man."[89] Thus, the Indians who did not disappear as a result of disease would disappear by way of education.

The churches already had experience delivering European Christian education to Indian communities because re-education had always comprised an important component of their missionary agenda. The churches had established both day schools and the first residential schools many years before the colonial regime considered positioning schooling at the centre of its Indian policy. Day schools had achieved a moderate degree of success, but church officials had difficulties persuading Indian parents to send their children away from their communities to attend the boarding schools. Indian parents wanted their children to attend school to learn the "cunning of the Whiteman"; however, they also wanted their children to be educated in their own communities where the extended family was the cornerstone of not only their societies but also their educational system. Furthermore, Indigenous people doted on their children and wanted to keep them at home where they would be safe, which was another thing that the colonial officials found problematic. Because of their strong familial ties, few students stayed for long at boarding schools where they experienced great loneliness. Some clergy, such as Father Lacombe in Alberta, recognized this as a problem and "did their 'best to prevent these departures,' but to no avail. The constant 'excuse to go,' rooted in the pain of separation, 'was and is always the same—We are lonesome.' Nothing would make them stay."[90]

In addition to being situated far away from the children's loved ones, residential schools had earned a poor reputation in many Indian communities. Former students returned with stories of inadequate food and abuse at the hands of the staff, and as a result many students refused to stay at school. Rather than improving conditions as a means to improve student retention, the churches complained relentlessly to the colonial regime. As a result, in 1920, the colonial regime amended the *Indian Act* to make school attendance mandatory for every Indian child between the ages of seven and fifteen. If the children did not attend, truant officers or police would investigate. The courts would fine or even incarcerate parents who did not comply.[91] From 1920 onward, the policy that created and regulated residential schools and their students would eventually affect every Indian in Canada.

Beneath their rhetoric of noblesse oblige and moral superiority, the colonial regime had other, more self-serving, motives for removing children
from their homes and placing them in the residential schools. By the time
of Confederation, Indian communities were in a severely weakened state.
Disease had reduced their populations while the number of European immigrants continued to grow. Indians had suffered severe economic losses
because the colonizers no longer needed them as important trading partners.
At the same time, their traditional economy was laid to waste as European
immigrants and their descendants claimed more and more land. Buffalo
herds on the Great Plains were shrinking in number. Indian nations were
concerned for their very survival. Yet, despite their weakened state, the colonial regime and their settlers still feared the Indians. A goal of the Canadian
government policy that mandated attendance at residential school was to
coerce Indian people to obey the dictates of the empire. Their means of
achieving this goal was to hold Indian children hostage during their stay in
residential school. Both churches and colonial officials agreed that Indians
would be less likely to engage in hostile and disruptive acts if their children
remained in the custody of the schools.[92]

Residential education became the keystone of the colonizers' Indian
policy, whose aim was to eradicate all things Indian in Indian children.
The classroom activities comprised but a small component of the over-
all assimilation strategies that the regime ordered the schools to employ.
Each school was to become "a circle—an all-encompassing environment
of resocialization. The curriculum was not simply an academic schedule
or practical trades training but comprised the whole life of the child in the
school."[93] Understanding culture as the complete life way of a people, the
regime mandated school officials to change every aspect of the children's
culture: their dress, food, language, religion, manner of working, and interpersonal relations. When they first arrived at school, school officials issued
new clothes to the children and destroyed their old ones. The next act was to
cut their hair. Agnes Grant, in her study of the effects of residential schools
on former students, describes how soul-destroying this seemingly trivial
alteration in appearance was to many Indian children.[94] But changing the
students' appearance was only the beginning. Understanding that language
is a critical vehicle of cultural transmission, colonial officials identified
eradication of the students' Native languages, followed by their acquisition of
English, as paramount to their resocialization efforts. Accordingly, colonial
officials developed a policy that ordered schools to prohibit students from
speaking in their Native languages with a goal of ensuring that students

spoke and thought in English. To achieve that goal, school officials punished students who they caught speaking in their Native languages. Often that punishment was swift and severe.[95] Many former residential school students talk about "losing" their ability to speak in their Native languages. What is more likely is that their language development was curtailed because they could only speak covertly and only to other children. By the time they left school, many students had forgotten some words and had never learned others. Speaking only to other children, except during brief holiday periods, these children had had no chance to expand and enrich their knowledge of their Native languages and to acquire the sophistication in language expected of adults.[96] They continued to speak as if they were children. Most of these children became only minimally proficient in English, often learning their new language from francophone priests and nuns who were barely conversant in English themselves. Although the students now dressed like White children and spoke a nominal amount of English, they still thought, worked, and related like Indians, albeit confused and frightened ones.

Colonial officials planned that the Canadian schools, like their US industrial counterparts, would teach basic literacy and numeracy for part of the school day with the remainder of the day devoted to instruction in the trades for boys and domestic education for girls, thereby applying the same gendered division of labour as was the norm of the colonizer culture. This segregation of the curriculum by gender as defined by European patriarchal conventions and its subsequent privileging of the masculine was very damaging to Indian students and to future generations of Indian people. Although the division of labour in Indian societies was typically gendered, the gender roles were not the same as those of European societies, and the masculine was not automatically privileged. In those nations that engaged in agriculture, for example, farming was typically women's work. Women from those nations would sneer at any men who attempted to usurp their role by attempting to farm. Indeed, some Indian societies considered the women to be the owners of the land.[97] How shocked young Indian boys were when school officials ordered them to work on the school farms. By attempting to make them over into farmers, the school officials effectively emasculated these young men.

Gender complementarity was more often the norm in Indigenous cultures than was the gender hierarchy that prevailed in colonial society. Often women were strong political leaders or healers, and nowhere in this country were women mere appendages to their men. Together, men and women formed the circle—a central symbol in many Indigenous nations—with each gender comprising and supporting one-half of the circle that was their community. Women and men were deemed to be of equal worth because, without the support of both genders, the circle would collapse. In the same way, women and men in Indigenous societies fulfilled roles and functions that were complementary in order to support their communities and, thus, ensure the survival of their people. By imposing a European patriarchal and hierarchical model of gender roles and values onto the curriculum of residential schools, the colonial regime committed another direct assault on Indian cultures. Through the curriculum, they taught Indian children to devalue their own societal norms and, worse yet, to devalue the women in their communities—their grandmothers, mothers, aunts, sisters, future wives, and daughters.

Because the colonial regime did not provide the schools with adequate funding, school officials had to find ways to make up the chronic funding shortfalls. Under the industrial school model, each student worked in a trade that supported the operation of the schools, which were designed to be self-sustaining. Boys worked in the barns and chicken coops, and girls worked in the tailor shops and kitchens. School officials sold agricultural produce to make ends meet rather than using it to provide students with healthy diets. Although their work supported the production of food, the students' diets were often poor, and the quantity of food they received was minimal.[98] Furthermore, because the colonial regime funded them on a per-student basis, the schools admitted as many Indian children as possible resulting in over-crowded conditions where diseases, such as tuberculosis, flourished. Because the students' diets were poor, their health care inadequate, and their living conditions cramped, the death rates of Indian students were inordinately high. Ironically, without the children's labour, the schools could not function as businesses, yet running the business of the schools became more important than providing a good, or even adequate, education for the students. At many schools, the students knew that food was available and were aware that the staff ate a much more substantial and appealing diet than they did. This has become a theme in literature about residential school, such as Maddie Harper's *Mush Hole*, Lee Maracle's "Charlie," and Oskiniko Larry Loyie's "Ora Pro Nobis," to name but a few. The children's awareness of this injustice—of how little value both colonial regime and churches place on them—caused them to feel enormous bitterness.

Perhaps it was the emotional starvation, rather than the physical, that has had the most damaging effects not only on the children who attended the residential schools but on their children and grandchildren as well. Students felt bitter about the absence of emotional support and the cruelty of the punishments that school officials meted out at school. Because many staff believed that Indians indulged and spoiled their children, school officials were very deliberate in their efforts to ensure that no form of emotional comfort was available for the children.[99] To that end, they instituted the truly mean-spirited policy of discouraging student contact with siblings of the same sex and prohibiting contact with siblings of the opposite sex.

Government policies of fiscal restraint resulted in the residential schools being rarely able to attract top-quality staff. Few teachers considered residential schools desirable places to work, and as a result most top-quality teachers, and indeed even mediocre ones, sought employment elsewhere. The challenges of resocializing a people whom most Whites thought of as savages while being housed in chronically underfunded, isolated institutions made residential school employment unattractive to teachers who had other options. Thus, residential schools became convenient "dumping ground[s] for less-competent church staff."[100] Not surprisingly, the teachers and staff who were hired often lacked the stock of educational resources and strategies that might have enhanced the prospects of success for the colonial regime's grand experiment in resocialization.[101] Without such resources to draw upon, teachers and staff often turned to violence—both physical and emotional—to coerce children to learn and obey. The schools' primary focus quickly shifted from resocializing Indian children into civilized people to enforcing order and discipline. School officials punished students cruelly in a variety of circumstances.

However, there was an even darker side to residential school staffing. Because they afforded staff unlimited access to children, absolute power over those children, and little scrutiny, residential schools attracted disproportionate numbers of pedophiles, who were free to wreak havoc on generations of Indian children. It should come as no surprise to learn that, as time progressed and students suffered physical, sexual, and emotional abuse at the hands of the school staff, some learned to abuse each other. This is part of the psychopathology of abuse. Children learned from example and experience. Often student abuse of other students was institutionalized and incorporated into the structure of the schools. School officials appointed children to monitor, and often discipline, other children—a practice that missionaries also employed with adult Indians to monitor the behaviour of their converts on the reserves.[102] In "Returning,"[103] Louise Halfe remembers "the girl with the big lips" who hit the other children with rules, abusing them on behalf of the nuns. By demonstrating favouritism to some children and not others, school officials effectively divided the students as a community and instilled fear, suspicion, and distrust. Many former students clearly remember learning to abuse each other, both verbally and physically.[104] As a result, the children learned to mistrust their classmates and isolate themselves from others. And, above all, the children felt anger but, having no outlet to express their anger, they repressed their feelings and suffered intense shame.

Shame had been part of the hidden curriculum of residential schools since their inception.[105] In the minds of the school officials, both teachers and staff, the Indian children in their care were savages from an inferior race in need of civilizing. They did not hesitate to communicate this to the children, and, not surprisingly, the children learned to feel ashamed of their very identities as Indigenous people. Shame and fear were also part of the missionary agenda of the schools. As part of the process of converting Indians to Christianity, school officials taught students that they were pagan savages and, therefore, would burn in hell if they persisted in practising their traditional ways. Beatrice Lavallee, an elder from the Piapot First Nation, told how, as a young child, she would on countless occasions come home from residential school terrified that her *Kohkom* (Nêhiyawêwin for "your grandmother") would go to hell because she was not a Christian.[106] Like Lavallee, the students were isolated from any alternative discourse and, as a result, believed their teachers.

Predictably, Indigenous children at residential school began to exhibit behaviour that today would be labelled post-traumatic shock response. PTSR coupled with cultural differences resulted in students being reluctant to make eye contact or speak up in class. Having experience teaching White children only, many staff members interpreted this behaviour as a sign of their students' inherent racial inferiority.[107] Rarely did these supposed educational experts bear in mind that the students were terrified. Students were not afraid to tell their families and communities about the physical and emotional abuse that they experienced at residential school, however. Stories of beatings at the hands of school officials were commonplace in Indigenous communities, and students learned quickly that their families had neither the power nor the influence necessary to protect them. In his memoir *Indian School Days*, Basil Johnston explains how students often felt shame for and anger towards their parents because they were unable to protect them from the agents of the colonial regime.[108] Neither the family nor the children had the power to stop the physical and emotional abuse that the children endured at school. Indeed, their powerlessness seemed to be proof of what the schools taught them. If the power to defend one's self and one's family is a measurement of worth, then Indigenous people had less worth than White people did.

The students who had been sexually abused were much more reticent to tell family members about their experiences—feelings of terror caused them to keep silent. The foundation of the contract implicit between sexual abusers and their victims is silence, and abusers use every method at their disposal to ensure that their victims keep the secret. Although stories of the sexual abuse of Indian children did not become public until well after the last residential school closed, the consequences of this abuse revealed itself in Indigenous communities where some children who had been abused grew up to abuse others. In "Nitotem,"[109] Louise Halfe describes how a young man rages against women on the reserve, raping them while remembering the nun who abused him.

Given the children's soul-destroying experiences at the residential schools, it should come as no surprise to learn that the students continued to suffer emotionally and socially long after they left school. The negative consequences of the education that students received at the residential schools became apparent as early on as 1913, when Indian agents began to notify the colonial officials that when the children returned to their reserve they did not display any of the positive effects of education that the officials had projected. Instead, they were "stranded between cultures, deviants from the norms of both."[110] The schools' wanton disregard for the identity formation of their students and the way that those students fit into their societies tore at the social fabric of Indigenous society and affected relationships within Indigenous communities and with settler society. In its 1992 memorandum to the deputy minister of Indian Affairs, the Assembly of First Nations explains: "The residential school led to a disruption in the transference of parenting skills from one generation to the next. Without these skills, many survivors had had difficulties in raising their own children. In residential schools they learned that adults often exert power and control through abuse. The lessons learned in childhood are often repeated in adulthood with the result that many survivors of the residential school system often inflict abuse on their own children. These children in turn use the same tools on their own children."[111] Therefore, the pattern continues so that, often, Indigenous people who did not attend residential school still exhibit the same behaviours as those who did. Both Vera Manuel in her play "Strength of Indian Women"[112] and Robert Arthur Alexie in his novel *Porcupines and China Dolls* [113] describe the intergenerational effects of residential schools.

By the second or third generation of Indigenous children attending residential school, "the Department [of Indian Affairs] had to struggle with the consequences for Aboriginal people of Canadian economic development and its own assimilative policies: broken communities, dysfunctional families, and their 'neglected' children."[114] Churchill points out that

> in the end, of course, the racial biases of the settlers were such that there were precious few jobs for graduates, even of those demeaning varieties. Thus "disemployed," they were mostly forced into a posture of seemingly immutable material dependency upon those who most despised them. What the residential schools in effect produced were generations of increasingly desperate and dysfunctional human beings, incapable of valuing themselves as Indians and neither assimilated nor assimilable into the dominant society which had rendered them thus. Given the sheer impossibility of their situation, the self-negating pathologies evidenced by residential school graduates were, or should have been, perfectly predictable.[115]

As part of the colonial regime's policy of assimilation, residential schools failed. Few students succeeded academically, and those who lived to return to their communities came home emotionally wounded and uneducated in the ways of both White and Indigenous societies. Residential schools, then, have contributed to the positioning of Indigenous people as an underclass in Canadian society.

The regime was well aware of the failure of its policy of assimilation as early as 1946, following receipt of a report on that policy written by a joint committee of the House of Commons and Senate.[116] Nevertheless, the colonial regime persisted with the policies with only minor revisions until the last school closed in 1986. Buckley writes that "the tragedy is the educational system that they got, which no way fitted them for Canadian society. It was a cheap and cheerless package judged good enough for an unimportant minority."[117] The damage that these schools inflicted on Indigenous communities is unparalleled.

Policies that Governed "Not-Indians"

By 1867, the year of Confederation, the halfbreed/métis/Métis/mixed-blood/country-born people, a segment of that collective of Indigenous people that

I have termed "not-Indians," had existed for generations in every area of Canada that had come into contact with the fur trade. For the sake of convenience, I will refer to these people as the Métis, which has become the "polite" term—apparently in contemporary Canada "halfbreed" sounds better in French—recognizing that not all members of this group historically referred to themselves as Métis. A significant constituency of Métis were almost impossible to distinguish from their Indian relatives, much to the dismay of the colonial officials charged with the responsibility of negotiating the treaties. These people made their living from the land either by hunting, fishing, and trapping in the woodlands or by hunting buffalo on the Great Plains. They spoke Indian languages, and although many were Catholic, some, such as renowned Métis leader Gabriel Dumont, followed Indian spiritual practices. Other Métis, typically but not always those of French descent, had developed their own unique culture and language and were practising Catholics. Most of this group worked as freighters or as free traders, although some engaged in agriculture or commerce. It would not be unusual for people belonging to either of these groups to be multilingual, speaking Michif, the language of the Métis, along with one or more Indian languages. Many also spoke French or English. The Métis who belonged to both of these groups were highly mobile, some living a nomadic lifestyle while others maintained a home base but spent most of their time travelling. Still others, especially those who had received European-style schooling, continued to intermarry with White settlers, both francophone and anglophone, and were well on their way to being assimilated into White society. Although this attempt to classify the Métis is an obvious oversimplification, it does provide the reader with some understanding of the people so as to better understand how different sectors of Métis society were affected by colonial policies.

Although the colonial policy-makers virtually ignored the Métis, they did not go away, and with no land or resource base, they posed as much of an obstacle to settlement as did the Indians, as the colonizers found out when they encountered Métis resistance.[118] Negotiating with the Métis might have saved the colonial regime enormous cost, both human and economic, but they balked at participating in such negotiations. An examination of prevailing attitudes of the time regarding miscegenation suggests an explanation for the colonial officials' reluctance to deal with the Métis. Characteristic of colonial thinking, these attitudes constitute yet another binary. Jacqueline Peterson describes how, in the nineteenth century, "the cultural classification system" that was dominant in the eighteenth century "was being challenged and supplanted by a system based on pseudo-scientific ideas about race."[119] These pseudo-scientific ideas about race created the attitude that constituted one pole of this binary: that the Métis, as people who were created when the civilized race mixed with the savage, would naturally inherit the worst characteristics of both parent races.[120] It is from this school of thought that the Métis came to be called the "One-And-A-Half-Men": half-Indian, half-White, half-devil.[121] On the other pole was the missionary way of thinking: that the Métis, like the Indian, could be saved. Their mission was dependent on this way of thinking, for if this were untrue, their evangelism would have no purpose. Sandwiched between these two poles was a school of thought that represented a synthesis of the missionary attitude and the pseudo-scientific: that the Métis were significantly more redeemable than the Indians because the superior White blood had diluted—over-powered if you will—the savage Indian blood.[122] Nowhere in an examination of the prevailing attitudes is there a suggestion that the colonizer culture might accept the Métis as equals or welcome them as neighbours.

Although mixed-blood people existed across Canada, it was in the Red River Settlement, in the area now known as the Province of Manitoba, that these people became, for a time, a political force that effectively resisted imperial expansion. To lead their resistance, the Métis of the Red River Settlement formed a provisional government in 1870 to protect their rights to the land and to join the new country of Canada on their own terms. The Métis who negotiated with the colonial regime to form the agreement that resulted in the creation of the Province of Manitoba were well educated according to European standards, and the result of their negotiations, the *Manitoba Act* of 1870, was a major victory for Indigenous rights. Although they received none of the meagre benefits that their Indian relatives received, their victory lay in the colonial regime's recognition that they did exist and that it had obligations to them as Indigenous people.[123] However, in the same way that the colonial regime failed the Indians in its implementation of the agreements made in the treaties, the regime failed the Métis in its implementation of the *Manitoba Act*.

Having no idea how many Métis lived in the area, colonial officials attempted to conduct a census of the area in 1870 and 1875. Unfortunately, a census can only be successful if the enumerators are able to find the people. Because many of the Métis did not live sedentary lives, they were elsewhere at the time of the census. It is difficult, and some would argue foolhardy, to live a sedentary life in a floodplain. As a result, the enumerators did not count all the Métis, which delayed the finalization of their land claims. The

Métis' rights to the land that was their home were further eroded when the colonial regime passed "a succession of amendments to Sections 31 and 32 of the Manitoba Act in the 1870s [that] altered the spirit and terms of the legislation, ultimately dispossessing the Métis or isolating them from land economy."[124] While Métis leaders engaged in sometimes heated negotiations with colonial officials in an attempt to protect the interests of their people—especially those who were illiterate and/or those who did not speak English—the colonial regime allowed White settlers to "pre-empt" land that had not been surveyed and before the Métis had chosen their land.[125] The process was riddled with tension.

The requirement that the Métis apply for their land must have been an affront to those Métis who had lived for many years on land that they considered their own. However, if they did not apply for their land, the colonial regime would grant it as homesteads to White settlers. In the end, although some Métis applied for land, many others did not.[126] Some Métis were intimidated by the requirement that they "make improvements" while others did not understand the implications of failing to apply. Still others found the prospect of settling down on one piece of land objectionable after having had a lifetime of freedom to travel at will and to reside wherever they pleased. The prospect of living in integrated communities with White settlers for neighbours was objectionable to many Métis, given the racist attitudes of the times, especially those from families who supported the Métis provisional government at Red River. As a result, many of these Métis migrated further north into the bush and far away from the farmland that the White settlers coveted. Sadly, they did not understand the future implications of their decision, in that the colonial regime would deem them to be squatters—on their own territory.

Other Métis moved further west into the North-West Territories hoping that White settlement would not follow them. That was not to be the case. In 1872 the colonial regime passed the *Dominion Lands Act*, which it designed to open the North-West Territories for settlement. Although the original Act ignored the Métis, in 1879 the colonial regime revised the Act to acknowledge that the Métis, as Indigenous people, had a legitimate claim to the land. By revising the Act, the regime granted colonial officials authorization "to satisfy any claims existing in connection with the extinguishment of the Indian title, preferred by mixed-bloods resident in the North-West Territories outside the limits of Manitoba...by granting land to such persons to such extent and on such terms and conditions, as may be deemed expedient."[127] While the colonial regime acknowledged that the Métis had valid claims to the land, it did nothing to settle those claims. The consequences of its inaction were tragic for both the Métis and their Indian allies.

To realize its "nation-building" scheme, the colonial regime needed to settle all the land from Atlantic to Pacific with White immigrants, and considered the Indigenous people, both Indian and not-Indian, impediments to its plans. For its scheme to succeed, the regime needed settlers. To that end, it advertised for immigrants throughout Europe and the United States, offering vast tracts of cheap, unoccupied land for anyone willing to work it. Scores of people responded. Thus, the Métis who moved west found only a temporary reprieve. Witnessing the deluge of White settlers moving west and settling the land, the Métis, in fear and frustration, took up arms against the colonial regime in 1885. Unfortunately, the Métis resistance failed, and as a result many Métis and Indians died in battle while others were executed or incarcerated. Only then did the colonial regime begin to settle their land claims by issuing "halfbreed scrip," pieces of paper that could be exchanged for land or for cash to be used to buy land.

The scrip system was a disaster not only for those Métis who did not speak or write English but also for many English-speaking Métis. Without fluency in English, many were swindled of their scrip. Others suffered extreme poverty and desperation both in Manitoba and in the North-West Territories and sold their scrip to land speculators and soon had nothing.[128] In comparison to these poor souls, Indians with status looked relatively affluent with land, rations, and assistance to start farming. Like their relatives in Manitoba, many Métis of the North-West Territories had no alternative but to become squatters on land ill-suited for agriculture because it was the only land not coveted by the White settlers at that time. (Later, when the Whites saw the potential for mining and forestry in this land, they would come to covet this land as well.) Other Métis moved back to the land that they had occupied before the Resistance, especially the rich farmland on the banks of the South Saskatchewan River, where they lived in relative comfort for decades until increased European settlement and its accompanying racism made their lives more difficult. Unlike their Indian relatives whose daily lives were controlled by colonial officials and their policies, the Métis had little official contact with the colonial regime, which believed that it had no responsibility for their welfare or for the welfare of those other Indigenous people it deemed "not-Indians."

Not-Indian Identity and the Policy Void

The colonial officials developed no policies to ease the Métis' transition into colonial society even though it was as foreign to many Métis as it was to the Indians. In her autobiography *Halfbreed*, Maria Campbell describes how the government offered no assistance to help them take up agriculture. They did not think about their education and health care until almost five decades had passed. By issuing scrip, the colonial regime regarded its responsibilities to the Métis as having come to an end, having determined that the Métis "held no special status" once their claim to Aboriginal title was extinguished.[129] It was not until well into the twentieth century that some provincial governments developed policies to address the well-being of the Métis. These policies, however, typically served the wants of those regimes, not the needs of the Métis. Indeed, few governments considered the Métis at all when they developed policies, only doing so when they occupied land that the regimes wanted either for settlement or for the exploitation of natural resources. To those Métis who were well on their way to assimilating into colonial society, this policy void had little effect, but these people were few in number. For those Indigenous people who were unable to assimilate and who were officially designated "not-Indian," this policy void was a catastrophe and, ironically, every bit as damaging as the regime's "Indian" policies.

Unlike the Indians who encountered a policy backlash in the form of the pass system, which the colonial regime imposed following the Resistance of 1885, the Métis had no oppressive policies created specifically for them. Living in the policy void, they did, however, encounter overt racial discrimination from both the settlers and the agents of the regime. Some time following the first Resistance at Red River, the word "Métis" became a pejorative term.[130] In many ways the Métis, especially those who were landless, were more vulnerable to the settlers' harassment than were their Indian relatives who lived in isolation on the lands reserved for them under the omnipresent watch of the Indian agents and the farm instructors. Furthermore, when the Métis became targets of harassment by the settlers, they could not count on the police and other colonial authorities for protection. Indeed, the agents of both the repressive state apparatus, the police and later the social workers, along with the ideological state apparatus, teachers and clergy, were often as guilty of persecuting the Métis as the settlers were. Thus, identifying as Métis became a passport not only to poverty but also to persecution. Not surprisingly, many Métis who were visibly and culturally able began to deny their identity because this was the only way to protect themselves and their children. In her study of the Métis of the Interlake area of Manitoba, Nicole St-Onge reported that although many Métis would admit to having Indigenous ancestry, they would deny being Métis.[131] In fact, this practice was common for many years, and it is only in the last three decades that many Métis have felt safe enough to acknowledge publicly their own identities. Clearly, denying oneself must come with an emotional cost, and that cost is shame of one's own identity and of one's people.

Still, the ranks of the "not-Indians" continued to grow as a result of the "success" of the *Indian Act* as an assimilationist patriarchal policy created to reduce the number of Status Indians. The *Indian Act* removed Indian "status" from Indian women who married Whites and not-Indians. In its implementation of the *Indian Act*, the settler government "automatically and continuously 'bled off' people from [Indian] communities without the need for other policies of removal."[132] This practice continued until Bill C-31 amended the *Indian Act* in 1985. Despite their numbers being radically reduced when Bill C-31 enabled many to apply for Indian status, it is the Métis, rather than the Indians, who today comprise the fastest growing ethnic group in Canada today, even though there are few tangible benefits to identifying as Métis. In his analysis of the Government of Canada census data as it pertains to Aboriginal people, demographer Andrew J. Siggner has observed a trend in which people who formerly admitted to having Indigenous ancestry but refused to identify as Indigenous people are now identifying as Indigenous people.[133]

Policies that Controlled the Education of Not-Indians

In their original plan, colonial officials determined that residential schools would educate both Indians and Métis children. Later they expanded their plan to include Inuit children. Because the Government of Canada claimed that Métis education fell under provincial jurisdiction, the schools became known as "Indian" residential schools, and few Métis attended. However, "if the government or churches perceived Métis children as living an 'Indian mode' of life, as savages or as un-Christianized, they were more likely to take the children into the residential schools."[134] The churches also created a few residential schools in remote areas of Alberta, Saskatchewan, and Manitoba[135] specifically for Métis and non-Status Indian children, but the federal government refused to pay for the education of these children, claiming that they fell under provincial jurisdiction. The students who attended these schools suffered the same abuses—emotional, spiritual, physical, and sexual—as did the ones who attended the Indian residential schools.[136]

Money, and the Government of Canada's unwillingness to invest adequate amounts in Indigenous education, has always influenced policy. Indian residential schools were chronically and consistently underfunded because colonial officials took the position that the churches could take care of the children for less money than they claimed they needed, and "belief became policy."[137] As a result, the per capita payments from the Government of Canada to the churches that ran the schools were set at an inordinately low rate.[138] Because funding for the Indian residential schools was always inadequate, the churches gave preference to funded students, the Status Indian children sponsored by the federal government. If churches wanted to educate Métis children, they had to cover the cost. Often, churches would accept Métis students into Indian residential schools as acts of charity only when there were vacancies; however, this charity ceased when there were paying students (Status Indians or Inuit) ready to fill the seats.[139] When there were sufficient numbers of funded students to replace the non-paying Métis children, the churches sent Métis students home.[140] In other instances, the churches accepted Métis children as "day students." In her story "There Is A Place,"[141] Tantoo Cardinal explains how Métis children were always aware that, as charity cases, they were of less value than the other children at the Indian residential schools. Because more Indian children than Métis attended, the policy that created and managed them had a larger effect on Indians than it did on Métis in that fewer Métis suffered the abuses that were common at residential schools and more Métis retained their Indigenous languages. However, because of familial relationships and frequent intermarriage with Indians, residential schools still had a profound and negative effect on Métis people.

Before Confederation, the Métis of the North-Western Territory controlled and managed the education of their children. Often the teachers were priests, but sometimes they came from the ranks of the Métis themselves. As a result, most Métis had some European-style schooling, and some had even gone to eastern Canada or to Europe for advanced schooling. This situation changed after the imperial powers passed the *British North America Act* in 1867, under which education was deemed to be the responsibility of the provincial governments while Indians were the responsibility of the federal government. Neither provincial nor federal governments acknowledged responsibility for Métis education until well into the twentieth century. As a result, as the Métis' economic and political situation deteriorated, so did their educational levels. Local school boards more often than not refused to admit Métis children from landless families because their parents did not pay taxes. And, even though the Catholic and Anglican churches built schools in some Métis communities, few Métis children attended school and illiteracy became endemic. Trish Logan reports that "the Métis who were turned away from the federal-run residential schools for being *too white* were often turned away from the provincial schools for being *too Indian*."[142] When the provinces did assume responsibility for schooling Métis children well into the twentieth century, the situation improved only slightly.

The northern parts of the provinces, where Métis and Indians comprise the majority of the population, were isolated, with few roads and services. Even though most Métis students were illiterate and spoke only their Indigenous languages, the provincially operated "day schools" imposed on them an English curriculum that had been created for the White children of the South. Indeed, the "assimilationist practices and abuses prevalent in the Indian residential schools were institutionalized in the day schools."[143] Furthermore, the provinces funded northern schools at a lower level than they did the White schools both in the South and in those few towns in the North that had a White majority population. Not surprisingly, being located in isolated areas with no services and conveniences and receiving lower levels of funding, the "Métis schools" found it difficult to attract qualified teaching staff. As a result, they attracted the same inferior kinds of teachers that the Indian residential schools hired. Teachers rarely had the same qualifications as those in the southern schools and were ill prepared to meet the educational needs of the Métis students.[144]

Things were not much better for Métis children in the South. Often these children represented the only racial[145] minority in the predominantly White schools in the towns and cities. In *Halfbreed*, Maria Campbell describes the overt personal racism of both teachers and students that was all too common. Frightened Métis students often attended school sporadically and left as soon as they were legally able to do so. Other Métis families that were culturally and visibly able moved to large urban centres and hid their identities in an attempt to make a better life for themselves and their children. There they could find opportunities for employment, often in low-paying labour or domestic work, but their children could attend school. However, there was a cost for this " better life," and that cost was a psychological one; those Métis who denied their identities experienced the continual stress that comes from living a lie. As a result, even today Métis educational levels are not at par with those of the White majority.

Policies that Controlled the Consumption of Alcohol by Not-Indians

Those people whom the colonial regime deemed to be "not-Indians" were excluded from many other privileges that the White majority enjoyed. One of these was the purchase and consumption of alcohol. Even though the *Indian Act* was designed to exclude many Indigenous people, in its 1894 iteration, the Act was revised to include the same people it excluded elsewhere but only in the section pertaining to alcohol. In the 1894 Act, the definition of "Indian" included persons who would otherwise be considered "not-Indian" for the purpose of prohibiting alcohol consumption. As a result, "any person, male or female, with or without Indian status who was reputed to belong to a particular band, or who followed the Indian mode of life, or the child of such a person" could be prosecuted for consuming alcohol.[146] Although this section was later removed, it clearly reveals how the colonizers found it difficult to distinguish Indians from "not-Indians," and how they did not welcome "not-Indians" into their society. (Colonial bureaucrats later solved the problem of distinguishing Indians from not-Indians by issuing identity cards to Status Indians.) Indigenous people's desire to consume alcohol, like their White neighbours did, remained a bone of contention for the colonial regime, however.

Under the Canadian Constitution, the provinces are responsible for passing laws and developing policies to regulate the sale of alcohol to everyone not legally classified as Indian. Although the provinces did not pass laws prohibiting those designated not-Indians from consuming alcohol, they found other ways to prevent them from purchasing it. The provincial governments grant licences to establishments that wish to sell liquor and for many years owned and operated all liquor stores in the country. By refusing to open liquor stores in predominantly Indigenous communities and by refusing to license establishments to sell liquor there, the provincial governments, in effect, denied access to alcohol to Indigenous people who lived off-reserve, for the most part not-Indians. Rather than enforcing sobriety, these mini-colonial regimes criminalized alcohol consumption for not-Indians who determinedly drank either bootleg liquor or alcohol substitutes.[147] In later years, many not-Indians died or were injured in automobile accidents because they had to drive long distances to drink.

Although alcohol ravaged Indigenous communities, people seemed determined to balk at complying with the patronizing policies of the colonial regimes. Walter Hlady, an anthropologist employed by the Government of Saskatchewan in the 1950s, suggested that Indigenous people consumed excessive amounts of alcohol to dull the pain of living in an apartheid-like situation and to help them forget that they were second-class citizens.[148] Hlady forgot that Indians were not considered citizens by law at that time and would not become citizens until twelve years later. They could not, therefore, be "second-class citizens," when they were not citizens at all. It would be an understatement to say that Indigenous people, both Indian and "Not," developed an ambivalent relationship with the law as a result of the policies that governed their access to alcohol.

Policies that Controlled Hunting by Not-Indians

That ambivalent relationship with the law is even more evident when we examine the policies that regulate hunting. Those Indigenous people deemed to be not-Indians were just as dependent on hunting and fishing for their survival as were their Indian relatives, perhaps even more so, since they had no land and received no rations. However, once the provinces developed policies regulating hunting and fishing, not-Indians lost their right to hunt and fish when they needed food. The colonial regime considered hunting and fishing suitable leisure activities to be licensed, with participation in those activities limited to certain times of the year.[149] Before the creation of the Canadian welfare state, obeying these laws could constitute a death sentence to the many not-Indians whose only food came from hunting, fishing, and gathering. As landless people living in extreme poverty, they had no alternative but to break hunting laws continually. In *Halfbreed*, Campbell describes how her father was incarcerated for six months for hunting without a licence, leaving the family teetering on the verge of starvation after government officials confiscated the meat that was to feed them through the winter. With their Indigenous way of life criminalized, crime and poverty became inextricably linked for not-Indians. Indeed, survival for the not-Indians became a choice of denying their ancestry—a choice for only those culturally and visibly able—or engaging in a traditional way of life that had now become a crime. Many Indigenous people deemed not-Indians developed a relationship with the law that could be described as profoundly antagonistic.

Policies that Controlled Child Welfare for Indians and Not-Indians

By the end of the 1940s, years of oppressive colonial policies had begun to take their toll on Indigenous families. Two to three generations of Indigenous people, the majority of whom were Status Indians, had spent their formative years becoming institutionalized in the residential school system. With only school staff, many of whom were abusive, as their only role models, children left the schools having neither observed nor acquired parenting skills. All had suffered cultural and spiritual abuse as a consequence of the imperial policies that prohibited the schools from allowing students to speak their languages and to observe their cultural and religious practices. In addition, many former students had been victims of sexual, physical, and emotional abuse. Thus the students left the schools emotionally scarred and culturally confused. Although the policies dealing with the schooling of children classified as not-Indians were much different, those children did not fare significantly better than their Indian relatives. With few exceptions, Indigenous people found themselves living in poverty as the result of racist colonial policies that prohibited them from engaging in their traditional economies while barring them from participating in the mainstream economy. As a result, many internalized the racist attitudes that engulfed them and learned to associate their Indigenous identity with poverty and powerlessness. Thus, the stress of dealing with the consequences of colonial policies began to cause a number of social problems in Indigenous communities.

Following World War II, the settler governments became more involved in child welfare than ever before. The country had become accustomed to increased government involvement in its affairs during the war, and social services in Canada had become almost exclusively dependent on government funding. In addition, social work was developing as a profession and, consequently, many of these new professionals were anxious to find problems to solve and people to help.[150] However, once again the complexities of Canadian federalism influenced all policy changes affecting Indigenous people.

In the Dominion of Canada, each province and territory was, and still is, responsible for its own child welfare, but the federal government held responsibility for policies governing Status Indians. Although provincial governments were legally responsible for those implicitly classified as not-Indians, many provinces lumped them into the same category as Status Indians and reasoned that the federal government should be responsible for them as well.[151] Before World War II, the child-welfare system had no jurisdiction over Status Indians and virtually ignored not-Indians. In the late 1940s, the Canadian Welfare Council (CWC) and the Canadian Association of Social Workers (CASW) decided to take action to address the social problems in Indigenous communities. Although they had easy access to not-Indian communities because they fell under provincial jurisdiction, federal law forbade social work professionals from entering Indian reserves to intervene in the welfare of Indian children. To overcome this problem, the CWC and CASW petitioned the federal government in 1947 to change policies to permit provincial and territorial social work professionals to intervene in the problems that they believed were occurring on Indian reserves.[152] Of course, their goal was laudable. Both social workers and government officials professed that they only wanted what was best for Indigenous people. In response to the brief and the resulting discussions, the colonial regime changed policies to grant them access.[153] Beatrice Culleton Mosionier explores the results in her novel *In Search for April Raintree*, which is discussed at length in Chapter 4.

Not coincidentally, the resulting changes in child-welfare policy were remarkably similar to the assimilationist policies that created the residential schools. At their core, both were "rooted in non-Aboriginal pride and intolerance and in the certitude and insularity of purported cultural superiority."[154] Neither policy-makers nor social work professionals thought to ask Indigenous people what their communities needed. Indeed, no one even asked them for their opinions regarding the proposed changes that were to have such a profound effect on their lives. Like the colonial regime, the social work professionals believed, without question, that they knew what was best for Indigenous people. Because of the changes in child-welfare policies, the numbers of Indigenous children involved in the child-welfare system mushroomed in a brief period of time from negligible to comprising the majority of children, especially in the areas of the numbered treaties and in British Columbia. Thus, social-service agents apprehending children and placing them in foster care became the norm in many Indigenous communities.[155] This dark period in Indigenous history has come to be commonly termed the "Sixties Scoop";[156] however, that label is truly a misnomer since the "scooping up" of Aboriginal children did not end with the 1960s, in fact, and continues to this day.[157] Once again, the colonial regime, using public policy as its vehicle, sent Indigenous people down another "road to hell [that] was paved with good intentions, [but this time] the child welfare system was the paving contractor."[158]

After 1951, social work practices changed dramatically, first for not-Indians and later on for Status Indians. The colonial regime based its child welfare policies on the same underlying philosophical foundation as it did the policies that established the residential schools—that is, it was their moral responsibility to elevate Indigenous people to the standard set by White society. And once again, they believed that Indigenous families were an impediment. Thus, colonial officials planned to save Indigenous children from their families and communities by relocating them to White homes where they could learn White behaviours, norms, and mores. Under the new child welfare policies, provincial social workers "would, quite literally, scoop children from reserves on the slightest pretext."[159] Ironically, the conditions from which these social workers wanted to rescue these Indigenous children were conditions that the discriminatory colonial policies had caused, the primary one being poverty and all of its by-products: malnutrition, poor housing, inadequate clothing, crime. These, in turn, begat other social problems, such as alcoholism and violence, but neither the social workers nor the colonial officials considered that colonial policies were at the root of these problems. Likewise, they did not anticipate the long-term effects of removing Indigenous children from their communities and relocating them into White homes, nor did they anticipate the effects of their actions on Indigenous families and communities when some communities lost almost a generation of their children as a result of them.[160]

The social workers imagined that middle-class, White, Christian families would adopt the children, and in some cases that did happen. More often, the social workers had no choice but to place the children in foster care, and the foster families were rarely middle-class. Although finding families willing to take in foster children has always been difficult, the shortage became acute in the 1960s as more and more women chose to work outside the home.[161] Foster families were often working-class White families in which the mother either wished to stay home with her own children or had little chance of finding employment herself. Suzanne Fournier and Ernie Crey note that "often the only difference between the parents whose children were stolen away and those who took in foster children for a little extra cash was the colour of their skin."[162] Still, the colonial officials who created the policies and the White social workers who enforced them took as a given that mainstream, White, Euro-Canadian standards were the standards to which every thinking person should aspire. Neither the colonial regime nor the social workers considered helping Indigenous people to address the problems that their communities were experiencing. As soon as the various governments came to agreements regarding money and control, the lives of Indigenous people underwent a radical change. In 1959, 1 percent of all children in care were Indigenous, but that number rose to 30 to 40 percent in the 1960s, even though Indigenous people represented less than 4 percent of the national population.[163] Despite the lofty principles that its rhetoric espoused, the colonial regime was neither kind-hearted nor benign.

To say that "the road to hell was paved with good intentions" presumes that the policies promoting the indiscriminate removal of Indigenous children from their families were, in retrospect, merely human errors made by naive policy-makers who always worked with the best interests of Indigenous people and their children in mind. In his study of the Indigenous child welfare in Canada, Patrick Johnston contends that the evidence refutes the claim "that the Sixties Scoop of Indian children by child welfare authorities was simply an accident or the consequence of social workers' increased sense of compassion."[164] The timing of the changes to child-welfare policies as they apply to Indigenous people is especially noteworthy. At virtually the same time as the Government of Canada was changing policies to allow social work agencies access to Indian reserves and Indian children, it was also involved in the creation of the United Nations Convention on the Prevention and Punishment of the Crime of Genocide. Indeed, on 28 November 1949, Canada became a signatory to the UN Convention, which it then ratified on 3 September 1952. It is significant that the practice of "forcibly transferring children of [one] group to another group" contravenes Article 2(e) of the Convention, if such act is "committed with intent to destroy, in whole or in part, a national, ethnical, racial or religious group."[165] The question, then, is whether the policies that allowed social workers to transfer Indigenous children from their homes to non-Indigenous homes was created with the intent to destroy Indigenous nations. The evidence suggests that they were. For more than a century, the goal of the policies of the imperial regime was to destroy Indigenous nations by forcibly assimilating Indigenous people into mainstream society by first stripping them of control over all areas of their lives. Clearly, the policies that gave social workers the authority to remove Indigenous children from their homes and place them into the homes of non-Indigenous people as foster children or adoptees were consistent with the regime's assimilationist Indigenous policies of the past hundred years. To claim that the changes to child-welfare policies that enabled this action were the naive errors of well-meaning people is contrary to the evidence and lacks credibility.

Why Respond in Literature?

Despite the ferocity of the colonial regime's attack on them using public policy as its weapon, Indigenous people have not assimilated or disappeared. Indigenous people have appropriated the language and literary practices of the colonizers, which they use to expose the consequences of imperial policies on their people. However, Indigenous literature is not merely an exposé of past and present injustices. The discussion of Indigenous literature and drama in the following chapters reveals that Indigenous people have learned that the creative process has restorative powers. Today's Indigenous writers use the power of narrative and drama to heal themselves and their people from the trauma that colonial policies have inflicted.

chapter 3

Personal stories, healing stories

In his study of personal myths and their role in the construction of identity, Dan P. McAdams writes that personal myths are the narratives "that each of us naturally constructs to bring together the different parts of ourselves and our lives into a purposeful and convincing whole."[1] All of us must, then, by necessity, craft our own personal myths to enable us to interpret and understand our lives. As such, a "personal myth is not a legend or a fairy tale, but a sacred story that embodies personal truth."[2] By studying the narrated discourse of personal myths, McAdams has been able to gain a better understanding of the narrator through his or her narrative: "Like all stories, the personal myth has a beginning, middle, and end, defined according to the development of plot and character. We attempt, with our story, to make a compelling aesthetic statement. A personal myth is *an act of imagination that is a patterned integration of our remembered past, perceived present, and anticipated future.* As both author and reader, we come to appreciate our own myth for its beauty and its psychosocial truth."[3] McAdams contends that often an inadequate or incoherent narrative of one's life—an incomplete personal myth—can cause mental and emotional illnesses and subsequent suffering.

Edward M. Bruner's distinction "between life as lived (reality), life as experienced (experience), and life as told (expression)"[4] is useful when we consider how humans "story" traumatic experiences. Traumatic events from our past can be our constant companion if we are unable to process those events and let them go. Converting the residual pain of traumatic events first into language and subsequently into text enables us to distance ourselves from the trauma. We can then examine the text of the traumatic event to understand the emotions it triggers, a process that allows us to diminish its negative effects.

During the process of storying traumatic events, we may re-experience those emotions associated with the original trauma. However, by re-experiencing these emotions in a safe environment and by expressing them in language, we are often able to come to terms with emotional injuries and then move our emotional lives forward to a place of health and contentment: "Stories help us organize our thoughts, providing a narrative for human intentions and interpersonal events that is readily remembered and told. In some instances, stories may also mend us when we are broken, heal us when we are sick, and even move us toward psychological fulfillment and maturity."[5] The focus of McAdams's research is the personal myths and the individual. His theories, however, also apply to colonial society and the storying of relationships between the colonizers and the colonized. One of the many functions of Indigenous people's autobiography is to respond to the settlers' authorized collective myth. By drawing attention to the sickness inherent in colonialism, Indigenous life writing challenges the settlers' delusions and prompts them to rethink their collective myth. McAdams's theories of the personal myth also shed light on some causes of postcolonial traumatic stress response in Indigenous people. Indigenous life writing helps Indigenous readers to heal from postcolonial trauma by helping them recraft their personal and collective myths.

Another factor that has contributed to postcolonial trauma for Indigenous people is our exclusion from the authorized story of the creation of the Canadian nation-state. The shared narrative of the settlers dominates the Canadian story, and it is this narrative that I will term the "national collective myth." The creation of a national collective myth bears a striking resemblance to the process that forms the narratives of the lives of individuals as Charlotte Linde describes it. Linde contends that a life narrative "consists of a set of stories that are retold in various forms over a long period of time and that are subject to revision and change as the speaker drops some old meanings and adds new meanings to portions of the life story."[6] A national collective myth, like McAdams's "personal myth," is "an act of imagination that is a patterned integration of our remembered past, perceived present, and anticipated future."[7] However, in the case of nations that were created by colonizing Indigenous populations, it is the colonizers, as the dominant culture, who invest in themselves the authority to story the collective myth. The national collective myth of a colonial state is the story that justifies the settlers' existence as a new nation and inspires pride in the settlers as citizens of that nation. In other words, the national collective myth is, in effect, the creation myth of the settlers' nation-state.

The stories of Indigenous people who have not vanished must necessarily be excluded from the national collective myth. Indeed, our continued existence is problematic since we are a constant reminder of those historical and contemporary events that call into question the settlers' pride in their nation. As a result, Indigenous people receive little mention in the collective myth of the Canadian nation-state. This exclusion has health consequences and has caused Indigenous people to suffer grievous emotional wounds. Implicit in our exclusion is the understanding that we are not noteworthy enough to remember, not significant enough to perceive, and not desirable enough to have a place in the future of the Canadian collective. The collective myth of the Dominion of Canada is the expression of the colonizers' experience, not the experience of the colonized.

In the authorized national collective myth, the colonizers function as both authors and protagonists. Their myth begins as a romantic adventure filled with heroic stories. It tells of courageous settlers who braved arduous journeys across the ocean to search for a better life in the vast, unpopulated New World. Those brave settlers endured untold hardships but ultimately prevailed to tame, civilize, and modernize this savage land, which they shaped into the best nation in the world. They believe Canada was created through peaceful negotiation with a weak and shrinking Indigenous population that was quickly dying from disease. This national collective myth culminates in the formation of the modern-day settler nation of Canada, a country that the United Nations judged the best in the world in which to live for seven consecutive years. The United Nations arrived at this determination using scientific indicators: life expectancy, education, and income. Canada held the distinction of being the best country in the world in which to live from 1994 to 2000, and this honour became the crowning achievement of the perceived present in the national collective myth.[8] Ironically, when those same indicators were used to study registered or Status Indians, they revealed that Canada ranks forty-eighth in the same list of countries, with registered Indians living on-reserve fairing even worse than those living off-reserve.[9] This information was news for a few short days and then forgotten. Significantly, it is not included in the national collective myth.

In the national collective myth, Indigenous people are sometimes cast as antagonists but more often dismissed as secondary characters who disappear partway through the narrative, and in general are worthy of mention only in relation to their interaction with the settlers. Indigenous people are minor characters in the remembered past, characters who disappear completely in the perceived present, and characters who have no place in the anticipated future. This casting is not without consequence. It conveys the message that we have outgrown our usefulness.

At the same time that the colonial regime was developing policies to coerce the assimilation of the Indigenous population, it was ostracizing us from having a place in the national collective myth. The result has been a sense of intense dislocation and alienation in the Indigenous population and subsequent injuries to both our individual and collective worth. Jeannette Armstrong challenges the settler population to imagine how this has affected the Indigenous population: "Imagine at what cost to you psychologically, to acquiesce and attempt to speak, dress, eat, and worship, like your oppressors, simply out of a need to be treated humanly. Imagine attempting to assimilate so that your children will not suffer what you have, and imagine finding that assimilationist measures are not meant to include you but to destroy all remnants of your culture. Imagine finding that even when you emulate every cultural process from customs to values you are still excluded, despised, and ridiculed because you are Native."[10] She goes on to point out that, despite all this, Indigenous people have not remained silent. Each Indigenous community across the land has its alternative collective myth to which only its people are privy. These alternative myths form the foundation of contemporary Indigenous literature in general and autobiography in particular.

When discussing the function of the personal myth, McAdams draws his readers' attention to the words of novelist Philip Roth, who contends that his objective in writing his autobiography was to "depathologize" his life.[11] In the context of Indigenous autobiography, depathologizing becomes synonymous with decolonizing. Colonialism is a pathological condition, a sickness that requires a cure, and taking the shared truths of the Indigenous people to the settler population comprises a component of that cure. Indigenous autobiography supplies those truths in that it illustrates "the structural relationship presently existing between the continent's immigrant (settler) society and the peoples indigenous to it. It follows that an honest accounting must be made of the flows of impact and benefit involved, as well as an unequivocal repudiation of the elaborate veils of evasion and denial behind which such unpleasantries are habitually concealed."[12] By writing the stories of their lives, stories that articulate Indigenous truths in the form of alternate collective myths, Indigenous writers not only fill in the gaps in the collective myth of the dominant, colonial society but also correct many of its falsehoods. These gaps and falsehoods have functioned as weapons that continue to injure the collective esteem of Indigenous people. By making public another story, Indigenous autobiography calls into question the veracity of the national collective myth to address the pathology of colonialism. There is pathology inherent in living in a position of privilege, ignorant of the price that others have paid for those privileges, and believing that those privileges have been earned and are deserved. If settler society persists in maintaining their ignorance of their society's foundation of unearned privilege, their society will remain sick.

In the process of writing their own personal myths, Indigenous writers turn the images in the larger collective narrative "around to mirror an image of the colonized to the colonizers."[13] By studying an image of the colonized that the colonized, themselves, have created, settlers learn that the national collective myth of their country, and by extension its societal foundation, is flawed and that its prosperity is built upon the suffering of others. Churchill contends that the personal stories of Indigenous people who tell, and I would argue write, about their experience under colonialism and its effects initiate "a process by which victims can be healed while perpetrators are cured of their psychoses presents itself as a dialectical unity (a 'reconciliation' of sorts). By speaking clearly, consistently and, above all, *publicly*, to the facts of what has been/is being done to us, and by whom, native people can force admissions from the perpetrators that they have done what we contend."[14] In other words, to cure the settlers from the pathology of colonialism, Indigenous people must make public the alternative collective myth that comprises our truths, and to heal the wounds that colonialism has inflicted on the Indigenous population, we must hear our truths in the national collective myth. Without truth there can be no reconciliation.

In addition to its socio-pedagogical aim of curing the pathology of colonialism, Indigenous autobiography has another aim: to help Indigenous readers heal from the trauma they have suffered as a consequence of the policies of the colonial regime. Having been denied access to the discourse of public policy, Indigenous people have made public their life stories as eyewitness accounts that critique colonial policies and record the effects of these policies. In the process of describing the colonial experience from the perspective of the colonized, Indigenous autobiography exposes the pathology of colonialism as it is experienced by the colonized. Indigenous autobiography is not merely a retelling of colonial horror stories, however. It also depicts the resilience of Indigenous people and articulates their emotions in a way that inspires hope in its readers.

Indigenous autobiography narrates experiences that have caused its characters to suffer some of the more common psychological consequences of colonial oppression, including anger, shame, and, all too often, self-loathing. By organizing their experiences and articulating their feelings about these traumatic experiences, Indigenous life writers help themselves and their Indigenous readers come to terms with these emotions. Transforming the emotional responses to colonial oppression into text validates emotional responses that readers might share with the writer but might not have been able to articulate. Gold explains:

> Life experiences are often confusing and make us feel trapped and overwhelmed. We are lost in content.… If during our growing up, for instance, we have suffered trauma…we can get locked into the guilt, anger, rejection and so on, that we felt at that time. To escape the feeling of helplessness and confusion that we carry with us we need to organize, package, index our experience, do what we mean when we say "get a handle on it," so that we can carry the baggage of our experience comfortably and not have bits and pieces falling all over the place. This is what we do when we "story" it.[15]

Through story, we are able to recraft a new and healthier personal myth.

When readers identify with a narrative that describes trauma, they often re-experience many of the feelings they had when they experienced a similar traumatic event. However, during the process of reading, they are able to organize their feelings in their own time in a safe environment comforted by the knowledge that they are not alone, that others have suffered the same experiences under colonialism, and, most importantly, that others have survived, overcome, and triumphed. Indigenous autobiography reveals to readers that Indigenous people have suffered greatly and that the road to healing is a difficult one. However, when Indigenous writers create compelling narratives about their life experiences, those narratives have the potential to inspire Indigenous readers to examine their own stories.

McAdams finds it helpful to examine the literary strategies that his patients employ when creating and recreating their personal myths. Tone, for example, which McAdams classifies as romantic, comedic, tragic, and ironic, reveals much about the psychological state of the narrator. The storyteller's choice of what McAdams calls "tone" reveals her outlook on the events that transpire in her life. The personal myths of optimistic storytellers, for example, tend to be romantic or comedic, while those of pessimists tend to be ironic or tragic. And, tone affects health. Psychologists agree that people with optimistic outlooks tend to be healthier. Choice of imagery and representations are also telling. Unlike tone, which is highly individualistic, one's choice of imagery is steeped in culture. Vital to comprehending Indigenous autobiography is an understanding of contemporary Indigenous cultures, especially those aspects of contemporary cultures that have come into being as the result of colonial oppression. Given the extensive oppression that Indigenous people have endured under colonialism and the profound shame that has been an outcome of oppressive colonial policies, it should come as no surprise that Indigenous writers often employ a tone and incorporate imagery that valorize their people and downplay the inevitable negative traits inherent in all communities. Their stories act as a counterweight to balance the negative discourse of the colonizers as it pertains to Indigenous people.

Indigenous autobiography goes beyond catharsis. It is an act of imagination that inspires social regeneration by providing eyewitness testimony to historical injustices. As such, it is intensely political. Ross Chambers distinguishes between political testimony, "which requires action," and ethical testimony, "which defers action but requires moral engagement."[16] Indigenous autobiography attempts to conflate these two kinds of testimony. By inspiring empathy in its readers and by appealing to their sense of justice, it engages them on a moral level. At the same time, it advances social change by challenging readers to take action to redress injustices. Indigenous literature, then, seeks to do more than heal individual readers—it also seeks to repair the damage that colonialism has inflicted on Indigenous communities by inspiring readers to seek social justice through social change. Testimonial stories are a particularly powerful tool to achieve these ends:

> Because effective stories have perlocutionary power, they can influence the subsequent actions of narrator and audience. Powerful stories can shape future actions in decisive ways, and this only increases the complex and intertwined relation between telling stories and taking actions. The study of narrative has invited investigation of social life as an interplay of differently positioned actors and different moral and persuasive voices. A story, especially a personal story, allows us to see that—from other perspectives and/or through alternative "editing"—other stories might have been told. Even the seductive powers of the compelling story cannot easily disguise its status as a positioned account.[17]

When Indigenous readers see themselves and their lives depicted in a positioned account written by another Indigenous person with whom they share similar experiences, the narrative becomes real to them, especially in light of the absence of Indigenous reality in the majority of published narratives.

Indigenous autobiography seeks not only to reconstruct from an Indigenous perspective the stories of our "remembered past and perceived present"; it also imagines "our anticipated future."[18] Through the process of reading Indigenous autobiography and empathizing with the characters, Indigenous readers acknowledge that they, too, bear witness to the effects of colonialism. In this collaborative process of making meaning, writers and readers engage in a process of conscientization[19] in which the colonized awaken to the political realities that surround them and become aware of the colonial dynamics and their effects. Conscientization makes it possible for Indigenous writers to take control of that portion of their personal myth that deals with the present, and through their imaginative and sympathetic participation in the experience of the writer, engaged readers are inspired to take control over their present. Furthermore, as a result of conscientization, Indigenous life writers have, without exception, imagined an optimistic future for their people, a future beyond mere survival. To that end, Indigenous autobiography motivates readers to seek social change leading to social justice and to engender optimism by the way that they choose to imagine a positive outcome of their collective myth.

Halfbreed: Where It All Began

Although Maria Campbell was not the first Indigenous person to publish a work of literature, her autobiography, *Halfbreed*, has certainly proved to be the most influential and is credited with giving birth to contemporary Indigenous literature in Canada. The popularity of this text can be attributed not only to the power of Campbell's narrative but also to the times in which it was published. In 1973, Western society was going through a period of social upheaval that had begun in the 1960s. With the advent of television, Canadians were inundated by stories of racial intolerance and inequities in the American South. Young people questioned societal structures. Some had begun to doubt the reliability of their own history, suspecting that colonialism to the north of the border might not have been as benign as government officials and authorized histories had led them to believe. The history that most Canadians learned referred to Indigenous people in the past tense and contended that, with the exception of a few atypical incidents, their country had been settled by way of peaceful negotiation. No mention was made of contemporary Indigenous people in the discourse of Canadian history. Apparently, we had just disappeared.

In 1973, most Canadians were smug and self-righteous in their belief in this biased history, a history that omits or downplays references to the exploitation and oppression that are central to the creation of Canada as a nation. However, there were other Canadians who were not satisfied with the official version of history and who sought the truth that Campbell's story supplied. Speaking with the authority of an eyewitness to the events that she recounted, Campbell explains: "I write this for all of you, to tell you what it is like to be a halfbreed woman in our country. I want to tell you about the joys and sorrow, the oppressing poverty, the frustrations and the dreams."[20] These are, without doubt, the most-quoted lines of her narrative text. *Halfbreed* quickly became a bestseller exposing the rot in the foundation of the Dominion, and has been one of the most widely read books in the Indigenous community. As such, it has inspired other Indigenous people to tell their stories.

However, Campbell did not set out to become a professional writer nor did she plan to share her story with the world. Like many of the Indigenous life writers who followed her lead, Campbell wrote because the ghosts of personal and historical trauma continued to haunt her, thereby impeding her ability to move forward with her life. At the suggestion of a friend, she began writing as "scriptotherapy" in an effort "to order and organize these experiences and thoughts so that [she could] get control over them."[21] Campbell writes: "Going home after so long a time, I thought that I might find again the happiness and beauty I had known as a child. But as I walked down the rough dirt road, poked through the broken old buildings and thought back over the years, I realized that I could never find that here. Like me the land had changed, my people were gone, and if I was to know peace I would have to search within myself. That is when I decided to write about my life" (2). Campbell's writing, at first, took the form of a personal journal following the advice of a friend who had suggested that she "write it all down," all of her memories, both good and bad.[22]

By writing her story as a personal journal, Campbell sought to gain perspective on her life, the choices that she made, and the outcomes of those choices—in other words, to craft her personal myth.[23] For most people, this process is reflective and oral, combining internal and external monologues with our dialogue with others. Campbell, however, chose to write her personal myth. It was only by chance that someone came upon her writings and read them. That first reader convinced her that she had, indeed, written a book. This was a shock to Campbell, who had set out to heal herself from postcolonial traumatic stress response and whose writing was a means to a therapeutic, not artistic, end. Yet, Campbell was persuaded to seek a publisher and that publisher, in turn, realized that her story was one which that the book-buying public wanted very much to read. In the process of preparing her personal writing in a literary work, Campbell's writings were necessarily transformed from "scriptotherapy" into testimony, which "works to establish meaning in ways that are external to scriptotherapy, indeed, in ways in which scriptotherapy cannot, and offers closure on matters that scriptotherapy keeps open."[24] Neither Campbell nor her publisher anticipated the effect that *Halfbreed* would have on its readers, both the Indigenous readers who could identify with Campbell's experience and the settlers who were complicit in the oppression that she describes.

Campbell clearly represents *Halfbreed* as a factual account of her life as she remembers it even though she begins with a qualifying note that informs readers that "names of persons and places have been changed in some cases" (7). Although *Halfbreed* is clearly an articulation and transcription of Campbell's personal myth, it is important to note that her community shares the role of protagonist in much of the narrative. As a writer of autobiography, Campbell "presumably wants to fix, establish, share, and historicize a particular version of the self. All this is done on the basis of selecting those aspects of the self that seem to matter most, those feelings that prevail for the writer at the time of writing, and so she records memories in a language that conveys those feelings and values most effectively."[25] By sharing the role of protagonist with her community, however, Campbell also writes to "fix, establish, share, and historicize of particular version of" the collective selves of the Métis people.

That is not to say Campbell claims that the Métis community has authorized her to tell their story. The Métis, first of her childhood community and later on the larger Métis community, play such an integral role in her personal myth that Campbell often seems to be a secondary character in her own story. She writes: "I grew up with some really funny, wonderful, fantastic people and they are as real to me today as they were then" (23). Because these people were so much a part of Campbell's formative years, she writes their stories along with her own. Perhaps that is why *Halfbreed* resonates with Indigenous people and why it has inspired so many to write their stories. Yet, many readers infer that Campbell speaks on behalf of the Métis community, a narrative practice that Susan Lanser terms "the communal voice." By writing in the communal voice, "narrative authority is invested in a definable community and textually inscribed either through multiple, mutually authorizing voices or through the voice of a single individual who is manifestly authorized by a community."[26] To infer that the Métis community has invested Campbell with the narrative authority to write its story would be a mistake, and Campbell has never made that claim.

Most Indigenous people have been asked, from time to time, to explain to the settlers what Indigenous people as a collective think or feel about a particular issue. To the settlers, each one of us is a trope, a living synecdoche, in that one of us inevitably represents the whole. Ironically, this, too, is a reason that *Halfbreed* has inspired other Indigenous people to write their stories. Cognizant that the settlers will assume that *Halfbreed* reflects the experience of all Indigenous people, other writers—Rita Joe, Basil Johnston, Lee Maracle, and Gregory Scofield, to name but a few—have written their autobiographies to reveal the diversity of cultures and experiences inherent within the Indigenous population.

Halfbreed is structured so that it contains two distinct unmarked sections with Campbell's marriage marking the end of the first section and her subsequent self-exile from Saskatchewan marking the beginning of the second. Having written the text when she was but thirty-three years of age, Campbell clearly has had time to process her memories of the events of her childhood and to incorporate them into her personal myth but is still coming to grips with the choices that she made since her marriage. Thus, the two sections differ radically. In section one, Campbell's personal myth is inextricably linked to the collective myth of her community, beginning with the history of the Métis who came to inhabit the land near Spring River. In section two, Campbell is physically and emotionally dislocated from family, community, language, and culture, which are necessary to attain the "psychosocial integration" required for emotional health. Without a sense of psychosocial integration, her narrative becomes individualistic, in comparison, and she focuses almost exclusively on herself clinging to the "substitute lifestyle"[27] that has replaced her childhood lifestyle.

In Chapter 1, Campbell makes use of a style of writing similar to those used in historical narratives, which enables her to appear to be narrating an objective account of the events that culminate with her ancestors relocating to the "Spring River," the fictional name that Campbell has chosen for her home community. In this chapter, Campbell decolonizes the history of the colonial regime and, by extension, the national collective myth, by retelling history from the Métis point of view. In the narrative of Canadian history, the very events that were catastrophic to the Métis and their First Nations allies were, until very recently, depicted as the story of the colonial regime's great victory against the treasonous halfbreeds. Furthermore, those historical figures responsible for causing the death, suffering, and persecution of the Métis continue to be valorized not only in history books but also in the physical world. Their names appear on streets, buildings, and even entire communities, and their likenesses are immortalized in statuary and on monuments. It is against the monolith of colonial propaganda that Campbell writes her history to disseminate and promote the Métis historical perspective. Simulating the "objective" discourse of history, Campbell tells readers what "the history books say" (6), listing several of the executions, prosecutions, and costs that followed the 1885 Métis Resistance. Unlike the historians, who write their narratives from the perspective of the colonial regime, Campbell relates this history from the point of view of the Métis recounting not only the events that transpired but also the motivation of the Métis involved. By retelling a well-known historical narrative from an alternate perspective, she calls into question the much-touted objectivity of colonial historians.

Yet, Campbell does not entirely valorize the Métis. Her historical narrative is a tragedy, and the tragic hero, in this case, is not a single flawed individual but the Métis people as a collective. Like tragic heroes of Western literature, the Métis possess a fatal flaw that brings about their inevitable downfall. Campbell explains that "after [the battle of] Duck Lake, Ottawa hastily formed a committee to examine Halfbreed grievances and issue land scrip to assure the Halfbreeds of their land claims. But these were issued purposely to a chosen few which caused a split within the Halfbreed ranks" (5). Throughout the first section of the narrative, Campbell repeatedly recounts stories of instances in which she believes that the colonial government, with promises of material reward, seduces significant numbers of desperate, poverty-stricken Métis and persuades them to betray their own people. This interpretation of events lays the foundation of Campbell's combined personal and collective myth as tragedy and becomes an emotional battleground upon which she wages war with her feelings of disempowerment and self-hatred, hopelessness and despair.

Although Campbell calls herself "Halfbreed," she is not half-Indian and half-White. Despite being of mixed race, her mother's family are registered Indians who live on "Crown" land reserved for them, while her father's family are landless Métis and non-Status Indians who live as squatters on the easement land set aside for future road construction. Campbell's mother loses her Indian status when she marries Danny Campbell and their children are legally not-Indians. The Métis depend on a meagre income from hunting, trapping, and berry picking, but that income does not begin to meet their needs. To ensure that his family survives, Danny Campbell, like many Métis men, engages in activities that the settler government deems criminal: hunting out of season without a licence in the national park, selling meat, and bootlegging. But, Danny Campbell has few choices if he is to bring his family's income up to a level that would have still been far below the poverty line at that time. Ironically, the land where Danny Campbell hunts was his family's traditional hunting territory long before the Government of Canada claimed it and converted it to a national park. Cheechum, Danny's grandmother, was an Indian whose family lived on the land that was to become the Prince Albert National Park. They were not present when the treaty-makers came and, as a result, did not sign the treaty or cede their land. Nevertheless, colonial officials charge Danny Campbell for hunting on his family's traditional territory and sentence him to jail for six months. Maria Campbell's Status Indian relatives, in contrast, have the legal right to hunt for food for themselves and their Status family members without the need of a licence and at any time of the year. Her Indian relatives would have had to limit their hunting to reserve land, however, since the "pass" laws were still in force when Campbell was a child.

Campbell's descriptions of her extended family illustrate how the colonial policies that grant Indigenous identities caused breaches in both family and community relationships. According to Campbell, *wâhkôtowin* is a multifaceted network of relationships and prescribed roles that comprise the foundation of Nêhiyawîhcikêwin (Cree culture). The colonial policies that governed Indigenous identity and attacked that foundation were, and still are, a form of genocide. When Campbell juxtaposes her descriptions of her "Métis" great-grandmother, Cheechum, the most influential person in her life, with those of her mother and Grannie Dubuque, she reveals how these policies operated in the daily lives of the Nêhiyawak (the Cree). There is an irony in her descriptions, as well. The colonial regime classifies Cheechum as not-Indian even though she is clearly more culturally and biologically Indian than Campbell's mother and her mother's family. Her description of Cheechum suggests that she is indistinguishable from any other Cree woman of the time: "I remember her as a small woman, with white hair always neatly braided and tied with black thread. She wore black, ankle-length full skirts and black blouses with full sleeves and high collars. Around her neck were four or five strings of bright beads and a chain made of copper wire. On her wrists were copper bracelets which she wore to ward off arthritis. She wore moccasins and tight leggings to emphasize her tiny ankles. These were covered with bright porcupine quill designs" (10–11). Cheechum speaks only Cree, eschews Christianity and practises her Cree spiritual traditions, and is able to live off the land. Yet it is Campbell's mother's Christian mixed-blood family whom the colonial bureaucrats deem to be "Indian" and accord Indian "status."

In the midst of the hierarchy of indigeneity that the colonial regime has engineered, Campbell constructs a personal myth in which she attempts to persuade herself that the Métis are superior to their Status Indian relatives and blames them for the colonial policies that have determined that the Métis are not worthy of "status." Speaking as if she is merely stating fact rather than expressing opinion, Campbell engages in subtle disparagement of "status" or "treaty" Indians, whose character traits she juxtaposes with those of the halfbreeds. She contends that "Indians were very passive—they would get angry at things done to them but would never fight back, whereas Halfbreeds were quick-tempered—quick to fight, but quick to forgive and forget" (25). Likewise, she contends that "Treaty Indian women do not express their opinions, Halfbreed women do" (26). She acknowledges that the antipathy is reciprocated, and says that "there was never much love lost between Indians and Halfbreeds" (25).

At the same time that she valorizes the Métis and argues for their superiority to the Status Indians, she betrays her feelings of inferiority to them. Campbell explains, "We all went to the Indians' Sundances and special gatherings, but somehow we never fitted in. We were always the poor relatives, the *awp-pee-tow-koosons* [which she translates as 'half people'].[28] They laughed and scorned us. They had land and security, we had nothing" (25; emphasis in the original).[29] The hierarchy in which she lives positions the settlers at the top, the Status Indians very low down, and the Métis and non-Status Indians at the bottom. Her narrative illustrates how "status" under the policies of the colonial regime has become status in society. Through her description of the relationship between the Indigenous people with "status" and those without, Campbell reveals how the colonial policies that determine and control Indigenous peoples' identities aid the colonizers in the acquisition of the land by breaching the social fabric of Indigenous communities and by inflicting psychological injuries on the colonized Indigenous people.[30]

Clearly, Campbell is hostile towards the settlers, but she does not argue that the Métis are superior to them. Although she is obviously aware that the settlers as neo-colonizers are her oppressors, she aspires to have the material goods and the freedoms they possess. At many points in her life, she wants to be White, which causes her to feel intense shame.

Confined within the lines of this emotional battlefield—her fight to be proud of her Métis identity in the face of the overwhelming pressure from without to feel ashamed—Campbell desperately attempts to remember and describe all that is good and beautiful from her years living in the Métis community of her childhood. Her description of these affirmative qualities serves a healing function not only for herself but also for her Indigenous readers. Campbell imbues her descriptions of home and community with vivid images that evoke feelings of warmth and belonging, safety and love. She constructs her remembered past to incorporate the beauty she perceived in her childhood, and that beauty forms a significant component of her personal psychosocial truth. In one of the few descriptions of her mother, Campbell remembers her laughter and her "clean spicy smell when she held [her] close and sang to [her] at night" (14). Her home exudes the aroma of "moose stew simmering on the stove blended with the wild smell of the drying skins of mink, weasels and squirrels, and the spicy herbs and roots hanging from the walls" (17). Campbell combines olfactory imagery with precisely detailed visual imagery of furniture, appliances, and household implements to create an idealized image of her family's living room, which in her memories was "one of the most beautiful rooms I have ever known" (17). Clearly, Campbell would have been aware of how bleak her family's circumstances were when she was a child and that what she is, in fact, describing is a family living in almost desperate poverty. Nevertheless, she chooses to emphasize the beauty of that world and the resilience and ingenuity of the Métis people, an image that had never before been depicted in Canadian literature or in the national collective myth.

Campbell writes: "A close friend of mine said, 'Campbell, make it a happy book. It couldn't have been so bad. We know we are guilty so don't be too harsh'" (9). The fact that non-Indigenous readers usually assume that the friend must have been White, while Indigenous readers believe that she was Métis, reveals how deeply Indigenous people have internalized the racist attitudes that engulf us.[31] Inundated with the negative attitudes of the settlers, many Indigenous people habitually see themselves "through White eyes"[32] and the image they see is one that provokes feelings of shame. Campbell's narration exposes her own internal conflict between the racist attitudes she has absorbed and her desire to feel proud of her people. As a result, her depiction of her childhood contains many contradictions, and these contradictions give an inkling of the battle that rages within her. On the one hand, Campbell clearly wants to present the Métis in a positive light to counter the racist discourse of the settlers. On the other hand, she is well aware that there

is a destructive side to life on the road allowance and that destruction mani-
fests itself in violence of Métis against Métis within her community.

In the early part of the narrative, Campbell downplays the incidents
of violence in her community. She barely mentions her uncle's suicide, for
example. It is only in the context of her discussion of Cheechum's "second
sight" (19) that she refers to his death even though the death of her father's
brother would have deeply affected her family and community. Likewise,
she dismisses the drunken fights at community parties as mere pranks,
explaining "there was never a good dance unless there was a good fight"
(56). Furthermore, when she describes how a Métis man named Gene was
murdered at a party, she focuses on how the community conspires to hide
the murder from authorities thereby protecting the murderer, who was also a
community member. In this anecdote, her tone is neutral, almost matter-of-
fact, and she concentrates on the community's solidarity against the colonial
legal system rather than the horrors of the murder. It is only when she describes the men's excessive drinking with the profits from the community's
berry picking and the subsequent violence against their wives, that she can
no longer repress her feelings of revulsion.

There are several reasons that Campbell might have for choosing to employ positive imagery when describing her childhood, not the least of which
is her guilt for feeling ashamed of her people. These feelings of shame begin
when she attends an integrated school. Although physically integrated into
the school, the Métis children are socially and psychosocially marginalized.
As a group, "they are dislocated from the myriad intimate ties between people
and groups—from the family to the spiritual community—that are essential
for every person in every type of society."[33] Rather than helping the Métis,
integration injures them emotionally. Before integration, the children are unaware that their people comprise an economic and social underclass. They do
not know that their parents are powerless to effect social change. The poverty
in which they live is normal for them. However, when the Métis children attend the integrated school, they learn that what is normal to them is not the
norm for the settler culture.

Campbell learns from the settlers that the Métis are poor and that "there
was no worse sin in this country than to be poor" (61). With the support of
parents and teachers, the settler children flaunt their material superiority; to
them, the Métis' economic poverty is evidence of a deficit in character. The
settler children ridicule them for eating gophers, thereby traumatizing the
Métis children. Campbell explains, "We would fight back of course but we
were terribly hurt and above all ashamed" (50). Paolo Freire writes: "In their

unrestrained eagerness to possess, the oppressors develop the conviction that it is possible for them to transform everything into objects of their purchasing power; hence their strictly materialistic concept of existence. Money is the measure of all things, and profit the primary goal. For the oppressors, what is worthwhile is to have more—always more—even at the cost of the oppressed having less or having nothing. For them, *to be is to have* and to be the class of the 'haves.'"[34] Campbell learns to conflate Christianity and capitalism when she equates "poverty" with "sin." The settler children also conflate their Christian value of charity with their capitalist scorn of poverty. Thus, at Christmas, the settler children, as part of their Christian duty, leave packages containing used clothing in front of halfbreed homes but then mock the halfbreed children when they wear their "gifts" to school. Still, in this milieu of oppression, the settlers set the standard of success for Campbell. As a result, she aspires to acquire "the toothbrushes, fruit and all those other symbols of white ideas of success" (134).

Campbell's feelings become even more conflicted when she reaches adolescence and attends her first school dance. At this point in her life, it becomes obvious that she has internalized the racist attitudes of the settlers. Thus, when her settler friends ask if her chaperone, Sophie, is her mother, she attempts to distance herself from the Indigenous community by flippantly replying, "That old, ugly Indian?" (103). Realizing that Sophie has heard her and that her words hurt Sophie deeply, Campbell feels both guilt and anger: guilt for her hurtful words and anger at her Indigenous identity as the cause of her inferior status. Soon after this incident, Smokey, who was once the love of Campbell's life, tells her that her father has given them permission to marry when she turns eighteen. Rather than responding with joy, she mocks him replying, "Marry you? You've got to be joking! I'm going to do something with my life than make more Halfbreeds" (117). Later, after she has spent time as a drug addict and a prostitute, she blames Indigenous men for not only her choices but also for the choices of all the other Indigenous women in similar circumstances: "The drunken Indian men I saw would fill me with a blinding hatred; I blamed them for what had happened to me, to the little girl who had died from an overdose of drugs, and for all the girls who were on the city streets. If they had only fought back, instead of giving up, these things would never have happened. It's hard to explain how I felt. I hated our men, and yet I loved them" (143–4). By mining her memories for examples of what was good and beautiful in her community, Campbell achieves balance and wisdom. By sharing stories of the beautiful aspects of her community, she atones for what she considers her betrayal of her people.

In the same way that she once lashed out at her people and blamed them for the injuries that colonialism had inflicted on them, Campbell now attempts to reframe the collective narrative of her people in a positive light. Looking back as an adult, she is able to have a more balanced perspective enabling her to select and describe those positive aspects of her childhood. She is also able to understand and articulate how colonial policies have dislocated her people physically, culturally, linguistically, and socially, recognizing that it is the cause of their self-destructive behaviour. In this way, she is able to lift the burden of self-loathing from her own shoulders and from the shoulders of other Indigenous readers who might have experienced the same feelings.

Indian School Days: A Study of Resilience

When Basil Johnston published *Indian School Days* in 1988, he was a very different person than was Maria Campbell when she wrote *Halfbreed*. Under the tutelage of the Jesuit Brothers, Johnston had successfully completed both the elementary and secondary programs at St. Peter Claver's Residential School for Boys (later known as the Garnier School) and had then gone on to earn a bachelor of arts degree at Loyola College in Montreal.[35] Johnston is one of the few Indigenous people whom the colonial bureaucrats could display, if they dared, as a residential school success story. Having worked at the Royal Ontario Museum since 1970, Johnston also taught history in secondary school and lectured at several universities. Accordingly, Johnston was no stranger to writing, having published numerous stories of the Anishinaubaek,[36] both contemporary and traditional. Not only was Johnston aware of the power of the printed word, he was also conscious that the personal is, indeed, political. By 1988, Johnston was a mature scholar who knew his history and could not be intimidated by politicians, scholars, or bureaucrats. He was, and continues to be, well educated, politically astute, and imbued in what David Newhouse terms "postcolonial consciousness."[37] When Johnston ventured into the world of autobiography, he was well armed with a caustic wit and an astute analysis of the Canadian political landscape.

Indian School Days describes Johnston's life at St. Peter Claver's Residential School in the town of Spanish, in the province of Ontario. Although his narrator Basil, renamed "number 43" by school officials, is a consistent figure throughout the narrative, the story is not Basil's alone. *Indian School Days*, like *Halfbreed*, is the story of a community rather than that of a solitary individual. The idea for the narrative was born in 1973, when Johnston and a group of former schoolmates spent "an evening of recollection, of reliving the days in Spanish by recalling not the dark and dismal, but the incidents that brought a little cheer and relief to a bleak existence":[38] "None of the stories recounted in the text will be found recorded in any official or unofficial journals of the Garnier Residential School for Boys. In setting down some of the stories I have had to rely on my own memory and on the memories of my colleagues: Eugene (Captain) Keeshig, Charlie Shoot (Akiwenzie), Hector (Kitchi-meeshi Hec) Lavalley, Cecil King, Maxie Simon, Ernie (The Wrestler) Nadjiwon, and many, many more. This account of Garnier covering two periods, 1939–44 and 1947–50, *is as accurate as memory and effort and bias will allow*. I hope as well that it is fair" (11; emphasis added). Johnston's account of the genesis the narrative implies that his former schoolmates have authorized him to convert their stories into text, and, therefore, the narrative voice of the text can be defined accurately as a communal voice. *Indian School Days*, then, is the collective myth of the boys of the Spanish residential school.

It is significant that Johnston does not claim that the narrative is completely accurate nor does he deny the bias that will inevitably surface in any narrative account. Keeping this in mind, he contends that he will recount, in a manner that attempts to treat all characters with fairness, the story of the students and staff at St. Peter Claver's/Garnier Residential School. However, his goal of fairness does not prevent Johnston, through his narrator Basil, from liberally editorializing to enable him to provide readers with both a historical context and political analysis of the events that transpire within the narrative.

Johnston's introduction to *Indian School Days* supplies the context for the story to follow. In it, he includes a socio-economic analysis and critique of the town of Spanish and an explanation of the role that the school plays in the town's economy. He describes Spanish as a small village with little development to sustain its townspeople and little hope of a future. Characteristic of Basil's narrative is his sense of irony. He describes, for example, how the town survived difficult times, such as the Great Depression: "What kept the village from extinction in the 1930s were 'the school' and the Depression; the residents had nowhere to go" (1). In 1939, there are, in fact, two "Indian" residential schools in Spanish: St. Peter Claver's for boys and St. Joseph's for girls. In Spanish, the schools are one of the few sources of employment for the settlers, so "helping the Indians" has become an industry replete with employment opportunities for the townspeople. "There were a few residents on the north side of the highway," explains Basil, "eking out a living on the outcrops of the Laurentian Shield in hillbilly style…. The lucky ones worked for the CPR, Hydro, the Department of Highways and 'the schools'" (3). In this way, the town is a microcosm of Canadian society where "helping the Indians" continues to be a multi-million dollar industry that provides employment for a multitude of government bureaucrats, third-party managers, social workers, and prison guards, to name but a few.

As well as employment, the students of the schools provide the townspeople with entertainment. Townspeople turn out in droves to watch the students play "baseball, softball, football and hockey games, or to attend *The Pirates of Penzance* and other dramas put on by the boys." Basil sardonically comments that "were it not for 'the school,' Spanish might have been as dull as [the neighbouring community of] Walford" (3). Thomas King also comments on how Indians have come to function as "the entertainment" for contemporary settler society. "Somewhere along the way," he writes, "we ceased being people and somehow became performers in an Aboriginal minstrel show for White North America."[39] Johnston reveals how the schools have significance for both Indians and settlers, but that significance differs radically from one constituency to the other. For Status Indians, the schools have more sinister implications.

For Status Indians, the schools are a source of neither employment nor entertainment. Rather, they are the cause of fear. Basil explains the connotations of the word "Spanish" for the children of his reserve:

> "Spanish" might seem to be no more filled with menace than any other word; but it inspired dread from the very first time that we Indian boys heard it. From the tone in which statements like, "You should be in Spanish!" or "You're going to Spanish! Mark my words!" were delivered, we knew that "Spanish was a place for miscreants, just as hell and purgatory were for sinners.... None of us wanted to go to Spanish any more than we wanted to go to hell or a concentration camp.

> Though we didn't know for certain what Spanish represented, our fear of it was not without foundation. Many of our parents had gone to the institution—or one like it. But they did not share with us their knowledge of Spanish or Mount Elgin or the Mohawk Institute or Shingwauk. (6)

Unlike the Prairie provinces and British Columbia where almost all Status Indian children were forced to attend residential school, only those children that the Indian agents "selected" were required to attend residential schools in the Province of Ontario. At first, Indian agents "selected" children "from those who had shown the greatest talent and were the most deserving," but by the 1940s and 1950s "the basis of selection was modified somewhat in preference of cast-offs" (9). In Basil's case, the Indian agent and the priest made the decision to send him and some of the other Johnston children to Spanish without consulting his parents. His parents had separated, leaving their mother and grandmother to care for Basil and his four siblings.

The narrative exudes sarcasm and disdain when Basil describes how, "with nothing but our welfare in mind, of course," the Indian agent and priest "decided that not even the combined efforts of Grandmother and Mother were enough to look after five children and that they ought to be relieved of two of their burdens" (19). In 1939, then, the Indian agent "selects" ten-year-old Basil and his four-year-old sister, Marilyn, to go to Spanish. Basil's mother had not foreseen that the Indian agent would select young Marilyn. The intended victim was an older sister, but when the agent arrives at their home, that child is sick. Unable to leave without fulfilling his quota—"gotta take two at least," he tells Basil's mother—he takes Marilyn even though she has never attended school and speaks no English (20). When Basil's mother protests, he threatens to remove all of her children.

Long after the publication of *Indian School Days*, readers learn that the root of Basil's sarcasm is not only the government policy that removed him from his family but also for the degradation that he experienced while at residential school. In his preface to Sam McKegney's *Magic Weapons: Aboriginal Writers Remaking Community After Residential School*, Johnston describes being sexually abused within his first month at St. Peter Claver's Residential School for Boys, abuse that continued throughout his time there. Johnston also describes the shame he felt, believing himself to be "damaged goods" not worthy of love.[40] For decades those feelings of shame haunted him and affected all his intimate relationships.

Basil's choice of the term "cast-off" to describe the children "selected" is significant because it implies that the children were unwanted or abandoned. This, however, is not the case—or at least not entirely the case. The children "selected" for Spanish typically came from broken homes where the fathers had moved away and had left mothers and grandmothers struggling to feed and care for the children. It is important to understand how the lives of Status Indian men of the time, having been emasculated by the terms of the *Indian Act*, were filled with frustration. Even those men who participated in local governments as "chief and council" were powerless because, as Johnston writes, their "affairs and prospects were governed by an 'Indian agent' who ruled with autocratic hand and ill-informed dedication" (4). Although Basil makes no further mention of his father, by using the term "cast-off," he implies that the children are not wanted. Yet, his description of his mother's and grandmother's responses to the Indian agent's pronouncement that he will be removing their children is not congruent with the response of women who wish to "cast off" their children: "The mothers and grandmothers cried and wept, as mine did, in helplessness and in heartache. There was nothing, absolutely nothing, that they could do, as women and as Indians, to reverse the decision of 'the Department'" (8).

Basil explains how vulnerable the mothers and grandmothers were to abuse by petty bureaucrats, such as the Indian agents. They were not fluent in English. They had little education. And, under Canadian law, they had no right to choose what schooling would be best for their children. They, and their children, "were 'wards of the Crown,' not citizens of Canada" (12). Still, Basil's choice of terminology betrays a profound internal conflict. On the one hand, he is fully cognizant that his mother was powerless to prevent the Indian agent from removing him and his sister from their home. When she protests that his sister is too young to be removed, the Indian agents threatens her, replying, "'Well! If you don't want her to go, we'll take the whole family'" (20). On the other hand, he feels that his family has abandoned him, that he has truly been "cast off." Evidence of this internal contradiction appears again and again throughout the narrative.

Also telling is Basil's terminology regarding the students and their tenure at residential school. Basil refers to the students as "inmates" who have been "sentenced" to Spanish, thereby drawing our attention to the school officials' efforts to disempower and institutionalize the boys by eliminating individual and cultural differences. To that end, when Basil first arrives at school, Father Buck, one of the prefects who were the boys' primary caregivers, orders another student to shave Basil's head. Then, Buck issues him a uniform identical to that of the other students and assigns him the number 43, which will identify him for the remainder of his residence at Spanish. In 1939, the curriculum at St. Peter Claver's Residential School for Boys was still partially based on the industrial school model that many earlier policy-makers had endorsed. The school had two primary functions: to train each student in a trade and to foster religious vocations. Students were not prepared for university or even secondary education until several years later. Basil points out that St. Peter Claver's was a failure in both of its mandates: "while there were some accomplished chicken farmers and shoemakers, no graduate went into business; the trades for which we had been trained were rendered obsolete by new technology…. The school produced neither tradesmen nor priests" (26–7).

When Basil enters St. Peter Claver's in 1939, the school offers only grades one to eight. However, colonial policy dictates that students were required to remain at the school until they were sixteen years old whether they had completed grade eight before reaching sixteen or not. To that end, school officials place Basil in grade five even though he had already been promoted to grade six at the day school on the reserve. He learns that this was common practice:

> For my appointment to Grade 5, as I learned years later, was not a product of misunderstanding but a coldly calculated decision made "for my own good." For if I had been allowed to proceed to Grade 6 as I should have been, it would have disrupted the entire promotion and graduation schedule that decreed that all boys committed to a residential school remain at the institution until age sixteen, or until their parents, if living together, arranged an early parole…The only solution was to have a boy repeat grades until grade 8 and age sixteen were synchronized. I was not the only one to be so penalized. (35)

Modelled after schools for incorrigible White children, residential schools were, indeed, like prisons.[41] At St. Peter Claver's, the inmates were responsible for all the work required to maintain the institution, including caring for livestock and poultry, gardening, blacksmithing, cooking, tailoring, shoemaking, and cleaning. Basil recalls that "there was little in the entire institution that was not done by the inmates" (26). The Government of Canada provided St. Peter Claver's with "forty cents per student per day." For any other expenditure, the school depended upon the labour of the inmates or the charity of its "donors" (26).

Although residential school life is, at first, a mystery to Basil, its daily routine soon becomes etched upon his psyche. Chapter 4, "A Day in the Life of Spanish," provides readers with a sense of that mind-numbing routine. It is important to note that implicit in the school's routine and its draconian enforcement of rules is the residential school policy that prohibited spontaneity and creativity. Beginning at 6:15 and ending at 10:00, the days are a repetition of religiosity, labour, and study, with only minimal time allotted for meals and play, and the omnipresent clanging of the bells marking the time for the boys to move from one activity to the next. Free time is conspicuously absent. Basil describes how the priests and prefects attempt to operate the school with military precision: "Everything was by the clock, by the book, or by regulations" (40). Important is Basil's analysis of the imposition of strategies to compel the children to adapt to life in an institution and its consequences: "Bells and whistles, gongs and clappers represent everything connected with sound management—order, authority, discipline, efficiency, system, organization, schedule, regimentation, conformity—and may in themselves be necessary and desirable. But they also symbolize conditions, harmony, and states that must be established in order to have efficient management: obedience, conformity, dependence, subservience, uniformity, docility, surrender. In the end it is the individual who must be made to conform, who must be made to bend to the will of another" (43). When priests and prefects attempt to force the children to move instantly from one assigned activity, the children resist.

Since the penalty for open defiance would be swift and painful, as would the penalty for running away, the boys learn to exercise "a form of quiet disobedience directed against bells, priests, school, and, in the abstract, all authority, civil and religious" (29–30). "Dawdling," in this context, becomes a political action constituting a show of passive resistance. Under normal circumstances, resistance would be predictable in children. However, these circumstances are not normal. The priests grant the children no autonomy and expect them to obey without question. Thus, the children's acts of resistance are testaments to their resilient spirits. It is ironic that school officials, whose primary purpose is to educate Indigenous children, value obedience more than inquiry.

Even more oppressive than the regimentation of the children's activities is the priests' and prefects' "never-ending surveillance" (139). It is significant to note that the hyper-vigilance that the priests and prefects display with regard to the boys' behaviour does not extend to their psychological health or to their diet. Sparse in quantity and inferior in quality, the meals at St. Peter Claver's reveal the miserliness of the administration. Meals consist of "mush" or baked beans for breakfast and soup—barley, pea, vegetable, or onion—for dinner and supper. Mid-afternoon the boys receive a small snack, which the administration bestows with the grandiose title "collation," a title larger than the meal itself. Collation consists of a wedge of raw cabbage, two raw carrots, or a raw turnip, and the boys consider it "little better than animal fodder" (38).

Food and its conservation become major preoccupations for the boys. At breakfast, each boy is allotted a tablespoon of lard with which he is to "butter" his bread not only at breakfast but also at dinner and supper. In an effort to conserve lard for their other two meals, the boys use it sparingly at breakfast and then cache it under the meal table to be retrieved at dinner and supper. Because of their scarceness, lard and bread become commodities for trade. Boys fortunate enough to have earned money purchase candies and then trade them for staples. "The going rate on the open market was seven jawbreakers for a slice of bread and five for a spoon of lard," explains Basil (96). Other boys supplement their diets by using slingshots to hunt small game when the priests take them out on excursions into the bush. Still, even with the supplementary food that the boys acquire with their resourcefulness, the quantity of food is inadequate: "in quantity served there was just enough food to blunt the sharp edge of hunger for three or four hours, never enough to dispel hunger completely until the next meal" (40). Precious by virtue of its scarcity, food becomes the object of reverence for the boys who eat in complete silence and savour every morsel: "'I'm full' was an expression alien in our world and to our experience" (40).

Throughout the narrative, Basil quotes the anonymous boy who is always present in the background verbalizing the words that other boys say only in their minds. When one of the boys leaves the school, the anonymous voice begs, "Tell everybody what it's like in here" (157). Clearly, the boys believe that, if only people knew how they were treated, things would improve. A visit from the school inspectors proves that they are wrong. When the school inspectors arrive at the school, the priests immediately improve the boys' diets. Gone are the lard and the thin soups, and in their place the boys find butter and soup so thick with meat and vegetables that it could almost be labelled a stew. The boys are momentarily dumbfounded but quickly grasp that the presence of the inspectors is the cause of their good fortune. However, when one of the boys tells the inspectors about their normal diet, they do not believe him. And, when the inspectors leave, so do the improved meals, and the boys' diet reverts to its former deplorable state. Clearly their behaviour reveals that the priests are aware that the meals they feed the boys are substandard. Were they not, they priests would partake of the same food as the boys.

Not only does the priests' menu differs radically from that served to the boys, the meals served to the priests and prefects are relatively lavish in both quantity and quality. Their breakfasts consist of bacon and eggs with toast, butter, and jam. For the priests and prefects, roast beef and pork are common fare. The boys are well aware that the relative abundance of the priests' meals is the direct result of the boys' labour in the barns, chicken coops, mills, and kitchen. Needless to say, the poor food and inequitable treatment trigger resentment in the boys. As a result, the boys engage in thievery to remedy this injustice by developing an elaborate system of signals that enable the kitchen workers to pilfer such items of value, such as eggs—scrambled, poached, or fried. More so than in the classrooms, it is in these attempts to get the better of an unjust system that the boys learn analysis and problem solving.

Although clearly inadequate, the meagre rations that the school provides are not the cause of the most profound pain that the boys suffer. Johnston believes that the boys' fixation on their inadequate diet provides them with a concrete focus for their emotional discomfort. The real source of their anguish, however, is less tangible. "Food, or the lack of it, was something that the boys could point to as a cause of their suffering," explains Johnston; "the other was far too abstract and therefore much too elusive to grasp" (137). The boys of St. Peter Claver's suffer the trauma of being removed from their families and confusion because few of their families come to rescue them. Because parents are all-powerful in the eyes of their children, the boys simply cannot comprehend that their parents are powerless to oppose the agents of the colonial bureaucracy. Thus, when the Indian agents and the priests "select" a boy to go to Spanish, that boy cannot help but suspect that his parents are complicit in the decision, that his parents do not want him. Most families live too far away to ever be able to visit the children and explain. The only strategy that the priests and prefects are able or willing to employ to address the boys' emotional needs is to keep them so busy with work, prayer, and study that they have little time to feel. Especially tragic are the very young boys whom Basil calls "the babies": "They were a sad lot, this little crowd of babies; they seldom laughed or smiled and often cried and whimpered during the day and at night. Having no one in this world, in this institution, except this young scholastic to look to, to call for, to touch, to hold, these little waifs were even more wretched than we were. If they weren't huddled around the young scholastic's knee, they were hunched in their wretchedness and misery in a corner of the recreation hall, their outsized boots dangling several inches above the asphalt floor" (60). Still, all the boys, not just the babies, suffer the effects of emotional starvation and their feelings cannot be repressed indefinitely.

The boys find it difficult to repress their feelings when they are in their beds at night or when holidays come. At these times when they are not distracted by the priests' never-ending activities, the feelings that they have repressed, feelings that their loved ones have deserted them, rise to the surface and incite resentment that is directed towards their families rather than the colonial regime and its minions. Johnston describes how, at Christmas, "the feeling of abandonment, never far from the surface, now welled up and intensified every boy's inability to understand why his parents had given him up and turned him over to the priests" (80). Likewise, Basil compares the emotional response of the boys who must stay at school over the summer when they witness their schoolmates' excitement about going home: "For them someone cared; for us...we were forgotten" (92). Although the boys feel loneliness for their family, they also doubt their family's love for them: "But thoughts of family and home did not yield much comfort and strength; instead such memories as one had served to inflame the feelings of alienation and abandonment and to fan the flames of resentment. Soon the silence was broken by the sobs and whimpers of boys who gave way to misery and sadness, dejection and melancholy, heartache and gloom" (45). Without some kind of plausible explanation, the seeds of resentment are thereby planted in that child, and many Indigenous families have been torn apart by this unresolved grief and resentment that all too many former students are unable to let go even when they understand the situation. By giving voice to feelings and responses that former students share, Johnston helps them begin a process of healing.

It is remarkable that Basil fails to mention his family again after he describes how the Indian agent removed him and his sister from his home. Indeed, he does not mention his mother again, not even when he narrates his return to the reserve. At that time, he states that his father has left the reserve to work in a lumber camp, but never talks about his mother. The absence of mention raises many questions. Did something happen to his mother? Was their relationship irreparably damaged? Could Basil ever forgive his parents? These are questions that *Indian School Days* does not answer.

Although it would be easy for Johnston to set up a simplistic dichotomy of evil priests and victimized boys, he resists. When Johnston published *Indian School Days*, he was almost sixty years of age, and his narrative reveals that the passing of time has given him enough distance to fairly appraise people and situations that caused him so much pain in his childhood. To that end, his characterizations of the priests are fully developed, perhaps even more than his characterizations of his schoolmates. He describes the clergy in a manner that emphasizes their human fallibility and de-emphasizes their self-appointed role as God's helpers on earth: "Like boys and girls, priests and nuns were subject to laws and passions, the rules and emotions that govern the religious and the secular; they were no more exempt, by virtue of their vocations, to accidents or misadventures or mishaps than anyone else, although their discipline may have ensured that they suffered fewer accidents than ordinary mortals" (123). By their nature, the more idio-syncratic priests are easily individuated, and Basil's descriptions of their peculiarities are highly entertaining.

Brother Jean-Baptiste Manseau, for example, is an eccentric and relatively tolerant character with one short leg and hair that resembles Harpo Marx's. He does not reprimand the students when they reverse his initials to bestow upon him the nickname "B.J." or "Beedj," which is short for "Beedj-mauss" in Anishinaubaemowin and is a play on words. "Beedj-mauss" translates as "he comes reeking of the smell of smoke," alluding to the Brother's habit of smoking a pipe (39). Although "he could deliver a mean kick, especially with the discarded Mountie's riding boots that he wore," the boys still like Beedj-mauss because he does not send them to the school administrator, Father Hawkins, for punishments (39). If Beedj-mauss's kicks are prefer-able to Father Hawkins's alternative, one can only wonder what kinds of punishment Hawkins administers. Basil suggests that the students consider Beedj-mauss a kindred spirit because he seems to spend as much time on the receiving end of Father Hawkins's wrath as do the boys. Beedj is unable to overcome his propensity for profanity—even habitually taking the name of the Lord in vain, a habit frowned upon by the Society of Jesus, especially in its priests. As a result of his habitual cursing, Beedj spends an inordinate amount of time "on retreat." Whereas the other Brothers go on retreat once a year, Beedj-mauss goes regularly. To the boys, going "on retreat" seems to be the Jesuit equivalent of detention. It is only in Johnston's preface to *Magic Weapons*, published in 2007, that we learn that he spent much of his time avoiding Brother Manseau's kisses, and about Johnston's resulting feelings of disgust for the man.

Basil also speaks fondly of Father Laflamme, who staffs the infirmary, and Brother McLaren, the school's "jack-of-all-trades." Father Laflamme cares for sick and injured boys with a demonstration of compassion that is rare at St. Peter Claver's. Unlike his colleagues, "Father Laflamme sensed that what a boy needed was not medical treatment so much as a kind word and a pat on the head before going to bed" (83). Rather than calling the boys by number, he calls them by pet names, "Doodlebug" and "Little Fathead," and gives them the attention they crave. Likewise, Brother McLaren—the school's shoemaker, baker, and gardener, amongst other duties—treats boys with compassion and generosity. An orphan who travelled the country as a hobo begging for food before joining the priesthood, Brother McLaren is not averse to supplying a hungry boy with an extra morsel of food. Basil also describes Brother McLaren as "odd" because of his habit of talking not only to himself but also to piano keys, cordwood, and whatever else thwarts him in the course of his duties. When he encounters difficulty inserting a piece of cordwood into the furnace, he speaks directly to the wood "delivered in a tone that was supposed to be soothing," saying, "You don't want to go in, do you? I guess I can't really blame you. I wouldn't want to go in there myself. I even hate having to do this to you" (69). Brother McLaren's antics, therefore, provide some much needed levity for the boys.

Basil's description of Brother Edmund O'Keefe, his intellectual mentor, reveals how much the boys flourished when treated with dignity. Although Brother O'Keefe does not lose his temper and punish the boys, it is not so much his gentleness that Basil remembers as his demonstration of confidence in the boys' ability to learn. Brother O'Keefe's manner implies that he respects the boys' intelligence, something absent in the other classrooms of the institution. A skilled orator and avid reader, Brother O'Keefe instills in Basil a love of literature and language that remains with him throughout his life. Basil describes Brother O'Keefe's impact on the boys in relation to their educational environment:

> By comparison with courses of study in other schools, our curriculum would have been regarded as below standard. It's true that we did not have access to a well-stocked library, or attend classes from 9:00 A.M. to 4:00 P.M. It's also true that we were taught to know what to do with what little we knew; we were taught to be resourceful. But unless one has a sense of worth and dignity, resourcefulness, intelligence, and shrewdness are of little advantage. Brother O'Keefe, in the little time he had to teach us, instilled in us intangibles that were far more important than mountains of facts. (66)

Not only does Johnston's characterization of the priests who did their best to educate the boys support his effort to provide a fair account of his residential school experience, it also gives credibility to his critique of the institution.

In contrast to Basil's characterization of the more kindly priests is his characterization of Father Buck, the prefect who oversees the "team" to which Basil has been assigned. The prefects treat the boys in a way that could only by described as cold, cruel, and inflexible, and, consequently, the boys do not trust them. As the prefect with whom he interacts most often, Father Buck becomes Basil's nemesis. Had Johnston chosen to relate the narrative from a child's perspective, he would have characterized Father Buck as a cold and callous man whose peremptory treatment of the boys in his care is inexcusable. However, because Basil narrates his story from an adult's perspective, he explores Father Buck's situation more thoroughly than he could have as a child. Father Buck's position is tenuous, indeed, because he has not yet been fully accepted into the Society of Jesus. The school is known as a proving ground for these young men, desirous of joining the Jesuits, and "during their regency, the prefects, sometimes called 'scholastics' by the priests, had to demonstrate that they had the stuff to be Jesuits" (44). Thus, in the same way that the prefects continually watch the boys, the more senior priests continually watch and evaluate the prefects. Their future is dependent on their performing in a manner consistent with the Jesuit code of conduct, an onerous undertaking for any young man, but even worse for Father Buck, who is a German national in Canada when those countries are at war.

The adult Johnston understands how difficult it must have been for Father Buck to be stranded behind enemy lines trying to gain the approval of senior priests from an enemy nation. Although Basil gives no indication that the other priests are prejudiced against the German prefects in their midst, the boys clearly are. When the lights go out at night or when Father Buck's back is turned, the boys take turns whispering the words "Nazi" over and over again. Father Buck demands to know "Who says thees?" but to no avail (46). The boys merely mock him. In retrospect, Basil understands how the boys' behaviour must have affected the young prefect: "he must often have wished he were elsewhere: Montreal, Kingston, Halifax, Winnipeg, Regina …India …Iran—any place but Spanish. Spanish was known as an institution that made or unmade priests, and young men who had just completed four years of their novitiate at Guelph must have dreaded assignment in northern Ontario" (54). Johnston's characterization of Father Buck also reveals his compassion for the man and understanding that there were more people than the students who were ensnared in the residential school system. He saves his real contempt for the politicians and policy-makers who created the system in the first place.

Johnston's treatment of Father Hawkins, the administrator of St. Peter Claver's school, whom the boys nickname "Thin Beak," differs from his treatment of Father Buck in a number of significant ways. Unlike Father Buck's rigidity and short temper, which could be linked to the stress that he is experiencing, Father Hawkins' cruelty is inexplicable to Basil. As administrator, Father Hawkins is the chief disciplinarian at the school. That is not to say that the other priests do not lash out in fits of anger, striking the boys with fists and feet; rather, it is Father Hawkins to whom the prefects send the boys when their "crimes" are most severe. The prefects' stock threat—"Just wait and Father Hawkins fix you"—strikes terror in the hearts of the boys: "Father

Hawkins became in our minds the Arch-Executioner and Flogger who 'just waited' for evildoers to be sent to him" (138). Father Hawkins does not lash out in anger like the other priests do. He is cold and calculating in the administration of punishments. He lashes the boys' hands with a razor strap, and the number of lashes depends upon the severity of the crime and the boys' willingness to confess to it. This is problematic for boys who are innocent.

Basil recalls a time when the senior prefect finds a cigarette under the desk where he is sitting with Kitchi-Meeshi Hec and accuses the two boys of smoking. Because the boys are innocent, they refuse to admit to the crime. The prefect sends them to see Father Hawkins. Since neither boy is a smoker, they are certain that justice will prevail and that they will not be punished. Their confidence reveals their naïveté; they do not understand how the Father perceives them. Father Hawkins has never taken the time to know the boys in his care and, therefore, is not aware that Basil and Hector do not smoke. Without even weighing the evidence, the Father judges the boys as guilty.

This incident teaches the boys three lessons. First of all, "it was better to tell a lie than to tell the truth when our teachers preferred to believe their own biases" (160). Secondly, persisting in proclaiming one's innocence will result in a harsher punishment. And lastly, the cost of personal safety is one's dignity and integrity. Father Hawkins will reduce the number of lashes for any boy who begins "howling and screaming and bawling and dancing at the very outset of a thrashing" (161). For most boys, this is a price too great to pay. Indeed, many boys, like Ben Shigwadja, would prefer to accept "a thrashing" in complete silence in order to maintain self-respect. Ben, in a show of resistance, would often thank the priest who inflicted the thrashing, stating, "Thanks, Father; gotta tough up my hands, might get sof', them" (107). Surely Father Hawkins's attempts to manipulate the boys to force them to behave as if they were cowards are the real cause of their scorn for him.

In the chapter "The Best Laid Plans…," Johnston alters his narrative strategy unexpectedly shifting from first-person to third-person narration, an unusual choice in an autobiographical narrative. In this chapter, the narrator describes events that transpire at a bazaar held in the impoverished parish of Mississauga. Presumably, this story is well known in the Anishinaubaek community, since none of the boys from the school, including Basil, are present to witness the events narrated. Father Hawkins from St. Peter Claver's Residential School is the visiting missionary pastor for Mississauga and organizes a bazaar where he will sell used clothing and glasses of root beer to raise money to support the parish. To that end, he persuades wealthy settlers from Toronto to donate clothing and persuades Miss Leutsch from the St. Joseph's Residential School for Girls to donate two barrels of her home-brewed root beer. Although root beer is supposed to be a non-alcoholic beverage, the root beer in one of the barrels has fermented, unbeknownst to the Father and Miss Leutsch. In a magnanimous gesture, Father Hawkins rewards each of the Indian men whom he conscripts to haul barrels and boxes into the church with a drink of now-fermented root beer and unknowingly sets off a chain of events both humorous and revealing. The narrator describes the events that transpire both in the physical world as they are focalized through Father Hawkins's perceptions and in the emotional changes that occur in Father Hawkins's inner world. This change of narrative strategy, the shift from first-person retrospective to third-person, is worthy of note because it departs from the narrative norm for autobiography and reveals the tenuousness of the boundaries between autobiography and fiction. This third-person narrator appears periodically for the remainder of the text.

When the men taste the root beer, they are surprised to discover that it has fermented into wine. At this time, it is still illegal for Indians to consume alcohol. One of the movers informs Father Hawkins that he is serving wine, but the Father, having never bothered to learn to speak the language of his parishioners, does not understand. The mover tells him, "'Gawaetaunih mino-waugummih maundah zhowmin-aubo,' which was to say, 'Mighty damn good stuff, this wine'" (124). That alcohol is prohibited makes it all the more desirable in the minds of many First Nations people of the time, and as a result, word that the Father is serving wine spreads rapidly throughout the Anishinaubaek. The narrator explains that the Father quickly becomes troubled and perplexed when he witnesses the once-sober men becoming inexplicably inebriated before his very eyes. The narrator reports that "Father Hawkins was getting anxious" and that "he didn't want a scandal connected with his bazaar" (124). Ever vigilant for signs of sin, the Father sets out to find the source of the liquor, unaware that he himself is culprit.

It is in the narrative rendering of Father Hawkins's inner life that we learn that the man whose name strikes terror in the minds of the little boys of St. Peter Claver's is himself a coward when he encounters adult Indian men. It seems that Father Hawkins is a diminutive man weighing no more than 150 pounds. The narrator tells us that Father Hawkins wishes that he could to chastise Nigunaub, a large Indian man who shows signs of intoxication; indeed, he "would have liked nothing better than to grab Nigunaub by the throat and shake the hell out of him" (125). However, although Father Hawkins shows no reluctance to grab the boys at the school by the throat and "shake the hell" out of them, he does not have the courage to do the same to Nigunaub. Not only is Father Hawkins afraid to "shake the hell" out of Nigunaub, he is even reluctant to reprimand him. The narrator describes the internal struggle that transpires within the confines of Father Hawkins's mind when he rationalizes his cowardly failure to reprimand a drunken Nigunaub who pledges to begin attending church:

> For some time afterwards Father was uneasy with his conscience. He could not forget Nigunaub. Putting off the man could well mean damnation for the man for non-attendance at Sunday mass, for intoxication, for swearing. The Lord only knew what other evil the man had done, but Father Hawkins could imagine. It could mean damnation for himself for passing up the opportunity to save Nigunaub's soul. Even if Nigunaub's penitence had been inspired by Four Aces or Slingers, particularly insidious wines, and would all be forgotten on the morrow, still the man deserved a chance. Providence operated in mysterious ways: it might even operate through wine. (126)

Many former residential school students are unable to rid themselves of the fears that school officials instilled in them. Fear of authority figures, such as priests, police, and government bureaucrats, to name but a few, hinders their ability to move forward as adults. Johnston's imaginative narration of Father Hawkins's inner life supports his endeavour to divest the priests of the excessive power that they wielded over the children charged to their care. By depicting them as mere mortals like the rest of us, Johnston shows those readers who were residential school students themselves that they have no more to fear.

In the second story in the chapter "The Best Laid Plans…," the story of Stingy's wedding, Johnston's third-person narrator continues to expose the fallibility of the priests in a seemingly humorous tale. Johnston begins the story with an editorial comment regarding the government's and churches' two-pronged attack on Indigenous cultures: "You can't live the way your ancestors did; you have to organize your time, your work, if you're going to get anywhere. You can no longer just move in together and live as husband and wife; you can no longer get names for your children from the first thing that you see or hear after the birth of a child; you can no longer…you can no longer…you can no longer…. From now on you must do things the civilized way, the lawful way, the moral, Christian way" (128). Johnston's commentary draws attention to the fact that the settlers did not consider any aspect of Indigenous peoples' ways of life acceptable. Colonial policies governed, and often banned, even the most intimate relationships. Johnston also emphasizes the soul-destroying nature of the constant criticism that the settlers and their government heaped on Indigenous people. And, when this constant censure becomes government policy, its oppressive nature becomes systemic.

This section of the narrative is focalized through the perceptions of Stingy, a graduate of St. Peter Claver's Residential School for Boys. Stingy's legal name is Harvey Ermitinger, and like many residential school graduates he lives between cultures. On the one hand, Stingy is the product of a Catholic residential school education and, accordingly, wants a priest to officiate over his marriage ceremony. On the other hand, he knows something of the traditions of the Anishinaubaek, and in that culture he and his fiancée belong to the same clan or totem. As members of the same totem they are, in effect, brother and sister, and a marriage between them would be tantamount to incest. The narrator accesses Stingy's inner life and reports that "Stingy was bothered by this relationship not a little" (129). However, like many former residential school students, Stingy has been taught to venerate the wisdom of the priests above that of his Anishinaubaek elders. As a result, he approaches Father Baker rather than his family elders to discuss his concern and ask for advice. However, Father Baker, whose world is comprised of binaries—good/evil, true/false, Christian/pagan—cannot tolerate any belief system other than his own. Thus, he dismisses Stingy's concerns as "part of old pagan primitive beliefs and practices" and chastises Stingy, who he contends "should know better than to believe in or worry about superstitious practices." The narrator, sardonically, makes note of how "with a wave of his hand the priest dismissed several thousand years of Anishinaubae history" (129). Despite Stingy's reverence of him, Father Baker proves to be fallible. He forgets his promise to preside over the wedding and leaves Stingy, his bride-to-be, and their guests waiting at the altar for seven hours. Many humorous events occur while the wedding party waits for the tardy priest, and by the time the priest arrives the father of the bride, best man, and most of the guests are falling-down drunk. But Stingy and his would-be bride are sober and waiting patiently. In the end Stingy marries his intended. Still, the wedding can only be described as a disaster. How can it be anything else when Stingy has married his sister?

The narrative shifts once more after a major change in Basil's life. With only a few hours' warning and no ceremony, Basil leaves residential school prior to turning sixteen years of age. Basil does not explain how he is able to leave prior to his sixteenth birthday and is silent about his homecoming. The narrative resumes several months later. Basil mentions that, after leaving residential school, he attended grade nine at Regiopolis College in Kingston, Ontario, which is a significant distance away from his home community of Cape Croker. Regiopolis is another school operated by the Jesuits, and its student body, although all-male, was not all-Indian. Basil notes that he dropped out three months before completion "to return to the sanctuary and comfort of Cape Croker" (174). Although he does not give an explanation for his early departure, his words suggest that life at an integrated school might have been challenging in a different manner than was residential school. And although he barely mentions this episode in his educational journey—one sentence in total—that one sentence is significantly more than he allocates to his mother and siblings, who are conspicuous by their absence from the narrative. Granted, Johnston's stated objective of this narrative is to tell stories of the resilience of the boys of the residential school. That he is so reticent about his immediate family is perplexing, nonetheless.

When the narrative resumes, Basil is back on the reserve living alone in an empty house that once belonged to his grandmother. He mentions that his father has recently vacated the house to pursue work in lumber camps but says nothing about spending any time together. Too proud to ask for social welfare, Basil tries to support himself by working in two occupations common to Indian men of his generation: logging and trapping. He lists the names of members of his extended family—aunts, uncles, and grandparents—as potential customers and advisors, but says nothing about his day-to-day relationship with them. Basil devotes a very short segment of the narrative to his next three years. He is silent about his family and says little about the people on the reserve. Instead, he only describes his labour. Although Basil works diligently, he has learned no useful skills that would enable him to be self-supporting. The situation in which he finds himself is common to many former residential school students: "because of their extended isolation from their families, the persistent denial of their culture and the abuse, many returned unable to lead any sort of productive life, old or new."[42] Basil's experience reveals how residential schools partially failed to achieve their goals. Had Basil been offered work as a toilet cleaner, he probably could have been successful, since that was the only occupation for which his residential school education has trained him. Ironically, there is no plumbing on the reserve and outdoor toilets are still the norm; therefore, there are no toilet-cleaning jobs to be found.

Residential schools did not prepare Indigenous children to be assimilated into settler society. Instead, they de-educated the children so that they were unable to engage in traditional ways of earning a living. One cannot help but wonder if the clergy and policy-makers considered the schools partially successful then? In Basil's absence, St. Peter Claver's has been renamed Garnier Residential School for Boys and its new secondary program is unique among Indian residential schools. When Basil tells his neighbour, Frank Nadjiwon, that he is considering returning to Spanish to enter the school's new secondary program, Frank exclaims, "Yes! You ought to go back, it's your only chance" (179). With no other alternatives, Basil returns on his own volition to Spanish believing that a residential school education will ensure his future. His decision seems reasonable under the circumstances.

In the three years he spends back at Cape Croker, it becomes clear that Basil would be incapable of supporting himself trapping or logging. Having spent his formative years at residential school, he has no training in those occupations; however, his inability to support himself working as a logger and a trapper is not the only explanation for Basil's decision to return to residential school. The school has become a source of physical and emotional security for Basil, and his easy re-entry into the world of residential school reveals how institutionalized he has become. When Basil faces the challenges of living independently, he struggles to survive. Although the food at the school was inadequate, it was served regularly. Furthermore, for almost six years, Basil lived without the right to make even the most minor decisions about his life. From the time he awakened in the morning until the time he went to bed at night, the priests scheduled his every move and made all decisions for him. Although the narrative emphasizes the few incidents of resistance, it is clear that the priests and prefects kept that resistance in check and effectively controlled every aspect of the boys' lives. Rather than teaching the students to be self-sufficient adults who were able to make healthy choices regarding their lives, the schools teach their students to be helpless and dependent.

When Basil returns to Spanish, he learns that the school has a new name and new administrator. Father Oliver has replaced Father Hawkins as school administrator and brought with him some relatively progressive attitudes. With a new administrator and with students attending of their own volition, the Garnier School acquires a new atmosphere, and Basil feels optimistic about his future. Even the food has improved, and the priests now grant the boys the freedom to go into the town of Spanish on their own and socialize with the young people from the town. Basil is careful to acknowledge the priests' hard work in their efforts to provide the boys with an education comparable to that of the settler children. Yet, some things have not changed.

Under Father Oliver's regime, food continues to be of supreme importance in the boys' minds and the priests continue to control the kitchen. Thus, when Brother Westaway removes the ever-popular baked beans from the menu, the boys are aghast. At first, they believe that this must have been an oversight and tactfully attempt to communicate the error to Brother Westaway. When hinting fails, they complain bitterly to each other and to Mr. McCart, one of the new teachers who does not belong to the clergy. The lesson that Mr. McCart imparts in response to the boys' complaints is a radical one in that it introduces the concept of equality among men, something that has been absent from the Jesuit residential school curriculum:

> "You know what's wrong with you guys? Too naïve! You're just too damned naïve for your own good. You act as if priests can do no wrong; that they're always right. You look on them as if they were tin gods. Come on guys, wake up. They deserve respect but not veneration. They are men just like the rest of us, with their share of laziness, envy and pride. They get angry like anybody else. Some of them are selfish, more selfish than ordinary laymen…and maybe they have a harder struggle by virtue of their vocation and vows than we have. Come on, guys, you're men just like them. Why don't you talk to them and look them in the eye while you're talking?" (223)

Having been taught to place "God's helpers" on a pedestal, the boys are dumbstruck at the thought of talking to the priests "man to man." Once spoken, McCart's ideas take root and, eventually, a delegation of boys, full of optimism, musters the courage to take their complaints to Father Oliver. By this time, the removal of the beans from the menu has come to stand for all of the boys' complaints. If Mr. McCart thought that Father Oliver would respect the boys for behaving as if they were equals and presuming to discuss their complaints with him, he was wrong. Father Oliver does not welcome the boys' challenge to his authority and gives them two choices: accept the priests' dictates without question or leave. Thus, the boys learn that even in a progressive school they will never be equal to the priests and that good treatment is dependent upon their never-wavering shows of gratitude.

The priests continue to control every aspect of the boys' lives and to inculcate in them the beliefs of the Catholic Church. Basil points out how ludicrous their need to control can be when the priests, who have taken vows of celibacy, take it upon themselves to teach sex education. Gathering together the boys from the Garnier School and the girls from St. Joseph's, Father McDonough lectures them about the protocol for intimate relationships and places full responsibility for sexual conduct on the girls. Addressing the girls as "My dear vessels of virginity," Father McDonough explains that it is the girls' responsibility to keep male sexual drive in check: "You…must help…boys…ahem… girls…Boys are…more…ahem…passionate than… ahem…girls…ahem" (231). The contradictions in these teachings have implications for the future social health of the children. On the one hand, the priests teach the children the Christian creation myth in which woman was created from the rib of a man, that she is responsible for original sin, and that God has punished her so that in sorrow she shall bring forth children. They also teach the children that a man rules over his wife. At the same time the priests teach the children that girls are responsible for controlling the boys' sexual drive, thereby implying that they will be blamed for any sexual misconduct. Clearly, these teachings contain mixed messages that have contributed to the domestic violence that has become epidemic in Indigenous communities.

Johnston uses the story of Stingy's marriage to his sister to explain how the clergy and government imposed Christian beliefs and values on the Indigenous children in their care in an effort to stamp out Indigenous cultures. Johnston continues to expose how the imposition of Christianity affects Indigenous people in the story of the Garnier sex-education class. It is clear in Basil's earlier description of his life on the reserve prior to residential school that Christianity was already well established in his community. In his story of Father McDonough's sex-education class, Johnston exposes how those Christian teachings have had a profound effect on the cultural health of Indigenous communities and, as a result of cultural disintegration, now affect Indigenous peoples' emotional and sexual health. Today, the First Nations and Inuit Health Branch of Indian and Northern Affairs Canada grapples with individual and community health issues directly related to the breakdown of the cultural conventions that once governed intimate relationships and the imposition of patriarchal Christianity. The rate of teen pregnancies, single-parent households, domestic violence, and sexually transmitted diseases, including HIV/AIDS, are all disproportionately high among Indigenous people. Yet, like the storytellers of the Anishinaubaek oral tradition, Johnston does not connect the dots for his readers to explain the cause-and-effect relationship between the imposition of Christianity and the health and social problems that plague our communities today. Instead, he tells the stories with humour and with confidence that his readers will reflect on the stories and learn from them.

The stories that comprise *Indian School Days* exist in the space between the priests' efforts to institutionalize and assimilate the boys and their resistance to institutionalization and assimilation. "Were it not for the spirit of the boys," explains Johnston, "every day would have passed according to plan and schedule, and there would have been no story" (47). Rather than reconstructing Basil Johnston's personal myth, *Indian School Days*, on its surface, seems to be a collection of humorous anecdotes, of *ācimowinan* or everyday stories in the Anishinaubaemowin. However, the seeming simplicity of the text belies its more complex functionality. *Indian School Days* is both a social commentary and a healing narrative. Under its humorous veneer, *Indian School Days* functions as a study of resilience in the face of colonial oppression. Johnston documents the oppressive nature of residential schools and illustrates how the boys resist victimization. He describes the character traits of his schoolmates that support and further their resiliency. In this way, Johnston encourages his Indigenous readers either to see themselves in the characters and celebrate their own resiliency or to emulate the characters and develop their own resiliency. One practice that reveals this trait is the boys' habit of laughing in the face of adversity. Johnston's narrative exemplifies this practice, which is common to contemporary Indigenous people, thereby transforming what could be a series of tragic stories into humorous ones. The humour in the narrative, therefore, becomes an extension of the students' resistance.[43] By relating these stories to a larger audience, Johnston celebrates the resilient spirits of the boys and immortalizes them in text. Rather than depicting the boys as victims, Johnston characterizes them as indomitable spirits, who are able to survive hardships and ultimately overcome them. Likewise, rather than depicting the government and school officials as invincible oppressors, Johnston depicts them as flawed human beings, replete with fears, weaknesses, and idiosyncrasies, who, therefore, can be defeated. Healing occurs when the spirit of the narrative enters the readers and forever transforms them.

From Autobiography to Fiction

Bearing witness through writing to one's experience as an Indigenous person can be a valuable healing exercise; however, autobiography has its risks and shortcomings. Gold explains: "In the case of [autobiography], the writer and the goal of the writing are the same. The process is self-reflexive and the writer is engaged in the activity of creating and communicating his own life. The "I," the perceiver, is at the centre of the perception and becomes one with the perceived. There is no arguing with the procedure or its result. The consequence of [autobiography] is a given, hardly open to criticism or review."[44] This could be the case if the writer is merely transcribing her personal myth, but it is not the case if the writer is an Indigenous person writing in contemporary times and constructing her own personal myth along with the collective myth of her people. Although the writer is the centre of perception in the writing process—how could s/he be otherwise?—the persons who were present and witnessed the events recounted have their own perceptions of those events. Early in my career, I taught *Halfbreed* to a class of new students, most of whom were Indigenous people from Saskatchewan. I was taken aback when one of my students remarked, "My dad says that's a lie because he was there, and it didn't happen that way." Apparently, her father's recollection of events did not correspond to Campbell's. Likewise, my mother tells me that when she and her siblings get together and reminisce, she wonders if they grew up in the home with the same parents.

In a small, close-knit community like the Indigenous community in Canada, readers may often disagree with the writer's perceptions of her remembered past and her interpretation of those perceptions. As a result, Indigenous autobiography is often subject to criticism by other Indigenous people who have lived through the same events but perceive them differently. Consequently, Indigenous life writers often find themselves in the unenviable position of being criticized not only by the settlers whose narratives they write to correct but also by their own people. Disguising one's autobiography in fiction is often a less risky choice, and it is one that Beatrice Culleton Mosionier made when she wrote *In Search of April Raintree*, arguably a work of Indigenous life writing that is as influential as Campbell's *Halfbreed*. However, the boundary between factual narratives and fiction is tenuous at best. Campbell explains that in the language of the Nêhiyawak (Cree), the word for truth, *tapwêwin*, is mutable rather than fixed. Although each of us has our own truth, which is part of the greater truth of the collective, those truths are constantly shifting as our experiences and our contexts change. As contemporary Indigenous literature develops, then, fiction has become an attractive option for writers whose goal is to produce narratives that express what is *tapwêwin* for them.

chapter 4

Moving beyond the personal myth

In the process of writing their life stories, Indigenous people form "personal myths" that describe the narratives "each of us naturally constructs to bring together the different parts of ourselves and our lives into a purposeful and convincing whole."[1] When published in the form of autobiography, these personal myths form a new mythology that challenges the veracity of myths of the new Canadian nation-state. "Myth," explains Ronald Wright, "is an arrangement of the past, whether real or imagined, in patterns that reinforce a culture's deepest values and aspirations. Myths are so fraught with meaning that we live and die by them. They are the maps by which cultures navigate through time."[2] The colonial creation myth promotes the belief that the good, brave, and enduring settlers battled the forces of nature to bring civilization and progress to a land sparsely populated by primitive people, and the settlers' hard work and diligence resulted in the building of a new nation-state. Its function is to bolster and protect the collective self-esteem of the settlers. The destruction of Indigenous nations and the theft of Indigenous land go unmentioned even by those who are well aware of those events.

In 2005, the provinces of Saskatchewan and Alberta celebrated their hundredth anniversaries. The year was a particularly difficult one for Indigenous people. Not only was it a reminder of all that was lost, the settler governments persisted in trying to involve Indigenous people in its celebrations as if we, in some way, had played a role in creating the provinces. On 15 October 2005, at the University of Regina convocation ceremonies, former Saskatchewan

Premier Roy Romanow was granted an honorary doctorate and Dr. Robert Hawkins was installed as the new president of the university. As legal scholars and constitutional experts, both men are more than a little familiar with Canadian history. It would be unfair to say that their mention of the large Indigenous population of the province was mere lip service since Romanow and Hawkins are well-known civil libertarians. Still, Indigenous people comprised a small portion of the speeches with the larger part taken up with extolling the virtues of "settlers" who "built" this province, as if the land had been unsettled before the colonizers arrived. By continuing to endorse the colonial creation myth, thereby implying that Saskatchewan had been *terra nullius* before the province's creation, these illustrious scholars and public figures unwittingly inflicted yet another injury on every Indigenous person present. The question that comes to mind is, can these competing myths coexist?

Choosing to write autobiography is often a double-edged sword for Indigenous writers seeking to attain the narrative authority needed to challenge the colonial creation myth. On the one hand, autobiography claims the authority of eyewitness to the events narrated. On the other hand, that same authority can be challenged when readers' memories and interpretations of events differ from those of the author. Literary scholars and psychologists who study autobiography understand the unreliability of memory and the subjectivity of interpretation; however, not every reader shares that understanding. Yet if the socio-pedagogical function of Indigenous autobiography as personal myth is to reveal an alternate creation myth of the contemporary Canadian nation-state, then it is more important that it contain Indigenous truths rather than comprising a mere assemblage of facts. Myth making, after all, is an act of the imagination.

"Fiction has a great power to assist us in seeing process," Joseph Gold argues, "in seeing order and relation, and when we have done so we can apply it to ourselves."[3] Indeed, reading fiction is as effective in assisting readers to see order and relation as is reading life writing, and many readers have difficulty differentiating between the two. Beatrice Culleton Mosionier's *In Search of April Raintree*, Shirley Sterling's *My Name Is Seepeetza*, and Richard Wagamese's *Keeper 'n Me* all blur the lines between autobiography and fiction. *In Search of April Raintree* and *My Name Is Seepeetza* are advertised and marketed as juvenile fiction, while Richard Wagamese's *Keeper 'n Me*, although not marketed as juvenile fiction, is accessible to both youthful readers and adults. It is important to note that all three texts appear on many provinces' lists of texts approved for teaching in Canadian secondary schools, especially in those provinces in which large numbers of Indigenous people reside.[4]

The writers' professional backgrounds are significant. As one of the first and most influential Indigenous writers of fiction in Canada, Culleton Mosionier is the only one of the three who began her career as a novelist. Sterling was first an elementary school teacher and later a professor of teacher education at a large Canadian university. Wagamese is an award-winning journalist. The success of *In Search of April Raintree* undoubtedly influenced Sterling's and Wagamese's choices of genre when they began writing fiction. Like Culleton Mosionier, Sterling and Wagamese made deliberate choices regarding the mode of discursive production so as to ensure that their novels were effective in their socio-pedagogical objectives by being accessible and appealing to a broad range of audiences. Clearly, it is important to identify and understand one's audience when constructing a personal narrative: "The telling of a personal story, as a selective and imaginative process, is also powerfully influenced by the audience one has or anticipates having: an inevitable and necessary tension results as the fictive (ultimately from Latin *fingere*, 'to form or fashion') process is imposed on real events in an effort to re-present the self to others with a suasory purpose. As the line between the imagined and the factual blurs, the difficult question of how to determine what makes a 'good' (e.g., coherent, organized, meaningful, compelling) personal narrative becomes crucial."[5] With every choice, however, come consequences.

In the same way that choosing the genre of autobiography is a double-edged sword, so is the choice to write discursively "uncomplicated" fiction. In her article "'Nothing But the Truth': Discursive Transparency in Beatrice Culleton," Helen Hoy describes how this choice has diminished Indigenous fiction in the esteem of many literary scholars while simultaneously enhancing the narrative authority of the writers:

> With the author function, the dimension of discursive production, erased from the text, the writer is restored ironically, not as author but as anthropological site, source of authentic life experience, that which is being viewed. Such a critical stance lends itself further to an epistemology in which not only the text but the reality it purportedly transmits so directly, a reality that can somehow be separated from its textual rendering, is no longer a matter of discursive consensus, but remains unmediated, singular, unproblematic. Clarity of language and form threatens to generalize to other critical perceptions, so that first other dimensions of the text and eventually

experience itself are understood as equally simple, manifest, and unequivocal.[6]

The ostensibly simple discursive production of many works of Indigenous literature has spawned a debate regarding the appropriate scholarly home for their study. Should Indigenous literature be housed in English departments or in Indigenous/Native Studies departments (or, more often, programs)? That this debate exists at all is telling. The implication is that English departments study and teach sophisticated literary productions that trace their lineage to the English literary canon. Unsophisticated stories and "folklore" of Indigenous people should be relegated to Indigenous/Native Studies departments or programs where they could be examined from an anthropological perspective. When Indigenous writers write fiction to reach a broad audience with the hope of achieving a socio-pedagogical goal, the cost they often pay is scholarly respect.

In Search of April Raintree: Giving Voice to the Voiceless

When Culleton Mosionier published *In Search of April Raintree* in 1983, she became the first Indigenous person to expose, in an original work of fiction, what many Indigenous children experienced while in the care of the settler government's child-welfare system. *In Search of April Raintree* publicly acknowledges and validates the experiences of those children. Even though she could have written an autobiographical account of her own experiences as a foster child, Culleton Mosionier made a deliberate choice to write the story of a fictional family, the Raintrees, who, like her own family, were torn apart by Canadian government policies. However, the fact that Culleton Mosionier spent her formative years in foster care is prominently noted on the book's cover, and thus, for many readers, confers the text with the authority of an eyewitness account, overriding its claim to be fiction.

Rather than assuming the role of "I" narrator herself, Culleton Mosionier creates two fictional characters—April Raintree and, to a lesser extent, her sister Cheryl—to narrate what is, in effect, a compilation of narratives of foster children, including the author, her siblings, and other former foster children. Fiction, then, becomes a vehicle that enables Culleton Mosionier to tell many foster children's stories, not simply her own. Culleton Mosionier dedicates the novel to her sisters, Vivian and Kathy, who were unable to heal from childhood trauma and committed suicide. Having experienced the foster-care system first-hand and having close personal contact with other foster children, Culleton Mosionier combines imagination with experience to give voice to the inner lives of her siblings and of the many foster children who are unable to articulate their own stories. Likewise, the adult Culleton Mosionier, a parent herself, is now able to imagine the trauma her parents must have experienced when the child-welfare authorities removed her and her siblings from their care. By exploring the imaginary inner lives of her characters, Culleton Mosionier is better able to grasp the effects of the foster-care system on Indigenous individuals and communities and to share that understanding with her readers.

Working within the genre of fiction affords Culleton Mosionier the freedom to delve deeply into her own inner life in a manner that is simultaneously private and public. Only she, not her readers, knows which parts of the narrative are fact and which are fiction. This allows her to explore, in safety, the residual pain of the traumatic dissolution of her family and her subsequent experiences in foster care while at the same time validating those experiences by making them public. "Key to her healing," writes Deanna Reder, "is her need to articulate her memories publicly, to provide a testimonial to her own life."[7] It is through her writing that Culleton Mosionier is able to transform residual pain into text, which she can examine and eventually understand. In this way writing can be therapeutic. Culleton Mosionier's understanding of writing as healing in the creation of this novel marks a turning point in the development of Indigenous literature. It is not surprising to learn that Culleton Mosionier has influenced many other Indigenous writers to tell their stories in fictional form.

Culleton Mosionier is cognizant of the healing potential of fictional narratives. "In April 1981, I narrowed my goal from finding solutions to world problems to trying to find answers to questions relating to my own family," she explains. "Writing *In Search of April Raintree* was, for me, therapeutic. Unfortunately, I still know of people who might have benefited from reading this book and others like it, but didn't."[8] By sharing her characters' experiences through their reading of this novel, readers share in both Culleton Mosionier's pain and her healing. For the Indigenous readers who share Culleton Mosionier's experiences in the child-welfare system, the novel has become a vehicle of healing that validates their experiences and provides an opportunity for critical reflection and catharsis. The novel helps other Indigenous readers understand how friends and relatives have suffered through traumatic events that continue to affect them and their communities. For settlers who rarely question the accuracy of the colonial creation myth, the novel provides a window into a world that many did not know existed. Through her narrators' descriptions of life in foster care and the destruction of their family, Culleton Mosionier debunks the portion of the national collective myth that claims that the child-welfare policies—policies that authorized and promoted the relocation of Indigenous children to White homes—improved the quality of life of Indigenous children. Furthermore, reading *In Search of April Raintree* ensnares these readers in the world of the Raintree family and provokes them to vicariously share the pain that generations of Indigenous people have felt. Settlers are forever transformed by the emotions that inevitably arise when they begin to understand that one of the legacies of colonialism is the position of unearned privilege that they enjoy in contemporary neo-colonial society. *In Search of April Raintree* engages its readers on an emotional level and then transforms their understanding of the world.

The novel begins in 1955 and is set in the city of Winnipeg, which has the largest population of Indigenous people of any city in Canada. Prior to the commencement of the novel, health officials relocate the Raintree family from their home in Norway House, a small Indigenous community in northern Manitoba, to Winnipeg. The move is necessary because the father, Henry Raintree, had contracted tuberculosis and, at that time, no medical treatment would have been available in an isolated Indigenous community. For the Raintree family, however, relocation becomes dislocation, and dislocation causes a breach in the extended family unit. This is significant, since extended families are the foundation of Indigenous communities. Furthermore, few visibly Indigenous people lived in Winnipeg in the 1950s, and those who did almost always lived in rented slum housing in the poorest areas of the city. In the 1950s, racism was endemic, since neither federal nor provincial governments had yet passed laws to protect people from racial discrimination. Indeed, the Canadian Bill of Rights did not receive royal assent until 1960, and Status Indians did not receive the right to vote in federal elections until 31 March 1960.

At first, Henry Raintree is unable to work because of his health. Yet, after he recovers, he is still unable to find work because of his distinctly Indigenous appearance. April describes her father as "a little of this, a little of that, and a whole lot of Indian...[with] black hair, dark brown eyes which turned black when angry, and brown skin."[9] In Norway House, Henry would have been able to build his family a modest log home with the help of extended family and could have supported them by hunting, fishing, and trapping. In Winnipeg, the Raintrees are without community; they have no home of their own, no extended family, and no employment. April remembers her father saying that tuberculosis had "caused him to lose everything that he had worked for" (9). Having lost everything, Henry and the family become trapped in the slums of the big city.

Although few settlers would consider Henry Raintree's life in Norway House as one with high status, status is a relative thing. In the context of an isolated northern Indigenous community at this time, Henry would have had the social mobility to achieve high status amongst his peers. Had he been a successful trapper and fisher, he would have had cause to be proud of his skills. In a large, predominantly White urban centre, however, Henry would have had no social mobility and, therefore, would have been stuck at the lowest social stratum. Having neither the skills nor the privileged skin colour necessary to secure employment, Henry becomes dependent on meagre social-welfare payments to support his family, and the Raintree family soon becomes mired in the culture of poverty. As welfare recipients, they live under the intense scrutiny of the child-welfare authorities, who consider poverty in itself a form of neglect. "When the goals of higher status are denied to people, other forms of adaptation are created—for example, withdrawal and rebellion—in order to deal with the despair and hopelessness that are central to the culture of poverty," James S. Frideres writes. "Once an individual is placed within the traditional culture of poverty, it is almost impossible for him or her to get out."[10] Inevitably, Henry descends into "despair and hopelessness," and turns to alcohol to dull his pain, and his wife, albeit grudgingly, accompanies him on his downward spiral.

Like her husband, Alice Raintree experiences personal, social, and spiritual dislocation in the big city. She does not know how to cope with the overt racism she experiences and adopts the same demeanour as that of the Métis described by Maria Campbell in *Halfbreed*, hanging her head in shame and fear when surrounded by settlers. Unable to defend herself, Alice Raintree is ashamed of her very existence. When she encounters overt racism, Culleton Mosionier writes, she "would get a hurt look in her eyes and act apologetic" (13). As a result, she avoids shopping in the large department stores where the clerks and other shoppers treat her with disdain. Rather than exposing herself to situations in which she might encounter racism, she isolates herself by staying home.

At home, however, Alice is a different person. There her love for her children motivates her to fight the feelings of hopelessness and despair that drive her husband to drink. Her oldest daughter, April, remembers how her mother does not succumb to alcohol to the same extent as her husband does and that she tries to be a good mother:

> she would clean the house, bake, and do the laundry and sewing. If she was really happy, she would sing us songs, and at night, she would rock Cheryl to sleep. But that was one kind of happiness that didn't come often enough for me…. My first cause for vanity was that, out of all the houses of the people we knew, my mother kept the cleanest house. Except for those mornings after. She would tell her friends that it was because she was raised in a residential school and then worked as a housekeeper for the priest in her hometown. (12)

Because of her substandard residential school education and the racism and sexism of the time, Alice Raintree's opportunities are few. Her only skill, and her only source of pride, is her ability to perform domestic work. In the 1950s, being a competent homemaker could have provided her with a degree of status, had her husband had an income. Unfortunately, he does not. The social-welfare payments that the regime provides them are barely enough to supply the family with the necessities of life. With no support, both financially and socially, Alice's life is bleak. When the social work professionals take away her children, her sole reason for existing, her life becomes unbearable. Alice Raintree and her husband are unable to achieve "psychosocial integration" because they "are dislocated from the myriad intimate ties between people and groups—from the family to the spiritual community—that are essential for every person in every type of society."[11] Without psychosocial integration, they develop a "substitute" lifestyle to which they cling "with a tenacity that is properly called addiction."[12]

April's description of her early childhood reveals how the Raintree parents combine elements of their traditional Indigenous lifestyle with the substitute lifestyle that their addiction dictates. Their parenting style, for example, suggests that they still adhere to many Indigenous traditions. April remembers how, as a very young child, she takes responsibility for the care of her even younger sister, Cheryl. Every morning throughout the summer, she helps Cheryl to wash and dress and then feeds her breakfast. In traditional Indigenous societies, giving young children this kind of responsibility would be normal, and indeed, caring for younger siblings was an important component of a traditional education. However, as Fournier and Crey point out, in the eyes of the bureaucrats who managed the child-welfare system, "the tradition of strong sibling ties, where an older Indigenous child took on lifelong responsibility for the protection of younger brothers and sisters, counted for little."[13] Following breakfast, April and Cheryl walk to the park where they play until they choose to come home. April remembers that their "daily routine was dictated by [their] hunger pangs and by daylight" (13). They learn from natural consequences rather than imposed ones. Still, although neither mother nor father dictates when the girls should come home, their father's stories about the frightening figure of the bogeyman who comes out at night persuade the girls to return before dark.

In Indigenous communities that follow traditional norms, children are accorded a greater degree of autonomy and self-determination than are children in mainstream Canada.[14] Hence, it would be normal for children to spend their days playing freely until they, not their parents, decided that it was time to come home. In Indigenous communities, the families' psychosocial integration within the web of extended family members would surround and protect the children, and the community itself would believe that the care of children is everyone's responsibility.[15] Social-welfare workers across the country have repeatedly interpreted this parenting style as permissive and, therefore, negligent and determined it to be sufficient cause for the apprehension of the children they would subsequently relocate and dislocate into foster care.[16] April's description of her life in foster care makes it clear that the regime's child-welfare workers have neither knowledge of nor interest in Indigenous peoples' child-rearing practices. To them, the Raintrees are merely morally deficient, negligent parents who fail to adequately care for and properly supervise their children.

Yet because of their lack of psychosocial integration and their subsequent addiction, Henry and Alice Raintree's child-rearing practices are also lacking according to the standards of traditional Indigenous communities. Like many Indigenous people who live with the consequences of assimilationist colonial policies, Henry and Alice Raintree have lost some of their cultural norms and distorted others. In Indigenous communities that follow traditional practices, children learn by imitating the behaviour of the adults. All adults, then, are teachers and, as such, are responsible for modeling socially acceptable behaviour. In Winnipeg, the Raintrees create community by finding other dislocated Indigenous people who become their surrogate extended family. This community of "aunties and uncles" substitutes for the extended family that the Raintrees left behind in Norway House. As an extended family, however, this motley array of "aunties and uncles" does not fulfill the responsibilities that they would have in a traditional Indigenous society because, along with the Raintrees, they self-medicate the pain that is the result of their despair by consuming alcohol excessively. Henry and Alice tell their children that the alcohol is their "medicine," which is correct in a distorted way. Alcohol functions as an anaesthetic to dull the pain that their hopeless situation causes them. Like the medicine that cures Henry's tuberculosis, however, alcohol is a double-edged sword. Henry must relocate to Winnipeg so that he can obtain treatment—and medicine—to cure his tuberculosis. Although the medicine cures the tuberculosis, the treatment, that is the relocation, becomes dislocation, which ultimately destroys his family and his life. In the same way, the alcohol succeeds in anaesthetizing both Henry and Alice's pain in the short term, but in the long term, it destroys their family and indirectly causes both Alice's and Cheryl's deaths.

Although the regime's social-welfare workers are aware that Henry and Alice have many problems, they do not try to help them. Instead, they focus on poverty and alcoholism as the cause of Henry and Alice's perceived neglect of their children, which is a gross over-simplification of alcohol's role in the colonial relationship with Indigenous people. As Patrick Johnston writes, "Rather than viewing alcoholism as a cause of child neglect in Native communities, it is more useful to think of it as a symptom of more fundamental and deep-seated problems. It is a consequence of a lack of employment opportunities and of the resulting despair experienced by many Native people. Alcoholism is a symptom of the powerlessness of Native people who are denied the right of self-determination."[17] The regime's social-welfare workers have no interest in assisting the adult Raintrees to take control over their lives and to reclaim their right of self-determination just as the health-care workers show no interest in the health of Baby Anna, whom they discharge prematurely from the hospital and who dies as a result. Indeed, the social-welfare workers demonstrate no interest in the welfare of the family unit as a whole. Instead, they dismiss the Raintree parents as incorrigible and focus their attention on "saving" April and Cheryl.

Like the colonial policies that held Indigenous children hostage in the residential schools to keep their parents in check, colonial policies permit the child-welfare authorities to take custody of the Raintree children to coerce their parents to modify their behaviour. In order to have their children returned, Henry and Alice must not only heal from the disease of alcoholism, they must also participate in the free-market society. Not surprisingly, this places Henry and Alice in an impossible situation. According to the prevailing beliefs of the time, alcoholism was a moral deficiency rather than an illness. The only support available to people who wanted to quit drinking would have been the fledgling fellowship of Alcoholics Anonymous, which was in its early stages of development. Alcohol treatment programs of the day would have only dealt with the addiction, not the dislocation that caused it.

Even if he had of dealt with his alcoholism, there is no way that Henry Raintree, with brown skin and a limited education, could have obtained the employment necessary to finance a middle-class lifestyle. Not surprisingly, then, the Raintrees fail to meet the conditions that the child-welfare authorities set. Not only do the child-welfare authorities blame Henry and Alice for their failure, Henry and Alice blame themselves. They believe that if they were only stronger, if they only loved their children more, they would be able to accomplish what the child-welfare authorities demand of them; they would have overcome their addiction and transformed themselves into members of middle-class society by the sheer force of will. Henry and Alice might have well tried to change the colour of their skin. In the end, the social workers apprehend April and Cheryl and relocate them to foster families as permanent wards of the state. Fournier and Crey write that "the white social worker, following hard on the heels of the missionary, the priest and the Indian agent, was convinced that the only hope for the salvation of Indian [and Métis] people lay in the removal of their children."[18] Rather than coercing social advancement in the guise of healing, the actions of the child-welfare agency rupture the family irreparably and cause even further dislocation.

Ironically, the removal of the children fails to modify the parents' behaviour or ensure the children's safety and well-being. April is five years old and Cheryl is three when the child-welfare authorities place them in separate foster homes. Not only do the child-welfare authorities separate the Raintree children from their parents, they separate them from each other, thus damaging their relationship forever. The practice of separating siblings was deliberate, "a bizarre holdover from the residential school days [that] dictated that native children could be better acculturated and assimilated if they grew up away from their brothers and sisters."[19]

The Children's Aid Society, the agency the regime has given responsibility for the care of Indigenous children in many provinces, places April with the Dions, a French Catholic family who live in St. Albert, a small French Catholic town in southern Manitoba. The Dions are April's first foster "family." The term foster "family" is an ironic misnomer. Child-welfare authorities contract foster "parents" to care for the children they apprehend and pay them for services rendered; either party can cancel this contract at any time and for any reason. In many cases, fostering children is merely an economic transaction, but even when foster "parents" develop an emotional attachment to their foster "child," they have no recourse if the colonial bureaucrats decide to move the child elsewhere. The Dions' foster home, like most White foster homes that take in Indigenous children, becomes the site where the process of acculturation and assimilation begins for April, thereby achieving the goal of the colonial policy. As a member, albeit transitory, of the Dion family, April learns to behave as if she were a French-Canadian child. Six-year-old April yearns for acceptance and, therefore, is eager to please. She attends Catholic Mass and learns to pray in French. Of course, since April is light-skinned and can easily "pass" as White, it is easy for her to blend into the community. At home, the Dions teach her the behaviours appropriate for a White girl. At school, a group of "bossy, even haughty" girls "had deemed [her] acceptable enough to take possession of [her]…they let the others know that they were going to show [her] the ropes" (25). Given the racism that April has experienced in Winnipeg, she is astonished that these people are friendly to her, and she is grateful to be taught "the ropes" of settler society. April tells the reader that, because of the Dions' kindness to her, she comes to consider the Dion home "as safe and secure as the [Raintrees'] tiny one on Jarvis Avenue" (26). This is important because it tells us that, despite the parties and the alcoholism, April did feel safe and secure with her mother and father.

Although April enjoys the secure feelings she experiences while residing with the Dions, it is their material wealth that truly seduces her. Given that one of the goals of the regime's assimilationist policies was to convince Indigenous people the benefits of materialism and individual ownership, its policies succeed in this instance. April remembers how, even before the child-welfare agents apprehended her, she came to equate White skin with material wealth during her visits to the park near her Jarvis Street home. To five-year-old April, the White-skinned children were beautiful and exotic and appeared rich while the brown-skinned children, the ones who looked like her sister, Cheryl, appeared poor. Of course, given that Jarvis Street is situated in the poorest area of Winnipeg, it is very unlikely that the White-skinned children would have been rich. April cannot understand that wealth is relative, so when the child-welfare workers place her with the Dions, who have a nice home and supply her with nice, albeit second-hand clothing, she thinks "that [she is] rich, just like those other white kids" (24)—the kids from the park. She believes that she has joined what Paolo Freire calls "the having class."[20] This thinking affects her relationship with herself as an Indigenous person and her relationships with other Indigenous people, including her family, throughout the novel. Through her description of April, Culleton Mosionier reveals one of the most problematic outcomes of transcultural adoptions and fostering. To many Indigenous foster children, like April, White customs and standards—especially of material wealth—are normalized. To most Indigenous people, however, poverty is the norm. As a result, reconnecting with their birth families becomes incredibly difficult because poverty, not material wealth, is still more likely to be the norm in Indigenous communities.

The objective of the regime's child-welfare policy in the 1950s and 1960s was to remove children from dangerous homes and then relocate the children in safe and secure ones; however, many foster homes were the antithesis of safety and security. Culleton Mosionier exposes just how tenuous April's, and by implication other Indigenous children's, safety and security really was. The plot shifts, when Mrs. Dion becomes ill and the Children's Aid Society relocates April to the DesRosier home. April's description of life with the DesRosiers is one that many Indigenous foster children recognize: a life of racism, abuse, and drudgery with foster families whose motivation for taking in children is monetary gain and free labour. Nevertheless, "most social workers, none of whom were Aboriginal at that time, felt little harm could befall an Indigenous child rescued from poverty and placed with a nice, middle-class, white family."[21]

Ironically, life with the DesRosiers merely reinforces April's belief that the Dions are the benchmark for all things good. And tragically, the DesRosiers' overt racism causes April to situate Indigenous people on the opposite pole as the Dions: "Being a half-breed meant being poor and dirty. It meant being weak and having to drink. It meant being ugly and stupid. It meant living off white people. And giving your children to white people to look after. It meant having to take all the crap white people gave" (47). Thus, April vows to hide her identity when she grows up to enable her to become rich. Feeling that she has to hide her identity to be accepted and to advance socially, April is unable to communicate honestly with family and friends. As the dark-skinned sister, however, Cheryl has no choice but to admit her indigeneity.

The Children's Aid Society places Cheryl with the MacAdams family, and although Mrs. MacAdams is Métis, Cheryl has little contact with other flesh-and-blood Indigenous people. As the secondary narrator, Cheryl does not speak to readers directly. We learn about the young Cheryl through her letters and essays in the first part of the novel and the adult Cheryl through her journal in the latter. We also learn April's interpretation of her sister through April's narration of their early years and of the sporadic visits that the Children's Aid Society arranges. Cheryl resembles their father in that she is visibly Indigenous and, therefore, cannot conceal her identity like April does. However, Cheryl becomes intensely proud of her Indigenous heritage while living with the MacAdams. Like the Dions' community of St. Albert, the community in which the MacAdams family lives is predominantly White, and because Cheryl is visibly Indigenous, she faces overt personal racism and has few friends. Thus, what she learns about Indigenous people, she learns from her liberal-minded foster parents and the books that they provide.

Wanting Cheryl to develop a positive self-image, the MacAdams provide her with books that show Indigenous people in a positive light, albeit a romantic one. Like many lonely children, Cheryl finds solace in books. She explains to April how Mrs. MacAdams gives her "books on Indian tribes and how they used to live a long time ago" as a substitute for friends:

> Mrs. MacAdams gave them to me to read because no one at school would talk to me or play with me. They call me names and things, or else they make like I'm not there at all. This one girl and her friends would follow me home and make fun of me, so I slapped that girl. So her Mom called Mrs. MacAdams. And Mrs. MacAdams says that all the bad stuff was 'cause I'm different from them. She told me I would have to earn their respect. How come they don't have to go around earning respect? Anyways, I don't even know what respect is, exactly. I just wanted to be friends with them. (43)

A bright child, Cheryl immediately perceives the injustice, and it angers her. The "Imaginary Indians"[22] whom she meets in books become her friends and her benchmark for all things good, and settler society becomes her benchmark for ill. And although her thinking is the polar opposite of her sister April's, it still affects Cheryl's relationship with herself as an Indigenous person and her relationships with other Indigenous people, including her family, throughout the novel. In the second half of the novel, we learn more about Cheryl through her actions and her journal writing. At this point in her life, her distorted thinking has tragic consequences. Rather than supplying Cheryl with a solid foundation, the romantic depictions of Indigenous people that she creates from her reading set up a false ideal. When Cheryl seeks out and locates her family, the reality is more than she can handle.

By creating her character Cheryl, Culleton Mosionier explores the psyche of Indigenous foster children who, like her sisters, commit suicide, with a goal of understanding how children with such promise are defeated. Culleton Mosionier writes that she wanted to create a character readers would love so that her suicide would affect them deeply. By encouraging readers to align themselves with a character, Culleton Mosionier works to effect social change by prompting them to examine the issues that defeat Cheryl and ultimately cause her death. In her article "The Special Time," she writes, "Both of my sisters were beautiful and special, and they had so much promise, as Cheryl did, and as do many others who commit suicide."[23]

An honours student and high-school graduate, Cheryl is intelligent and shows potential. She begins attending university and plans to study social work. Despite her negative experiences with the child welfare system, social workers have had an enormous influence in Cheryl's life, so she sets out to learn the profession and to become a better social worker than the ones with whom she has had contact. Full of high ideals, she begins to spend time at the Indian and Métis Friendship Centre, where she befriends Indigenous girls, girls whom April calls "strays" because of their tragic circumstances—although their lives are not unlike those of Cheryl and April.[24] Yet, because the child-welfare system denied Cheryl contact with Indigenous people in her formative years, she is unable to relate to these girls and behaves as if she were from middle-class, settler society. Rather than treating them like friends, Cheryl behaves as if she is a kindly social worker or foster parent. The language that she uses when writing in her journal betrays the gap between the Indigenous world and her own; she refers to Indigenous people as "them" and "they" rather than "us" and "we," evidence that the assimilationist goals of the colonial policies have succeeded.

The primary reason that Cheryl is a sympathetic character is her determination to take pride in her Indigenous heritage in the face of the overt racism she encounters as a brown-skinned person. April, in contrast, is an unsympathetic character because she denies her identity to make her life easier and becomes as bigoted as the racist settlers are. Although they seem to be polar opposites, the sisters have much in common as a consequence of their foster-home upbringing. For both April and Cheryl, there is no room for diversity in Indigenous people, who are either "gutter-creatures" or "princesses" if female, and "chiefs" and "warriors," if male. These are the only identities their foster families taught them, so these are the only identities that they are able to see. Finding no princesses, chiefs, or warriors, Cheryl becomes despondent, and her thinking and language come to resemble that of her sister. In her journal, she writes: "I feel like April does, I despise these people, these gutter-creatures. They are losers" (196). Still, she persists in her effort to cling to her ideals. She defends her Indigenous "strays" to April and takes them to middle-class restaurants even though they meet overt racism and feel desperately out-of-place. Having been socialized away from the Indigenous community, she unconsciously mimics the behaviour of the White people who have tried to civilize Indigenous people by making them adopt the mannerisms of White society. Cheryl's foremost goal is to help Indigenous people become the people she imagines they once were, the idealized images she has gleaned from the books of her childhood. Her other goal is to find her birth family.

Once she connects with the Indigenous community, it is not difficult for Cheryl to find her father, who has never escaped the city. Trapped in the culture of poverty and his own addiction, Henry Raintree returns to his home community periodically but never remains there for more than a few months. Armed only with fantasies, Cheryl is unable to cope with the reality that her father is an indigent alcoholic. Having learned that alcoholism is a moral deficiency, she is unable to have compassion for him:

> All my dreams to rebuild the spirit of a once proud nation are de-stroyed in this instant. I study the pitiful creature in front of me. My father! A gutter-creature!
>
> The imagination of my childhood has played a horrible rotten trick on me. All these years, until this very moment, I envisioned him as a tall, straight, handsome man. In the olden days he would have been a warrior if he had been all Indian. I had made something out of him that he wasn't, never was. (198)

Still, Cheryl is unable to leave her father, even though he disgusts her, es-pecially after she learns that her mother has committed suicide. Unable to come to terms with the loss of her children, Alice Raintree has surrendered to hopelessness and despair. She retreats further into alcoholism and, when she can bear the pain no more, throws herself off a bridge. A despondent Cheryl follows in her footsteps. She begins drinking with her father, and her life quickly deteriorates.

Despite having shown so much promise, in a short time, she too becomes a gutter-creature. This is most perplexing to readers who have come to align themselves with her because we admire her pride and determination in the face of adversity. Cheryl tries to understand the damage that colonialism has caused Indigenous people but, in the end, sounds more like a frustrated White liberal than an Indigenous person. She writes: "the white bureaucracy has helped create the image of parasitic natives. But sometimes, I do wonder if *these people* don't accept defeat too easily, like a dog with his tail between his legs, on his back, his throat forever exposed" (196; emphasis added). It bewilders readers when Cheryl seems to make a conscious decision to behave like *these people* herself, the people that she condemns. However, many former foster children who have grown up in loving middle-class homes have done the same thing.[25] In the end, Cheryl, like her mother before her, commits suicide by jumping to her death from the Louise Bridge. Although Cheryl's rapid descent is perplexing for readers, the act of imagining it is healing for Culleton Mosionier. Imagining narratives that give voice to the voiceless can provide answers. Culleton Mosionier's siblings cannot explain their suicides to her, but by creating Cheryl, she gains a better understanding of them. To imagine a convincing character, a writer must have empathy. Likewise, Culleton Mosionier is able to empathize with her parents after walking, for a time, in their shoes through the narrative. Healing, for her, comes through empathy and understanding.

My Name Is Seepeetza: Through the Eyes of a Child

Although clearly based on the author's experience at residential school, *My Name Is Seepeetza* is classified as juvenile fiction. Motivated by socio-pedagogical objectives, Shirley Sterling makes a strategic decision to choose juvenile fiction as the genre in which to write her story. As an educator, Sterling would, undoubtedly, know that the history of residential schools is rarely taught in Canadian schools. And, although the history taught in Canadian schools no longer contains disparaging comments about the supposed savagery of Indigenous people, Indigenous people are still worthy of note only in relation to their contact with the settlers. There is no mention of the brutality of colonization and its continuing effects on the Indigenous population. In the authorized curricula of both elementary and secondary schools, the colonial creation myth is taught as fact while Indigenous history—if it is taught at all—is marginalized. To teach young people about the history and effects of residential schools would incite them to question the veracity of the colonial creation myth.

As an educator, Sterling would also be aware that when literary texts are being evaluated for inclusion in the curricula, they are scrutinized less stringently for their factual accuracy than are historical ones. Furthermore, as a result of ongoing pressure from Indigenous political organizations, provincial departments and ministries of education have been aggressively seeking teachable literary works written by and about Indigenous people for inclusion in the curricula of elementary and secondary schools in areas with high Indigenous populations. As a result of this political lobbying, *My Name Is Seepeetza* has been included in the official curriculum for courses in language arts in several provinces, and students who might otherwise have never learned about residential schools have come to understand the callous brutality that Indigenous children experienced while they were in the care of the government and churches who operated the schools. Also, by narrating from the perspective of a young person, Sterling encourages the novel's young readers to see the world through Seepeetza's eyes and share her emotional responses to that world. In this way, young readers come to empathize with Seepeetza and, as a result, align themselves with her. Indigenous readers come to understand what their parents and grandparents might have endured when they were young. Settler readers experience vicariously what many Indigenous children experienced and realize that there is another version of Canadian history. As an educator, Sterling aims to reach young people, teach them about this alternate history, and recruit allies in the fight for social justice for Indigenous people.

My Name Is Seepeetza is the journal of twelve-year-old Seepeetza, whose English name is Martha Stone. At the beginning of the 1958 school year, Seepeetza commits to writing a secret journal in which she will chronicle her life for a full year. The result is a complex narrative that combines fact and fiction interweaving the life of the author with that of her narrator, and pictures of the author as a residential school student appear on both the front and back covers of the text. Sterling and Martha Stone share the same Indian name, "Seepeetza," and the adult Sterling, a professor of education at a prominent Canadian university, "calls herself Seepetza, the name given to her by her father, with students and colleagues."[26] Reder poses the question, "Is it Martha Stone, disguised as Shirley Sterling, or Sterling posing as Martha Stone?"[27] Like Martha Stone, Sterling attended a residential school whose acronym is KIRS; however, whereas Stone attends the fictional Kalamak Indian Residential School, Sterling attended the Kamloops Indian Residential School. Although *My Name Is Seepeetza* is categorized as juvenile fiction, it is clear that this novel has more psychological complexity than appears on the surface.

Sterling dedicates her novel to "all those who went to residential schools"[28] and expresses her hope that former students will be able to recover those essential elements of their lives that residential school took away from them. She advises former students that healing from trauma means recovering the lost children hiding deep inside them. For Sterling, healing from trauma involves recovering Indigenous languages and cultures. Healing from trauma entails recovering "the mythology by which you can pick up and rebuild the shattered pieces of the past" (7). Her poem "Coyote Laugh"—her gift to former students, "in celebration of survival"—is itself a reclamation and adaptation of her Indigenous culture. Coyote is also the trickster hero/anti-hero in the mythology of many traditional Indigenous cultures. By foregrounding him in her dedication, Sterling emphasizes the need for reasserting Indigenous mythologies.

It is important to note that coyotes are extremely resilient and, as a result, have survived where other more ferocious animals have not, having either been hunted to the point of extinction or having been unable to adapt to the changing environment. Although smaller and less ferocious than wolves, for example, coyotes survive and even thrive in areas that were once wolf territory but where no wolves live today. Coyotes have even migrated to large urban centres, such as Vancouver and Calgary, where they have established themselves as a new urban species.[29] By foregrounding Coyote in a poem written in English, Sterling emphasizes the resiliency and adaptability of Indigenous knowledges and people who, like the coyote, continue to survive and adapt in the face of adversity. Also by writing in English, Sterling implies that although former students might not be able to speak their traditional languages, they can still access the traditional knowledges that will heal their wounds.

Sterling tells the story of the residential school experiences from the perspective of twelve-year-old Seepeetza, a naive narrator whose narrative is filled with dramatic irony. Seepeetza's journal contains detailed descriptions of both her internal and external life at residential school, which she juxtaposes with descriptions of life at home on an Indian reserve situated in the mountains of British Columbia. The novel is set at a time when people with "status" under the *Indian Act* were not Canadian citizens but were still considered wards of the federal government and, therefore, were denied both the right to vote and the right to manage their own affairs. Although the number of children attending day schools on reserves was increasing, most Status Indian children attended residential school for some or all of their education. The novel not only educates Indigenous youth about what past generations of their people might have lived through; it also shares with former residential school students that they are not alone in their

experiences and pain. Seepeetza does not dramatize the things that happened at residential school. Rather, she describes them as children who keep
journals typically do. Given the hardships, the brutality, and the terror that
Seepeetza suffered at residential school, her choice of narrative might lack
excitement for readers, who are often accustomed to sensationalized descriptions of these kinds of events. Yet, by refusing to dramatize situations that
clearly have sensational potential, Sterling subtly executes her socio-pedagogical goals. What Seepeetza portrays is her norm, and readers are forced
to look beneath the matter-of-fact descriptions to understand how the events
described would affect a child.

My Name Is Seepeetza highlights for White readers the disparities between their lives and the lives of Indigenous people. Although the world that
Seepeetza describes is normal for her, White readers understand that this
world has never been normal for them. In Seepeetza's world, it is normal
for siblings, cousins, and neighbours to be removed from their families and
placed in residential schools. No one likes the schools, but with few exceptions, such as her brother Jimmy who is White in appearance, people with
Indian status have no other choices. White readers, in contrast, are aware that
other children would have a multitude of choices—if they were White.[30] If a
school did not meet the needs of a child, parents would be able to complain
to the teacher—if they were White. If the teacher could not or would not
resolve the problem, parents could take their concerns to the principal—if
they were White. If a principal was unable or unwilling to resolve the matter
to the parents' satisfaction, they could turn to their elected school board—if
they were White. If the school board did not help them, parents could take
their concerns to the press or to their elected representatives—if they were
White. As well, parents might have chosen to relocate the child to another
school—again, if they were White. Seepeetza's narrative reveals that, in 1958,
people with "status" under the *Indian Act* had no choices. And, although
the young narrator does not know that others have choices, the readers do.
Seepeetza's attitude is fatalistic. She accepts her residential school attendance
as inevitable, much like the sun rising in the east or the birds flying south in
the autumn, but she yearns for something different: "I wish I could live at
home instead of here" (14).

In the same way that forced attendance is normalized for Seepeetza, so is
the hard labour and hunger that is part of her residential school experience.
By 1958, the focus of residential school curricula had shifted from instruction in the trades to academic instruction; however, students at KIRS continue
to perform all the domestic work required to maintain the institution. School

officials force the children to prepare food, clean lavatories, dust halls, sweep stairs, and scrub and polish floors all the while feeding them poor-quality food in quantities sufficient to ward off starvation yet still keep the children in a continual state of hunger. "Supper," Seepeetza writes, "is usually cabbage soup, two slices of bread with margarine, and wrinkled apples for dessert" (25). The children attempt to subvert the system either by caching food for later or by stealing. Although margarine has replaced the lard, little has changed since Basil Johnston and his classmates attended residential school twenty years earlier. In 1959, Seepeetza and her classmates stick their mea-gre allotment of margarine under the dining table for use at their next meal and hide bread in their underclothing to be retrieved when hunger strikes at night. Seepeetza recalls, "Sometimes Cookie and I get so hungry at night we eat her toothpaste" (87). The most daring children—or perhaps the hungri-est—steal potatoes and carrots from the root cellar to satisfy their hunger. Yet, the nuns and priests expect students to be grateful for their paltry ra-tions. When Seepeetza informs Sister Theo that there is a worm in her soup, the Sister berates Seepeetza for not being suitably grateful and tells her that "there were starving children in Africa" (25).

The inequity between the children's rations and the staff's also resembles the situation at Spanish twenty years earlier. At KIRS, the children's break-fast consists of "gooey mush with powdered milk and brown sugar," while the nuns and priests eat "bacon or ham, eggs, toast and juice" (24). Food allocations come to signify value and suggest that the nuns and priests judge their lives as being more valuable than those of the children in their care. The attitudes of the nuns and priests who operate the school are fur-ther revealed in their choice of transportation for the children. Although the schools have buses, the children are loaded into a cattle truck that the school sends for them. Like cattle being transported to a slaughterhouse, Indigenous children are shipped to KIRS to kill the Indian within them and replace it with the ways of the Whites. Not surprisingly, the absence of fair-mindedness gives rise to feelings of anger and resentment in the children, and often they vent their anger on fellow students. As a result, there is no safe place within the walls of KIRS, so Seepeetza must learn survival. After two years at school, she comments: "I am mean now too" (98).

Residential school terrifies Seepeetza, but the only escape she can imag-ine is one that would lead to her death. She writes: "Sometimes I look out the dorm window at the Tomas River and I wish I could hide under the water and never come out" (20). Seepeetza does not dwell on these daydreams and moves on to other things before her fantasies develop into thoughts of suicide. The fear does not leave her, however, and its physical sensations manifest themselves in Seepeetza and her siblings when they think of returning to school:

> We get stomach aches when we have to come back to school after summer. It starts when we see the first leaves turning yellow at the end of August.... We look at each other with sick eyes and then we walk home so we can be near Mum.

> When I hear the red doors slam behind me at school it's like I get a numb feeling over my whole body and I'm hiding way down inside myself. I don't really hear or see what's going on around me. Just sort of. It's like a buzzing that's far away. I wake up when Sister calls my name. By then she's mad and I'm in trouble, and I feel awful. (36)

Seepeetza copes by repressing her feelings and dissociating from the situation. Although this strategy momentarily eases her anxiety, it incurs the wrath of Sister Theo, who is easily roused to anger. Not only does Sister Theo forbid displays of affection; to her, illness is also a punishable offence. Seepeetza describes Sister Theo's reaction to her becoming infected with influenza: "Sister Theo yelled at me and kept punching me on the back until I almost fell. Once she punched me and I got a boil on my back. I was scared to tell her, so I didn't" (64). Like all children living in abusive environments, the children at KIRS understand implicitly that "you don't tell on anyone here," especially the nuns and priests (21). The children who bear the brunt of this anger find no succor at KIRS where shows of affection, even between siblings, are forbidden. The students, however, resist when possible. Seepeetza and her sisters refuse to comply with this dictate and covertly hold hands while walking back to their dormitories from recreation—the only time that they elude the Sister's watchful eyes.

Given Ireland's history of oppression at the hands of the British, it seems incongruous that the Irish nuns and priests at KIRS would not only be cruel to the Indigenous children in their charge but would impose a curriculum whose goal was to obliterate their culture. Culhane explains that when the English first colonized Ireland, they had to find some way to rationalize subjugating their neighbours. The result was a novel "social theory" that judged the Irish as near savages at the same stage of development as were the ancient Britons prior to being "civilized" by the Romans. This social theory included a plan to guide the Irish to a stage where they would be worthy of civilization:

"The Irish should therefore be made subservient to the colonizing English (the true inheritors of Roman civilization) so that, through subjugation, they could come to appreciate civility and thus eventually achieve freedom as the former Britons had done. This belief that meting out punishment to subordinated peoples and individuals 'for their own good' will result in their eventual emancipation, while an enduring one, is belief by the historical record which offers more support for the theory that cruelty breeds brutality."[31] Seepeetza's narrative suggests that the nuns and priests at KIRS were instilled with this attitude. Thus, in the same way that abused children often grow up to be abusive adults, so do the Irish nuns and priests who likely immigrated to Canada to escape oppression. By comparing themselves to the Indigenous children in their care, the Irish nuns and priests elevate their status by altering their positionality. At home in Ireland, Catholics occupied a position of racial, religious, and social inferiority in relation to their British Protestant masters. In Canada, although they might not be considered equal to the British Protestants, as White Christians they still occupy positions superior to that of the Indigenous children in their charge. The Status Indian children occupy the lowest position in society, being inferior according to the doctrine of White superiority and without rights under Canadian law both as Indians and as children. Thus, the Irish nuns and priests whom the British had once treated as less than human now treat the children in their charge the same way. Abuse breeds abuse. With no legal rights, the children are easy targets on whom the nuns and priest are able to unleash their repressed rage without fear of retribution or penalty.[32]

The nuns and priests force the children to practise Catholicism and turn their backs on their traditional spiritual practices. They also compel selected students to participate in Irish folk dances in competitions across the province, a seemingly benign activity that they force upon the children in a merciless fashion:

> This year my group has learned how to do the Fairy Reel, an Irish dance with fancy foot work. We do square, line and star patterns as we are dancing. We have to keep straight backs and lift our legs high to do it well. And smile, of course. We wear green kilts with big silver pins, white satin shirts, black sequined boleros, black dance slippers and green hats.... Some dress up like boys, but we all wear make-up like rouge for our cheeks, eyebrow pencil, mascara, blue eye shadow and bright red lipstick.

> We sing a lot of Irish songs in the concert. We harmonize in alto, tenor and soprano. We practice so much on Sunday afternoons that I sometimes almost fall asleep on my feet, and my whole body aches. (73–4)

Thus, if the children are less than perfect in their performances, they feel the fury of Sister Theo's shillelagh. Worse yet, the children are compelled to smile even when they are tired or afraid: "Sister makes us smile all the time when we are dancing. If we don't she punches us on the back or hits us with the shilayley [sic]" (63). Rather than allowing the children their right to healthy emotional expression, the staff at KIRS teaches them to repress their emotions, a practice that has had far-reaching consequences for former students. James Pennebaker discusses the health consequences of repressive coping, which is "characterized by high levels of inhibition and the refusal to admit to feelings of anxiety."[33] He goes on to explain that repression causes elevated cholesterol levels, hypertension, and lowered immune function. Pennebaker cites a broad array of research that suggests that women who utilize repressive coping strategies "may be at a greater risk for early death due to breast cancer."[34] In 2005, author Shirley Sterling died from breast cancer at age fifty-seven.

Another consequence of the seemingly benign folk-dance program is its contribution to the destruction of Indigenous cultural practices. This program is part of a larger Canadian government program that is both self-conscious and deliberate and that constitutes cultural genocide. When Seepeetza and her siblings begin school, their cultural foundation has already been severely weakened. Although their parents are multilingual, they do not teach their children how to speak even one Indigenous language because they believe that having the ability to speak their mother tongue will make the children even more vulnerable to abuse at residential school. For three years Seepeetza's mother attended the Kalamak School, where she endured continual acts of brutality. "The nuns strapped her all the time for speaking Indian, because she couldn't speak English," Seepeetza writes. "She said just when the welts on her hands and arms got healed, she got it again. That's why she didn't want us to learn Indian" (89). Seepeetza's parents believe that by teaching their children English rather than Indian, they can protect their children in absentia. The cost of protecting their children was to severely hinder their ability to gain access to important traditional knowledge of the culture and the environment, which is transmitted in the language. This loss is exposed in Seepeetza's narration of childhood trips into the mountains with her community, which worked together to hunt game and pick berries. During these excursions, she listens to adults telling stories and talking about business, and infers from their tone that the business discussed is serious. With sadness, Seepeetza observes: "they talk in Indian so I don't understand what they are talking about" (91). By 1958, this community's cultural traditions have been severely eroded. Many of the men are military veterans and have travelled the world.[35] Agriculture is now the community's primary economic activity. Although still illegal for Status Indians, the excessive consumption of alcohol is increasing. There is no mention in Seepeetza's narrative of traditional songs and dances. As a result, when her father asks Seepeetza and her sisters to sing for him, they are unable to sing songs from their peoples' traditions. Instead, they serenade him with a Scottish folk song, "Ho Ro My Nut Brown Maiden," or a Christian hymn, "Bless This House" (74). Ironically, "nut brown" Indigenous girls serenade their "nut brown" father with a song that venerates a "nut brown maiden" at the time that they face discrimination and oppression because of their "nut brown" skin. In the end, the only difference that Seepeetza can observe between the reserve people and the settlers is their connection to the land: "Real Indians are just people like anyone else except they love the mountains" (90).

Throughout her journal, Seepeetza continually juxtaposes her life at home on the reserve at the Joyaska Ranch with her life at Kalamak Indian Residential School both visually and in narrative. She writes: "I can't help it. I can't stop thinking about home" (35). Immediately after the dedication can be found two diagrams that Seepeetza has drawn to map the physical features of her two residences. The two are not dissimilar. Located beside the highway to the town of Firefly, the ranch is virtually indistinguishable from any other ranch of its period. It contains two corrals, a granary, blacksmith and wood sheds, and hayfields. Seepeetza even indicates the place where "Dad's truck" is parked (8). There is nothing in the diagram of the Joyaska Ranch that would indicate that it is situated on an Indian reserve. KIRS, too, borders the road to the highway and along with school buildings features a barn and farm buildings, potato and vegetable fields, an orchard, a playground, a soccer field, and houses for the teachers. Seepeetza's narrative reveals that, although clearly preferable to life at residential school, life at home is not idyllic.

At home, Seepeetza feels loved and accepted, and at home, she is free to have fun, something that is strictly forbidden at residential school. Most of the time she feels safe at home. Although both mother, Marie, and father, Frank, treat their children with gentleness and love punctuated by spontaneous shows of affection, Seepeetza's mother is the source of her security. Seepeetza describes Marie as an attractive woman with big brown eyes and long black hair that she braids and wraps around her head in a crown. Knowledgeable in the traditional medicines of her people, Marie is generous with her praise in contrast to the nuns at KIRS who "punish [the children] when [they] make a mistake, but never say a word about the good things [they] do" (106). Although the Stone family is poor, Marie works hard to ensure that her children are adequately clothed. She is an inventive and resourceful seamstress who makes clothes out of flour sacks and old hand-me-downs from which she designs new creations, such as Seepeetza's blue satin bathing suit. Seepeetza has fond memories of falling asleep on the floor beneath her mother's sewing machine while Marie works late into the night. Living in poverty might not have been easy for Marie, but she is unfailingly cheerful, according to Seepeetza's recollections. She even allows her children to climb in bed with her when her husband is out late and warm their feet against her legs. As a result, when Seepeetza receives a package of candies from home, it is not so much the sweetness of the treats that thrills her as the fact that the package is itself a tangible connection to her home and to her mother. "Just a few days ago this parcel was at home," Seepeetza exclaims. "My Mum must have touched it!" (27). The maternal bond is so strong that separation causes severe trauma, and Seepeetza cannot allow herself to experience the pain that it causes: "Then Mum turned and left. I looked at her walking away from me. I heard her footsteps echoing, and I was so scared I felt like I had a giant bee sting over my whole body. Then I stopped feeling anything" (17). To forestall the pain of separation, Seepeetza inhibits her natural emotional responses. It is only when she is home and safe in her tree perch that she considers permitting herself to feel: "Maybe I'll cry now" (102).

Still, it is important to note that that Seepeetza's sister Dorothy does not share Seepeetza's and the other children's antipathy for KIRS. Seepeetza hints that life for her older siblings is not as carefree as it is for the younger ones: "I think [Dorothy] got tired of babysitting Benny and Missy and me when we were little. May be that's why she likes school" (30). Seepeetza's older brother Jimmy, who is eighteen, works hard chopping wood for the family and helping his father on the ranch. Frank has other plans for Jimmy, however, and emphasizes the importance of a White education. When Jimmy tries to stay home from school and sleep, Frank pours a bucket of ice water on him. Clearly, he does not want his children's lives to replicate his. Thus, when Jimmy graduates from high school and wins a scholarship, the family supports his plans to go to university the following autumn. Given the dearth of

Indians in Canadian universities in 1959, however, Jimmy is likely to have a challenging time.[36] The likelihood of his succeeding is further compromised by the fact that Jimmy drinks.

Although Marie is Seepeetza's security, it is her father, Frank, whom she resembles both in appearance and interests and with whom she has the most fun. Marie has black hair and brown eyes, while Seepeetza has light hair and "grey-green eyes with yellow near the irises" (110), eyes like her father Frank's, "wolf eyes, yellow eyes" (111). Likewise, Seepeetza does not aspire to be like her mother when she becomes an adult; she wants to live on a ranch and drive horses, like her father. Frank teaches his daughter to be a horse-lover, and she rides with absolute comfort and abandon. When her teacher, Mr. Gorky, invites Seepeetza to ride his horse, Penny, at residential school, she is astonished at the privilege but not intimidated by the horse. Clearly, she understands horses, quickly identifying Penny as a "dainty walker" with "a sensitive mouth" (95). Seepeetza throws caution to the wind and takes Penny for a run until both rider and horse are hot and tired: "I had a hard time getting her back under control," Seepeetza writes. "By then she was mad, so I turned her home and brought her past the barns and up towards the mountains. I rode in the hills all afternoon" (96). Although Sister Theo is angry that she does not return in time to complete her ironing, Seepeetza does not care. Suffering Sister Theo's rage is a small price to pay for the opportunity to ride a horse, which provides her with an emotional connection to her father and their life together on the ranch. Like Seepeetza, Frank is a storyteller and is also the person who gives her the Indian name "Seepeetza" along with her nickname "Tootie McSpoot," in fond remembrance of her infantile attempts at language: "My Dad gave me my Indian name, Seepeetza. I am named after an old lady who died a long time ago. My dad laughs when he says my name, because it means White Skin or Scared Hide. It's a good name for me because I get scared of things like devils" (77). Reder accepts Seepeetza's reporting of her father's translation as correct. She contends that "it is a mistake to look at the title of the novel, *My Name Is Seepeetza*, and read it as a rejection of her 'White' name and an affirmation of her First Nations' identity.... [Seepeetza] doesn't link this name with the fact that she looks white, although clearly this is significant to her identity."[37] However, Seepeetza is unable to speak her language, and consequently, must accept her father's translation because she does not have the ability to examine the connotative and denotative meaning of the name as she might have, had she been a speaker of the N'laka'pamux (Thompson) language.

A linguistic analysis of Frank's English translation of Seepeetza's Indian name (as Seepeetza reports it) reveals a problematic understanding of its meaning and its implications for Seepeetza's identity. Linguist Jan Van Eijk explains that the name "Seepeetza" contains a common Salish suffix "-eetza" (in the anglicized version) that means "hide, skin, sheet, blanket"[38] and that, the root "sip-" means "startle, frighten, scare s.o.; worry s.o."[39] Linguist Brent Galloway notes that there are two N'laka'pamux (Thompson) roots of the shape that would be anglicized "seep." The former means "scared" and also "rush," while the latter means "shake or knock down." The name "Seepeetza" most likely refers to the latter since the Thompson dictionary gives what would be anglicized as "seep-um" meaning "shake (something) (for example, a blanket, mat, cloth, clothes, rug, mattress)" and the Thompson suffix IPA=ic'e (anglicized -eetza) means "outer covering, blanket, clothes, garment, hide, pelt, etc." and can be suffixed to the root to mean "shake blanket/clothes/hide/etc." and have exactly the form anglicized as "Seepeetza." In other words, "scared hide, scared clothes" is possible, but "shaken clothes/hide" is more likely.[40] Neither Van Eijk nor Galloway can find any reference to "white" in this name. Van Eijk posits that there might be an association with turning white when one is scared. Galloway points out that if there were some local or family-specific interpretation that would include "white," it would not necessarily be derogatory, since people of the area traditionally decorated blankets by whitening them with diatomaceous earth mixed with mountain goat wool and dog wool. Jeannette Armstrong, a N'laka'pamux speaker, understands the name as having the connotative meaning of an "adept" hide or blanket, that is, one imbued with a spirit light.[41] Clearly, the name Seepeetza contains multiple layers of meaning that the young narrator is unable to comprehend with her limited knowledge of her mother tongue.

Although Frank is genuinely fond of his children and his wife and is full of fun, he is also an emotionally troubled man and living with him is not always easy. Frank is haunted by memories of the war and the young men he was required to kill as part of his duties as a sharpshooter. Seepeetza remembers, "He said once that the Germans they killed were just boys" (103). Because there were few mental health services for World War II veterans and even fewer for Indigenous veterans, alcohol became a common mode of self-medication when painful memories became too much.[42] Frank has learned that alcohol is an effective sedative and drinks to the point of blacking out: "When Mum tells him how he was acting he doesn't believe her" (103). But it is not only the war that haunts Frank. Although she does not know its cause, Seepeetza observes her father's antipathy directed at the Catholic Church and clergy. "My dad won't go inside a church. When he sees the priests he spits," Seepeetza writes. "He doesn't like priests. He says priests are not as holy as they like us to think" (122). Still a troubled Frank asks the Christian god for forgiveness, rather than the god of the N'laka'pamux: "But once when I was walking by the barn I heard Dad crying and saying sorry to God when he didn't know anyone was around" (119). Like Frank, Marie's brother, Seepeetza's Uncle Tommy, who is also a veteran and also a drinker, has bad feelings towards Catholic priests. In this case, Seepeetza knows the cause of Tommy's hostility: "Uncle hates priests since the time one of them tried to do something wicked to him" (117). Still, her father's and uncle's excessive consumption of alcohol is also normalized for Seepeetza, and her descriptions of their behaviour are unemotional and almost matter of fact. Although it is normal, indeed even fun, when Seepeetza and her siblings wait in the truck outside a beer parlour or hide in the bush or flee to her uncle's home when their father drinks, she is frightened of her father's drunken rages and compares Sister Theo to him: "The way that Sister Theo yells at us reminds me of my dad when he's drinking. It scares me" (63). It is ironic that Seepeetza turns to the residential school's Christian teachings when she attempts to persuade her father to stop drinking and threatens him with hellfire and damnation:

> Last night I talked to my dad about God. He came home drunk and he was hollering around as usual, so I got mad at him. I told him not to drink. I told him to pray. He looked at me for a long time. Then he sat down and looked at me with his face in his hands. At first I thought he was laughing. Then I thought maybe he was crying.
>
> After that I didn't know what to do so I jumped up on a chair and got the holy picture down from the little shelf in the living room. It was a picture of Jesus dying on the cross. There, I told Dad, look at Jesus. He died on the cross for you, for all of us. Pray, and stop your drinking. Stop cussing. Stop fighting with Mum. Dad, bad people go to hell. (117)

It appears that the Christian propaganda that the nuns and priests at KIRS mete out has penetrated Seepeetza's psyche and become a part of her world view.

My Name Is Seepeetza is an intensely political novel disguised as juvenile fiction. As a consummate educator, Sterling teaches her readers about residential schools and their effects without resorting to plodding and patronizing didacticism. Even though she is a fictional character, Seepeetza, as narrator, claims the authority of eyewitness to the events that she describes in her journal. This narrative authority is bolstered by the fact that the narrator and the author share the same Indian name and the same image as presented on the novel's cover. This novel is more than a mere exposé, however. It is also a vehicle for healing for both author and readers. Through her depiction of Seepeetza and the narration of the journal, Sterling is able to revisit a time of childhood trauma armed with an educated adult's ability to transform residual emotions into language. By translating the emotions of residential school experiences into language—something that many former students are unable to do—Sterling helps those readers distance themselves from their pain. When traumatic feelings become text, they can be examined and understood and, consequently, their power to cause pain is diminished.

Keeper 'n Me: Imagining a Better Ending

For Richard Wagamese healing is a more difficult process. Like Culleton Mosionier, Wagamese was removed from his family by the child-welfare authorities who placed him in foster care. His first foster "home" was with the Wright family who fostered him and his siblings. A short time later, the child-welfare authorities relocated him to the home of a Ukrainian-Canadian family, the Tacknyks. After spending five years with the Tacknyks, the authorities once again relocated Wagamese to the home of a White, middle-class family, the Gilkinsons, who adopted him and changed his surname. At age nine, Richard Wagamese became Richard Gilkinson. Forced dislocation caused Wagamese enormous and long-lasting trauma, and like Culleton Mosionier, he creates works of imaginative fiction to help him to come to terms with his experiences and his pain. In 1994, Wagamese published his first novel *Keeper 'n Me*, which tells the story of a young Anishinaubae[43] man, Garnet Raven, who, like the author, was taken from his home by child-welfare authorities and placed in foster care. Unlike Wagamese, the fictional Garnet, like many Indigenous children, was not adopted and spends his childhood moving from one white foster home to another. The psychosocial dislocation and resulting trauma that Garnet suffers mirrors that of his author, however. Rather than compiling and fictionalizing the stories of many foster children, Wagamese synthesizes his lived experience with his deepest desires: to connect with a healthy Anishinaubae family and to find a way to heal from the pain of residual trauma that continues to afflict him. The novel is a retrospective, and in the first part, Garnet remembers and describes his experiences in foster care and in the years that precede his reunification with his birth family. The larger part of the novel, however, deals with Garnet's subsequent life with his family, his healing journey, and his reclamation of his identity as an Anishinaubae man.

Eight years after publishing *Keeper 'n Me*, Wagamese published *For Joshua: An Ojibway Father Teaches His Son*, an autobiographical narrative, in which he endeavours to explain to his son how his childhood dislocation continues to affect them both. Wagamese establishes a cause-and-effect relationship between his childhood experiences, his feelings of insecurity and self-doubt, and his subsequent and continuing battle with addiction. This autobiographical work not only helps us understand Wagamese, it also informs our reading of *Keeper 'n Me*. *For Joshua* reveals that much of the fictional narrative is based on the author's lived experiences and that there are many parallels between the lives of Richard Wagamese, the narrator of the autobiographical narrator, and Garnet Raven, the narrator of the fictional narrative. We learn that *Keeper 'n Me* constitutes Wagamese's first attempt to use his writing to recall, examine, and divest himself of his painful memories and that many kernels of the fictional narrative come directly from the author's life. The scene that precedes Garnet's removal from his first foster home, for example, is identical to Wagamese's lived experience as told to him by his sister, Jane. Garnet's sister, who is also named Jane, tells him that the last time she saw him she was looking out the window of the school bus and saw "a little Ojibway boy hunched over in the sandbox with a little red truck with one wheel missing, growing smaller 'n smaller."[44] Like Richard, the "I" narrator of *For Joshua*, Garnet is well into adulthood before he sees his birth family again.

Garnet's discursive representation of his childhood reveals much about the trauma that he—and by extension his creator—has suffered and describes the consequences of the policies that are the cause of his suffering. Garnet's description of his experiences in foster care reveals how the colonial child-welfare system and its policy of placing Indigenous children in White foster homes have been inherently damaging to those children. When the child-welfare authorities move Garnet from one foster "family" to another, they prevent him from achieving the psychosocial integration necessary for healthy emotional development. Garnet's childhood, then, is an insecure one, as he explains: "I mean, being from a nomadic culture is one thing but keeping a kid on the move for twelve years is ridiculous. I was in and out of more homes than your average cat burglar" (*Keeper* 12). Given that Wagamese was not on the move for twelve years, having been relocated only three times, one wonders why he deliberately created Garnet's fictional experience as worse than his own. Could it be that he imagined that his readers would not have thought his experiences sufficiently traumatizing? Could it be that he thought himself undeserving of readers' sympathy? Clearly, the consequences of forced relocation were traumatic and long-lasting for Wagamese. When the child-welfare authorities removed him, at age nine, from a foster family with whom he had spent five years of his life, Richard is clearly devastated. Richard's Ukrainian-Canadian foster family felt like family to him because they were the only one he could remember. He explains that "when you're nine, five years was a lifetime in itself." [45] He remembers how when he leaves on the train with his new family, his foster mother, heartbroken, runs alongside with "huge tears rolling down her face" (*For Joshua* 42). Despite his witnessing her vivid display of grief, Wagamese believes that the bureaucratic decision to move him is somehow indicative of his inadequacy as a human being. The words that he hears over and over in his nine-year-old mind convince him: "There's something wrong with you that makes you unlovable, that makes no one want you, that makes them give you away to someone else. If there wasn't something wrong with you they wouldn't let you go" (43).

Richard leaves the home of his adopted family at a young age and spends several years wandering the country, sometimes leading a criminal life, before reconnecting with his birth family. Richard describes his life on the street, where he uses alcohol as a source of false courage: "The alcohol gave me the courage to do things I wouldn't normally do—things I felt I had to do to ensure that my street buddies would continue to accept me. Things like car theft, cheque fraud, and breaking and entering. I drank to get brave enough to break the law. I was addicted to the esteem of others and I was addicted to the alcohol it took to do the things it took to earn me the esteem. I absolutely needed both" (85). Later, however, alcohol becomes an anesthetic with which Richard deadens his pain. Because of his criminal activities, Richard is regularly incarcerated; however, unlike the fictional Garnet, who is sentenced to five years in the penitentiary for trafficking cocaine, Richard's longest sentence is six months. Again, Wagamese finds it necessary to ensure that Garnet's life is somehow even more tragic than that of his creator. Nevertheless, at a deeper level, both Richard and Garnet suffer from the same "soul wound,"[46] which is responsible for their self-destructive behaviour. Here, the narrator of the autobiographical narrative and the narrative of the fictional one seem to be on the same emotional level. The lack of psychosocial integration, the dislocation/displacement combine to convince both Richard and Garnet that they are inherently unlovable and, therefore, responsible for

their own pain. Garnet describes "how all those things [the multiple reloca-
tions] leave little holes in your gut and how eventually they all turn into one
great big black hole in the middle of your belly" (*Keeper* 23).

As the only Indigenous person in all-White communities, Garnet, like
Wagamese, spends his formative years not seeing himself reflected in the
faces of his foster family, friends, neighbours, and teachers. Garnet explains
how the experience of being a racialized (visibly non-White) minority caused
him to lose himself: "Growing up in all-white homes, going to all-white
schools, playing with all-white kids can get a guy to start thinking and react-
ing all-white himself after a while" (12). In *For Joshua*, Richard explains that
his experience as a racialized minority in a society that tolerates and often
condones expressions of overt racism resulted in chronic stress, which he
describes as "a belly fully of fear" (*For Joshua* 45). Protected by the privilege
that their whiteness provides, Richard's adoptive parents are incapable of understanding his reality and the fear that it causes. Consequently, he suffers in
silence: "I couldn't tell them how afraid I was to walk out the door every day
and be the only brown person I saw" (45). Furthermore, in Richard's mind,
his visible differences prove that he does not belong, that he is "the attachment, the afterthought, the grafted limb on the family tree" (48).

Garnet shares Richard's feelings of isolation and, with no Indigenous
direction, learns to see himself through White eyes. Garnet's foster "father,"
in an effort to frighten him into obedience, takes Garnet to the poor area of
town to observe the Indigenous people who live there drunk and destitute.
His foster father tells him, "See. Those are Indians. Look at them. If you don't
start shaping up and doing what you're told around here, that's what you're
going to become!" (*Keeper* 13). Implicit in this commentary is that Garnet
has the ability to choose his identity. He can choose to be "Indian" and accept the poverty, violence, addiction, and despair that his "father" insinuates
would inevitably accompany that choice. Or, he could choose to be "White"
and garner the affluence, enlightenment, civilization, and progress that his
"father" suggests go together with that choice. The foster "father" clearly
believes that to choose whiteness is the rational decision and attempts to coerce Garnet to believe likewise.[47] As a consequence, Garnet Raven, like April
Raintree, comes to understand that Indigenous identity is not only suspect
but is a deficit, and that he should regard all Indigenous people critically
and as a source of embarrassment. Obviously, those who choose Indigeneity
have made an imprudent choice and deserve the suffering that is the result of
their lapse in judgement. Unfortunately for Garnet, however, genetics have
already made that choice for him no matter what he decides: "this brown skin

of mine was always a pretty good clue to most people that there must have been a redskin or two creeping around my mama's woodpile" (13–4). Unable to "pass" as White and unwilling to acknowledge his Indigeneity, Garnet is filled with shame.

What is surprising, then, given the gravity of the subject matter, are Garnet's comical descriptions of episodes in which he attempts to deny his Indigenous identity. In what is, in fact, a confessional narrative, Garnet explains how, at various times in his youth, he endeavours to persuade people that he is either Hawaiian or Chinese or Mexican. His descriptions are extremely funny, for example:

> after seeing a couple of episodes of "Kung Fu" on TV I became a half-Chinese guy looking for my father all across North America. He was supposed to be some Canadian businessman who knocked up my ma, little Wing Fey, while on a trip to the East. I was going to use my considerable kung fu skills on him when I found him and avenged the death of Wing Fey, who'd succumbed to malaria finally after putting me through some monk temple in the mountains. That one ran pretty good in a few towns until I got too drunk in Sudbury and gave a traditional Chinese name to a big biker named Cow Pie. Guess he didn't like being referred to as Sum Dum Fuk. My kung fu skills failed me utterly. (15–6)

Garnet also explains that "anytime you had to be an Indian, see, anytime that other shtick wasn't a go, well, you had to be one of top-rated prime-time kinda Indians" (16). That Wagamese creates words for Garnet that are humorous, albeit in a tongue-in-cheek fashion, is significant. Wagamese understands that the colonizers' popular culture has created a hierarchy of Indigenous people based on the Indigenous nations that Hollywood movies feature: the Sioux, Cherokee, Comanche, and Apache. In the absence of a supportive Indigenous family or community, Indigenous identity as depicted in Hollywood movies has become, by default, the determiner of Garnet's worth.

It is also significant that the humour that predominates Garnet's confessional in Wagamese's fictional narrative is absent in his autobiographical one. As a confessional itself, *For Joshua* continues to shed light on Wagamese's fiction in that Richard's description and analysis of his earlier behaviour helps us better understand Garnet's humour in the portions of *Keeper 'n Me* that he narrates. Richard reveals that he learned how to employ humour strategically in his adolescence to conceal his feelings of worthlessness while seeking the approval of others: "I chose to be the class clown and with every laugh I got I felt more like I was accepted. I began to believe that all I had to do was get a reaction from people, that getting attention was the same as getting recognition" (*For Joshua* 51). Not only does Wagamese revert to this same strategy when writing *Keeper 'n Me*, he bestows the same narrative strategy to Garnet. Humour, then, provides Garnet with the means of endearing himself to the readers while detracting from the feelings of shame that are the inevitable consequence of denying his true self. Humour also helps Wagamese minimize the pain that he must have felt when writing such a deeply personal confession if we accept, and the evidence in *For Joshua* suggests that we should, that much of Garnet is Richard Wagamese. It is significant, as well, that this type of humour also anticipates reader responses. If readers criticize Wagamese for denying his identity or committing crimes or criticizing society or a host of other things, he can always say, "I was joking. It's fiction."

To guide Garnet on his healing journey, Wagamese creates a secondary narrator, Keeper, an Anishinaubae elder who is a storehouse of traditional knowledge. Modelled after John, Wagamese's own spiritual teacher, Keeper becomes Garnet's teacher, mentor, and ally. Like John, Keeper has also suffered dislocation and is on a healing path that runs parallel to, and often intertwines with, Garnet's. Where Garnet's narrative relates the events and actions that make up his story, Keeper's provides context and social commentary while moving Garnet's healing journey forward. It is through Keeper that Wagamese delivers a scathing critique of both colonial policies and, to a lesser degree, of the attitudes of some of his Indigenous contemporaries. Keeper speaks in the vernacular addressing readers directly to teach Anishinaubae history from an Anishinaubae perspective to help readers understand how the colonial policies that relocated Indigenous children first to residential schools and later to foster homes damaged the same children that they were ostensibly created to help:

> *They been comin' for our kids long time now. Nothin' new. Not for us. I always thought it was us Indyuns supposed to do all the sneakin' and creepin' around. But those white people, boy, they got us beat when it comes to sneakin' through the bushes. May be we taught 'em goo much. Heh, heh, heh.... In the real world it's the white people kept sneakin' off with our kids. Guess they figured they was doin' us a favor. Gonna give those kids the benefit of good white teachin', raise them up proper. Only thing they did was create a whole new kinda Indyun. We used to call them Apples before we really knew what was happenin'.*

Called them Apples on accounta they're red on the outside and white on the inside. It was a cruel joke on accounta it was never their fault. Only those not livin' with respect use that term now. (Keeper 37; emphasis in the original)

Notice that not only does Wagamese use Keeper to criticize the colonial regime whose policies caused him such trauma, he also criticizes those Indigenous people who, we can infer, mocked and rejected him when he attempted to reconnect with his community. Still, to defuse tension—and perhaps to prevent readers from abandoning the novel and by implication its author—Wagamese intersperses Keeper's narrative with ironic quips followed by Keeper's distinctive laugh—"Heh, heh, heh"—throughout the many critical passages. Thus, Wagamese employs humour both to avoid his own pain and as a strategic device to educate his readers in the gentle manner of the Anishinaubae so that he might teach them in much the same way that the people of White Dog teach Garnet.

Throughout Keeper's narrative, we learn that Wagamese has, indeed, reclaimed much of his stolen heritage. Keeper speaks at length and in detail about Anishinaubae culture and tradition. In *For Joshua*, however, we learn that, although Wagamese had learned about the teachings at the time he was writing *Keeper 'n Me*, he was unable to apply them to his personal life and healing. Ironically, Keeper's words apply to his literary creator: *"lotsa people think that just learning the culture's gonna be their salvation. Gonna make them Indyun.… But there's still lotsa people out there drinkin', beatin' each other up, raisin' their kids mean. All kindsa things. That's not our way. So doin' the culture things don't make you no Indyn"* (38; emphasis in the original). Failing at being Anishinaubae is Wagamese's greatest fear. He tells us that, when John leaves him alone on a hill to complete a ceremonial fast, he is afraid that he will fail: "Failure at this ceremony would mean that I didn't have what it took to be an Indian, to be an Ojibway. It meant that I belonged nowhere and that I would be alone forever" (*For Joshua* 30).

It is noteworthy that, when Wagamese imagines Garnet reconnecting with his birth family, the narrative veers away from Wagamese's lived experience. In *For Joshua*, Wagamese is uncharacteristically silent about his birth family. He mentions that alcohol "was a titanic influence" (33) that resulted in the Children's Aid Society placing him and siblings in foster care. He mentions a sister, Jane, and two brothers, Jackie and Charles (not Stanley), but they play no meaningful role in the narrative and are conspicuous by their absence. In *Keeper 'n Me*, in contrast, Garnet's birth family is key to

Garnet's subsequent healing. Remarkably though, his siblings—Stanley, Jane, and Jackie—are one-dimensional characters who bear little resemblance to Indigenous people. Stanley, for example, has a degree in social work but seems to have no employment. Jackie's only distinguishing characteristic is that he was involved with the American Indian Movement for a time. And, there is no mention of Jane doing anything. Furthermore, although all are Garnet's senior, they have no spouses and no children, which is highly unusual for Indigenous people of their age. Thus, Garnet's siblings seem con-trived and have no other function in the narrative but to wait for his return to enable them to fill in the gaps in those parts of the narrative that occurred when Garnet was absent.

Likewise, although Garnet alludes to social problems on the reserve, he minimizes them by focussing on the positive and the humorous. Seeing the world of the narrative through White eyes, Wagamese avoids including material that might reinforce some White readers' negative stereotypes of Indigenous people. It is only when Garnet goes on the land to fast that he again becomes Richard. Importantly, in *For Joshua*, we learn that, although Wagamese is able to imagine healing for his fictional twin Garnet, he is un-able to heal himself. He explains that his feelings of inadequacy as a human being and as an Anishinaubae man have undermined his attempts to heal himself from his addiction. He also explains that, at the time of his writing, he has been unable to face the whole truth of his past: "As I sat on the hill and looked around I thought that perhaps when you're hurt it's easier to mythologize the past than to explain it, easier to find a source of blame than a source of truth" (33)

In *Keeper 'n Me*, Wagamese attempts to reframe his personal myth by creating an alternate narrative, a narrative of healing. Wagamese uses his imagination to reinvent the narrative of his subsequent reunion with his birth family and home community. It is unfortunate that, because he continues to respond to the postcolonial traumatic shock that he experienced as a child, Wagamese is unable to apply that narrative of healing to his lived experience. Living vicariously through his fictional alter ego, Wagamese imagines for himself and for many of his readers a healthy family and community along with an intact sense of identity as an Indigenous person. Indeed, the family that Garnet describes bears a striking resemblance to Cheryl Raintree's fanta-sies of her birth family but little resemblance to the many real-life Indigenous families that the child-welfare system has affected. According to Native American psychologist Terry Tafoya, the act of storytelling is a powerful healing device: "Stories are a way to understand what's going on around us.

If people become storytellers, they can change their own story."[48] Rather than considering *Keeper 'n Me* an escapist novel, it is more productive to consider it but one in a series of attempts by its author to reframe his own narrative.

Putting Community First

When I began teaching Indigenous fiction from Canada, many colleagues told me that it was too simplistic to study in a serious manner. In their opinion, it just wasn't very good. Some dismissed it as mere "protest" literature, literature about "issues" rather than aesthetics, and therefore more suitable for study in Native Studies programs. These colleagues preferred the literature of the Indigenous people of the United States, which they considered more sophisticated and, therefore, more suitable for scholarly work. If opaqueness and linguistic complexity are the markers of suitability for scholarship, then there is a grain of truth to their opinion. The US writers N. Scott Momaday, Gerald Vizenor, Louise Erdrich, James Welch, and Leslie Silko, whose works had made their way into the canon, are academics and understand scholarly expectations themselves, while the early Indigenous writers from this side of the border write primarily for their communities, with academia relegated to second place. Today, many scholars have come to appreciate the complexity that lies under the surface of Indigenous literature in Canada. I am thankful that things have changed.

Some Indigenous writers, such as Dr. Shirley Sterling, deliberately sacrificed status in academic and literary circles to increase accessibility for Indigenous people. These writers understand that literacy is not necessarily a marker of intelligence and that many of their relatives suffered horrific experiences in the educational system and, consequently, have low levels of literacy. With this in mind, Culleton Mosionier, Sterling, and Wagamese write for a broad readership, and the narratives discussed in this chapter are designed to reach readers of all ages on a variety of levels. These writers create works of fiction that function as counter-stories to heal community, as implements of social justice, and as tools of anti-racist education. In the next chapter, we will see how Indigenous theatre not only serves these functions, but also creates community.

chapter 5

Theatre that heals wounded communities

In First Nations cultures, stories are never "just stories." They are essential ways of communicating memory, history, belief, and tradition, and they require what Ojibwa critic Christine Lenze has called "response-ability" to material that is not understood to be "just" fictional. To use theatre for First Nations artists, then, is always to be translating, transforming, transposing (in terms of the integrity of the work itself), and negotiating, or accommodating (in relation to external contexts).

— Monique Mojica and Ric Knowles[1]

Adapting European Theatre to Indigenous Contexts

Unlike other literary forms, theatrical productions are not the creation of solitary individuals working in isolation. They are communal both in production and in performance. A community of actors, designers, and technicians work cooperatively to fashion productions that will be worthy of the communities that constitute their audiences. Furthermore, theatrical writing is not always a solitary endeavour; in many instances a collective rather than an individual creates theatrical productions. And, in some contemporary productions, members of the audience participate as characters/interveners in the play. The inherently communal nature of theatre makes it a particularly attractive genre for Indigenous people looking for a creative outlet for their stories because one of the values common to the many diverse Indigenous cultures is the value of community. As Lauri Seidlitz points out, "many Native theatre artists note that their choice of medium is well suited to the political goals inherent in reaching both their [Native and non-Native] audiences, and that the medium fits comfortably with their traditions, culture, and ways of expression."[2]

Theatre artists Geraldine Manossa and Floyd Favel Starr take that argument further. They assert that contemporary Indigenous theatre is not merely an adaptation or appropriation of European theatrical tradition; they maintain that it fits comfortably with Indigenous traditions because it is rooted in traditional Indigenous performance arts. Manossa compares contemporary Indigenous performance with Western performance and notes that "a main distinction between contemporary Native performance and colonial Western theatre is that the roots of contemporary Native performance can be traced to the lands of this country."[3] Examining traditional Indigenous performance arts, Favel Starr claims that "the concept, Native Performance Culture, could be described as developing practices of our ancestors. It came about not as a clearly formulated plan based on a clear vision, but as a feeling and intuition born out of personal, cultural and universal needs."[4] Monique Mojica and Ric Knowles, however, take an opposing view and write: "Although performance has always been a fundamental aspect of First Nations cultures, drama and theatre as they are currently understood are European forms. They are not indigenous to Turtle Island, and they are not traditional performance forms for First Nations peoples. The act of writing and staging 'plays,' then, necessarily involves Native theatre artists in simultaneous activities of protection and translation; but this is why theatrical forms are so useful and necessary for contemporary First Nations artists."[5] In other words, although contemporary Indigenous theatre is as different from traditional performance arts as contemporary Indigenous people are from our ancestors, it can still be compatible with Indigenous performance traditions. This quality inherent in theatre coupled with its communal nature and its ability to create an immediate intimacy are some reasons why Indigenous theatre in Canada has grown rapidly over the last twenty years; however, that growth has developed into two distinct, although often converging, streams: community and professional theatre. As a result, many Indigenous people who would not normally go to theatre have not only attended theatre but have participated in it.

Theatre can be transformative, and Indigenous people have come to recognize theatre as an art form that they can utilize to examine and address the unresolved grief and trauma present in our communities. Applied theatre functions as a catalyst for healing because "it helps people reflect more critically on the kind of society in which they live."[6] Indigenous community theatre is not as intensely political as other minority theatre, such as Chicano theatre among migrant farm workers, nor is its focus on aesthetics. Instead, Indigenous community theatre is more likely to be found in healing and educational venues rather than in purely aesthetic ones. Across the country Indigenous organizations hold numerous conferences designed to find solutions to the many social problems that plague our communities and that are the legacy of colonial policies. Ironically, the colonial regime whose policies were the cause of these problems is typically the major funding agent for these healing conferences. The agendas of these conferences almost always feature community theatrical productions that confront and explore these issues. Phillip Taylor defines "community theatre" as "an applied theatre form in which individuals connect with and support one another and where opportunities are provided for groups to voice who they are and what they aspire to become."[7] In the case of Indigenous community theatre, the style of each production might vary, but the subjects of the plays are consistent in their relevance to the audience. All are designed to reflect the audience's reality back to them. To that end, Indigenous communities often partner with professional theatre companies to create applied theatre, thereby acknowledging what Mojica describes as the healing potential of the arts:

> It is significant that the healers as artists are in the vanguard of this critical time. We are fertile minds from a living culture—ancient as well as contemporary.
>
> We are caught up on a wave of the cycle where, in our own words, we can approach the preservation, recognition, and continuation of our cultures with de-colonized minds.[8]

It is also significant that Indigenous communities partner with theatre companies, both Indigenous and non-Indigenous, that believe in the transformative potential of theatre and advance issues of social justice. It is also noteworthy that the most effective partnerships with non-Indigenous companies are with those companies that recognize and acknowledge their positionality and its implications.

Adapting Augusto Boal's Theatre of the Oppressed

Vancouver's Headlines Theatre for Living is a professional theatre company that has a history of effectively collaborating with Indigenous communities to effect healing through the arts. Headlines employs the Forum Theatre model created by Brazilian theatre innovator Augusto Boal and described in his groundbreaking text *Theatre of the Oppressed*. Headlines partners with communities to create theatre that meets needs that the communities have identified rather than creating theatre for them. Artistic Director David Diamond explains Headlines' philosophy: "We work only with people who have invited us to work with them. We never tell them who they are, but instead allow the process of them telling the group who they are guide how we facilitate the workshop."[9] Diamond describes his position as settler and artist:

> I consider myself part of an aberration on the planet. A new, mobile, essentially rootless culture the likes of which the Earth has never seen before.... As an artist in this new, mobile culture, I have a great hunger for the kind of rootedness that many Aboriginal people have through their cultures. But I can't have what they have. I am who I am and must take on the task of inventing my own culture—putting down my own cultural roots to investigate, change, and celebrate my community. I must also face the certainty that this process will take many, many generations to bear fruit.[10]

Diamond's understanding is the foundation of Headlines' partnerships with Indigenous communities. Like Boal's Theatre of the Oppressed, Headlines creates forums that empower the community by transforming spectators into "spec-actors," meaning that they become "engaged participants rehearsing strategies for personal and social change."[11] Taylor believes that "applied theatre works best when participants are actively engaged in critically exploring the implications of their own and others' actions."[12] Headlines has adapted Boal's model to fit into the Canadian environment and has adopted the name "Power Plays" for its rendering of Theatre of the Oppressed.

The process of creating a Power Play begins with the community partner identifying an issue, which its members have identified as significant and problematic for its members, such as racism or violence. The actor/participants, who are community members, then extract images from their reality. During the creative process they use their imagination to transform these images into the Power Plays, which represent acts of imagination based on the lived experience of the participants. During the production, the actor/participants reflect the images back to the community members in the audience for critical examination, thus creating a forum for critical examination and discussion. After first performing a Power Play in its entirety, the company then repeats it and invites the spectators to become "spec-actors" who participate in the performance by stopping the action when they identify a crucial moment in which they think that a character could behave differently and intervene with a view to effecting positive change. After the audience member stops the action, she or he physically replaces one of the actors and adds his or her own words with a goal of changing the outcome. The scene might be repeated several times in an attempt to change the outcome for the better. After each attempt, "the Joker," an unaligned character who acts as director or master of ceremonies, invites the audience and cast to critically examine and evaluate the changes:

> A Power Play offers an audience the chance to use the theatre as a concrete tool for creating alternative role models. The theatre or community hall is transformed into a laboratory. The forum play itself does not fight oppression, it simply exposes it, asking the audience to become activated and fight oppression themselves. In this way activated audience members become positive role models in their own communities, taking on a struggle that is directly relevant to them. The forum play does not have to provide the answers. In fact, it is better if it does not—the more answers that it provides, the less chance there is for audience participation.[13]

In the end, the images that make up the Power Play inform reality by expanding the participants' repertoire of choices.

One of Headlines' successful partnerships with the Indigenous community resulted in a Power Play entitled *Out of the Silence*. The idea for the play began with a series of conversations in 1989 between Diamond and Ron George, president of the Native Nations, which led to a formal partnership with Headlines, the Urban Representative Body of Aboriginal Nations (URBAN) and the British Columbia Association of Native Friendship Centres. The partners envisioned creating a healing-centred Power Play about urban Indigenous people, which would explore issues of family violence. The initial production took place in Vancouver with an Indigenous cast and Indigenous participants. In the process of developing the Power Play, however, it soon became apparent that family violence was merely a symptom of much deeper issues facing the community. The participants discovered that much of the family violence in their community could be traced back to racist oppression their people face. It also became apparent that, for many participants, family violence could be traced to the trauma they experienced and behaviours they learned while they, or their parents and grandparents, attended residential schools.

Clearly these issues were not unique to the urban Indigenous people of Vancouver, and after witnessing the success of the play in Vancouver, many other Indigenous communities sought to partner with Headlines to do the same healing work in their communities. The result was a very successful tour of Indigenous communities in British Columbia. After the tour was complete, six of the communities employed Headlines to conduct Theatre for Living workshops for their people. Diamond observes: "The richest and most productive way to work with oppressed groups is to help them find their own voice, not to speak for them. When individuals don't express themselves emotionally for long periods of time they get sick; communities are the same. One way for our communities to heal is for all of us to take back our rights of healthy collective expression."[14] Headlines has trained an enormous number of people from across the country, many of whom are Indigenous, in using Forum Theatre for healing. Some Indigenous theatre companies, such as De-ba-jeh-mu-jig Theatre on Manitoulin Island in Ontario, utilize Boal's Theatre of the Oppressed as well.

Community Plays Uncover Community Histories

Another theatre company that has partnered successfully with Indigenous artists and communities is Regina's Common Weal, which works "to connect artists with communities that may not normally have access to the arts."[15] Created in 1992, Common Weal's first production was *Ka'ma'mo'pi cik/The Gathering*, which used the community play form to tell the history of the settlement of the land from both the Indigenous and settler perspectives. The company contends that "the community play and its process empower[s] individuals and communities to embrace and rewrite their own histories."[16] Two professional theatre artists, one Indigenous and one not, Rachel Van Fossen and Darrel Wildcat collaborated to create *Ka'ma'mo'pi cik* with input and guidance from the people of the Fort Qu'Appelle town and district. Community members comprised the cast of the play. Fort Qu'Appelle is a small settler community in southern Saskatchewan with a large Indigenous population both in and surrounding the town. There are eight Indian reserves[17] and one Métis community in the immediate area, and Fort Qu'Appelle has the reputation of being a town divided by racism and social inequality. Van Fossen explains that when writing a community play, she tries "to capture the 'spirit' or 'essence' of the community" and that "a community play is written with the audience of the community in mind. The community must see, and recognize itself, in the play—and in the production."[18] To that end, the writers research extensively, examining both the historical archives and the oral history of the community.

In the case of *Ka'ma'mo'pi cik*, the settlement of the land, clearly the most contentious issue for this community, became the central theme of the play, and the signing of Treaty Four became the turning point of the first act. To witness its alternative collective myth/history told publicly to a mixed audience was incredibly healing and empowering for the Indigenous community. And to see its history—one that they had accepted as the "authorized" (read true) national collective myth—juxtaposed against that of the Indigenous community was educational and humbling for the settlers. Like the theme of Headlines' *Out of the Silence*, the theme of this play extended beyond the boundaries of the specific community for which it was created, which was unusual for a community play. Normally community plays are performed for a limited time and are not published; however, *Ka'ma'mo'pi cik* has become an exception and has been published and distributed extensively.

Common Weal has grown since 1992 and has extended beyond community plays into a variety of forms of theatrical expression all applied to issues of social justice. Today, a large number of Indigenous artists belong to that company. To accomplish its stated goals of working for "positive social change through the arts," Common Weal has developed collaborative works with people living in poverty, sex-trade workers, inner-city youth, prison inmates, a disproportionate number of whom are Indigenous. They also continue to work with Indigenous communities, community health centres, and many other groups. Common Weal is part of a growing movement to heal communities by promoting social justice and reconciliation through the arts.

Saskatchewan Native Theatre Company—Healing Through the Arts

Funding projects designed to heal the effects of the government and church-run residential schools has been a priority of the colonial regime today. To that end, the regime has created the Aboriginal Healing Foundation, which operates at arm's-length from the colonial government and which funds projects that help to heal Indigenous people and communities who suffer unresolved trauma as a result of being victims of physical and sexual abuse while attending government- and church-run residential schools. (It is important to note that the regime has restricted the mandate of the foundation, forbidding it from funding projects that deal with the trauma inherent in the loss of Indigenous languages and cultures that was the mandate of the schools.) The foundation's "mission is to encourage and support Aboriginal people in building and reinforcing sustainable healing processes that address the legacy of Physical Abuse and Sexual Abuse in the Residential School system, including intergenerational impacts."[19] One project that the foundation deemed suitable is the Saskatchewan Native Theatre Company's Healing Journeys Through the Arts Program. A recipient of a grant from the Aboriginal Healing Foundation, the Healing Journeys Through the Arts Program was designed to utilize theatre to "(a) empower and support youth and elders in acknowledging and discussing their life experiences as intergenerational victims and survivors of the residential school experience, (b) bring youth and elders together for a common purpose to share their stories and their family's [sic] stories through the creation of a unique cultural/theatrical presentation and (c) educate the Aboriginal and non-Aboriginal communities on the intergenerational impacts of the residential schools."[20] By removing Indigenous children from their families and placing them in residential schools, the colonial regime effectively removed children from their role models of culturally appropriate emotional expression. Unfortunately, the schools did not provide healthy role models from whom the children could learn emotional expression appropriate in any culture. Worse yet, the rules of the institutions prohibited them from expressing their emotions and expected the children to behave as if they were little automatons. Discipline took precedence over emotional health. As a result, residential school survivors returned to their communities experiencing feelings of discomfort with overt displays of emotion and unable to teach their own children to express their emotions in a healthy way. In the Healing Journeys Through the Arts Program, young Indigenous people are encouraged to explore their feelings and learn to articulate their emotions through artistic expression.

Even though it is a professional theatre company, the Saskatchewan Native Theatre Company clearly believes that it is responsible for using its art to help Indigenous people, especially Indigenous youth. This is not unusual. Daniel David Moses explains that Indigenous artists are hyper-aware of the pain in their communities and believe that they are responsible for using their art to contribute to the healing of these communities: "one of the words that always comes up in Native gatherings, and particularly among Native artists, is that it is part of our jobs as Native artists to help people heal."[21] To that end, most Indigenous theatre companies offer youth mentorship programs, and most Indigenous theatre artists state outright that their art is inextricably linked to the healing of their people and communities. Lauri

Seidlitz draws our attention to the pragmatic aspects of healing by pointing out that another function of Indigenous theatre is to provide employment to fight the poverty rampant in Indigenous communities. This is significant since poverty is one of the prime indicators of ill health. She writes that "theater requires actors, administrators, and various other dramatic works in a way that poetry and novels do not, benefiting Native communities in an immediate and tangible economic sense as well as by providing positive role models for the future."[22]

Almighty Voice and His Wife: Healing Historical Wounds

A first step towards healing is creating awareness and understanding. Because Indigenous theatre companies do not only perform for Indigenous audiences, they are always aware of those members of the settler population who attend their plays. Yvette Nolan argues that "healing can't happen without understanding. Once there's an understanding among the people themselves, like Aboriginal people doing Aboriginal theatre, then maybe the white audience will get some understanding of people's feelings, history, and situations. Then there can be some sort of understanding between the two groups."[23] The settlers cannot be cured from the pathology of colonialism unless they understand the damage that colonialism and colonial policies have wrought and the privileges they enjoy as a result.

Colonial agriculture policies seem to be far removed from theatre and healing, but because these policies have had such a profoundly negative impact on First Nations[24] communities, many people feel a need to relate the many stories of the effects of these policies. Although colonial agricultural policies do not normally provide the inspiration for literary works, they have inspired several works of Indigenous literature. Daniel David Moses's play *Almighty Voice and His Wife* is one such work. Agricultural policies comprised one component of the programmatic approach to the colonization of North America which the colonizers employed and which would irrevocably and fundamentally alter the lives of First Nations people. In *Almighty Voice and His Wife*, Moses uses drama to expose the madness of Canada's agricultural policies as they applied to the First Nations people who signed treaties on the Canadian Plains in the latter part of nineteenth century. He bases his play on a historical event that embodies the very worst possible outcome of colonial policies.

Almighty Voice is the English translation of *Kisê-manitô-wêw*, the name of a young Cree man who lived on the One Arrow reserve in Central

Saskatchewan, a short few miles from Batoche, the site of the 1885 Resistance. In 1895, Kisê-manitô-wêw killed a steer on the reserve, not to sell but to eat. Given the communal nature of Cree society at that time, it would be safe to assume that Kisê-manitô-wêw would have shared the meat with other hungry people in his community, and there were many. In his opinion, the steer belonged to his father. Unfortunately, his opinion differed from that of the colonial bureaucrats, who held firm to the position that all cattle given the First Nations under the terms of the treaties remained property of the Crown as represented by the Department of Indian Affairs. Indeed, they often decreed that hunger among First Nations people was not sufficient cause for slaughtering livestock. Believing that Kisê-manitô-wêw had committed a crime by killing the steer, colonial officials ordered his arrest.

On 22 October 1895, Sgt. Colin C. Colebrook of the North West Mounted Police (NWMP) arrested Kisê-manitô-wêw for theft and incarcerated him in the nearby town of Duck Lake. Kisê-manitô-wêw argued that the steer belonged to his father, not the government, but to no avail. The events that followed could easily be described as a comedy of errors had they not ended in tragedy. Thinking himself funny, one of the jailers told Kisê-manitô-wêw that the construction that was taking place outside the jail was, in fact, to build a scaffold for his execution. Kisê-manitô-wêw failed to see any humour in this statement and escaped from the guardhouse sometime during that night. Given that only a short ten years before, the colonial regime had executed eight First Nations men a short distance away in North Battleford, escaping custody seems a prudent course of action.[25] The North West Mounted Police claimed that they probably would have released Kisê-manitô-wêw the next day because of insufficient evidence, but that did not stop them from setting out to recapture him.[26] Colebrook and a tracker eventually located him, but when Colebrook tried to apprehend him, Kisê-manitô-wêw—after warning Colebrook to leave him alone—shot and killed him. Again, Kisê-manitô-wêw believed that he was acting in self-defence. A tasteless joke set in motion one of the biggest manhunts in Canadian history.

When the escape of Kisê-manitô-wêw came to the attention of the colonial regime in Ottawa, Secretary of State for the Government of Canada Sir Charles Tupper offered a $500 reward—an enormous sum of money at that time—for information leading to his apprehension and conviction. The description of Kisê-manitô-wêw on the wanted posters reveals the prevailing attitudes of the time: "He was described as a young man of about 22 years of age, 5′10" in height, of fair complexion, 'slightly built and erect' with 'neat small feet and hands . . . wavey dark hair to shoulders, large dark eyes, broad forehead, sharp features and parrot nose with flat tip, scar on left cheek running from mouth towards ear, feminine appearance."[27] Since many people at that time still considered physiognomy a credible branch of science, this description is telling. Typically having smaller hands and feet and less facial and body hair than did men of European ancestry, First Nations men's physical appearance did not then—nor does it still today—conform to the European notion of masculinity. For colonial officials to label his appearance as feminine connotes homosexuality and suggests that he was not a "manly" man. This, in conjunction with their description of his facial scarring, suggests that Kisê-manitô-wêw was likely treacherous and untrustworthy—certainly not a worthy opponent. Yet, for two years Kisê-manitô-wêw proved to be just that as he continually eluded the efforts of the North West Mounted Police to recapture him. When the NWMP did find Kisê-manitô-wêw near the One Arrow reserve, two young men, his cousin and brother-in-law, accompanied him. The gun battle that ensued resulted in the wounding of two NWMP officers and the death of two others as well as the postmaster from Duck Lake, one of the many civilians who had been appointed as special constables to reinforce the professionals in this great manhunt. In the end, it took twenty-four NWMP, an artillery team with a nine-pound gun, and hundreds of settlers to finally defeat the three young men, whom they killed while the mother of Kisê-manitô-wêw watched helplessly—all because of one dead steer.[28] Moses writes that "in the Cree communities of Saskatchewan, the story still has a life that's almost mythical because Almighty Voice…became a symbol of resistance."[29] Robert Appleford writes that Moses's "work reflects a desire to fully explore the nature of such 'wounds' [that colonialism has inflicted] and dramatize the process through which people can begin to heal."[30]

Moses relies heavily on his own historical research in his creation of *Almighty Voice and His Wife;* however, the play does not merely retell historical events. In the first act of the play, Moses augments history with imagination—a theatrical version of historiographic metafiction, if you will—thereby enabling his audience to experience history from the perspective of the Cree who lived through it. Rather than focussing on Almighty Voice as a historical figure who has acquired mythic proportions, Moses portrays Almighty Voice as a rather ordinary young man with a wife. Appleford contends that "Moses undertakes the difficult task of exhuming historical figures and stripping away the layers of romantic elegy which shroud them like winding-sheets."[31] The historical Almighty Voice is reported to have had four wives—evidently, he was not a Christian—but nothing is known of them.[32] Those who have authored the documents that form the historical record have rarely considered First Nations women sufficiently important to record their names and stories. In the absence of historical record, then, Moses imagines a wife for Almighty Voice, a young First Nations woman whom he names "White Girl." Cognizant of the position of First Nations women in history, she speaks directly to the audience saying, "I am the wife of Almighty Voice. You don't know my name. You don't even wonder if I have one. I'm only a crazy squaw."[33]

The play begins with Almighty Voice courting White Girl. Through his characterization of Almighty Voice and White Girl, Moses adds a human dimension to history by challenging the stereotypes of the silent, stoic warrior and the squaw drudge. The fact that Almighty Voice is in his early twenties while White Girl is only thirteen challenges the sympathies of twenty-first-century readers, especially the liberal-minded ones who want to sympathize with the mythical warrior but, because of the disparity between his age and hers, consider this relationship tantamount to child abuse. Yet, through his characterization of White Girl, Moses proves that she is no naïve child nor is she a passive drudge. Indeed, White Girl proves to be more than a match for the much older Almighty Voice. When Almighty Voice approaches her playfully, calling "Hiya. Hiya. Hey, girl. I said 'Hiya,'" she is not impressed, and her sardonic reply is, "I heard you the first time" (3). Almighty Voice's banter is laden with thinly veiled sexual innuendo, and his intentions towards White Girl seem less than honourable. However, she has no difficulty taking care of herself and talks circles around the man destined to become history's mythic warrior. Indeed, by the time their conversation has ended, Almighty Voice has not only committed himself to asking White Girl's father for permission to marry her, he has also agreed to send his current wife, known only as the Rump's Daughter, back to her father whether she wants to leave or not. White Girl quickly takes charge and becomes Almighty Voice's fourth and last wife and the mother of his son. Moses's White Girl is a formidable character indeed.

The function of the character White Girl in Act I is not merely to endow the play with a simple love interest. Hers is a complex character through whom Moses explores the rapid changes that the First Nations people of the Plains encountered at the end of the nineteenth century. He also explores their consequences, especially the effects that the government-controlled, church-run residential schools had on First Nations people. At the age of thirteen, White Girl is a fugitive from one of the early schools, then called industrial schools. Belonging to the first generation of Plains people to attend residential schools, White Girl would have had no previous generation to warn her about the loneliness and culture shock she would have to endure at school, a place where colonial officials would send a First Nations girl so that she could refashioned into a "white girl." No strangers to trauma, the Cree had experienced war with the Dene, Blackfoot, and Dakota, and they had experienced famine. However, the trauma that cultural and spiritual dislocation would cause was unknown to them. Accordingly, after her escape, White Girl continues to suffer severe emotional injury directly related to the trauma she experienced at residential school.

Most noticeable are the spiritual wounds that White Girl displays and which are the result of the school officials' attempts to force her to convert to Christianity. Although she is able to escape the White man's school, White Girl believes that there is no way to escape the White man's god, who is omnipresent. As a result, she thinks that she is incurably "crazy." We can hear the echo of Christian teachings when she says that she fears the White man's god, who is "jealous" and "like the glass. He's hard. He cuts you down" (16). Fear, then, is her constant companion and affects every aspect of her life, including her relationship with her husband. Frightened by her husband's bravado, White Girl explains her understanding of Christianity to Almighty Voice in an effort to persuade him to fear the White man and the power of his god:

GIRL   They called me Marrie. It's the name of their god's mother.

VOICE   What's wrong with White Girl? White Girl's a good name. They're so stupid. That agent has to call me John Baptist so I can get my treaty money.

GIRL   John Baptist. That's the name of one of their ghosts.

VOICE   I'm no ghost. I'm Almighty Voice. Why can't they say Almighty Voice?

GIRL   I'll call you John Baptist too.

VOICE   You're not the agent! You're my wife.

GIRL   It's so he'll kill the ghost instead of you, husband. That god won't know it's us if we use their names. (8)

Unable to understand Christianity as just another belief system that she may accept or reject, White Girl accepts it as truth and synthesizes the residential school's Christian propaganda into her existing belief system, thus adding a layer of complexity and confusion to it. Like Cree poet Louise Halfe, who describes the Christian god of residential school as having "the eyes of a roving fly,"[34] White Girl believes in the omnipresence of the White man's god. However, White Girl does not believe in his omnipotence, although she does fear him as vindictive and cruel. Thus, in her multi-dimensional spirituality, she believes that she can evade this god by assuming a Christian—and by definition false—name. Through his depiction of White Girl, Moses reveals how fundamentally foreign the White man's world would have been to the Cree only a short time ago.

White Girl's distorted understanding of Christianity is not the only reason that she has to fear the white man's god, however. In her monologue in Act I, Scene 6, she reveals that she is also the victim of sexual abuse at the hands of one of "god's helpers," the priest at the residential school:

> Mister. Mister! Mister God! I see your glass eye. Eye-eye! Stinky breath. It's me. Marrie! Marrie, your wife. Wife wife wife! God, look at me like before. How they taught me at school. How how. Here's my hair. Look. Here's my skin. How how, husband god, see what a little girl I am. Great husband god, see what a little girl I am. Great White God of the ghost men, mother is here. Blood blood blood between my thighs. Yes, gimme, gimme, gimme something sweet. Oh yes, yes, you're rotten, rotten meat, but wifey wife will eat you up. Mister God, god, stupid god, this is what you want! Come on! Come on, don't leave! I'm your little squaw. Eye-eye! See! Eye-eye, Mister God, Eye-eye! (19–20)

Her "marriage" to god, then, takes on another dimension when god's helper, as husband by proxy, is the one who consummates that marriage. The result is unresolved trauma that White Girl self-diagnoses as craziness. Living in a time before the invention of the term post-traumatic stress disorder, White Girl tries to explain her mental condition by theorizing that the school has put "bad medicine" in her.

In contrast to White Girl, Almighty Voice has spent his life in the relative safety of his community surrounded by a loving extended family and adored by women. Thus, his character is full of confidence, bravado, and lust, but lacks the analytical skills and political astuteness necessary for him to understand and cope with his situation. Although he is nearly ten years older than White Girl, Almighty Voice seems to be the younger of the pair. Born too late to have had an opportunity to prove himself as a warrior, Almighty Voice is frustrated and full of disdain for the life under the colonial regime.

Educated by his father, mother, and grandfather, One Arrow, who resisted signing the treaties, Almighty Voice grew up listening to stories of warriors and buffalo hunts. He yearns to emulate what he believes to be his ancestors' glorious deeds but cannot. The colonial policy-makers have determined that he is a child in an adult's body—albeit a dangerous and unpredictable one—so he must live as a ward of the state. He cannot provide his family with food because there are no buffalo and little game for him to hunt. He cannot fight his traditional enemies, the Blackfoot and the Dakota, because they, too, live under the regime's control, imprisoned on reserves. Moreover, the greatest enemy of all, the colonizers, now command the cultural hegemony and, accordingly, have decreed that the movements of the Indigenous people be kept in check. As a consequence, Almighty Voice cannot move beyond the boundaries of the reserve without permission of the Indian agent. In Almighty Voice's world, the White man has even "turn[ed] the prairie into a jail" (12). Finding the events that are taking place around him incomprehensible, Almighty Voice, had he a choice, would not be living in the post-treaty world of 1895. He cannot understand the White man's ways, is not interested in learning them, and dismisses anything that he cannot understand as "stupid": the White man's religion, customs, and laws. He cannot understand why he would be required to go hungry when there are cattle to eat, and he cannot understand why he should remain in jail when the authorities are planning to hang him.

The fictional Almighty Voice, like the historical figure, is a strong man and a skilled athlete, having swum the freezing North Saskatchewan River in late October. An expert marksman, he boasts about his hunting prowess. And, at age twenty-two, the fictional Almighty Voice has already secured and discarded three wives. What else would there have been for him to do to prove that he is a man? He can neither provide for his family nor can he protect them, so he must prove himself through displays of hyper-masculinity within his community. Through this characterization of Almighty Voice, Moses illustrates how colonization usurped First Nations men of their function in society, thereby robbing them of their self-esteem and effectively emasculating them. In addition, by depicting Almighty Voice as a character more noteworthy for his womanizing and athletic prowess than for his wisdom, Moses challenges the contemporary myth of the Almighty Voice, which depicts the historical figure as a mythic warrior endowed with superhuman qualities. Appleford contends that "there is a heightened awareness in Dan Moses' recent work of the gaze of the mainstream culture, and how this gaze often desires a 'real' Native present to be (re)presented for its view."[35] Deliberately refusing to satisfy the settler audience's desire, Moses characterizes Almighty Voice as a mere mortal, a flawed human being like the rest of us, struggling to survive the insanity of colonial oppression: "Our pursuit of Almighty Voice is the pursuit of the 'almighty Native voice,' and Moses' play emphasizes the chimerical nature of such a pursuit."[36] Yet, while the settler audiences pursue the "almighty Native voice," Indigenous audiences yearn for a homegrown superhero to offset the Hollywood images of bloodthirsty and/or noble savages. Thus, in the Almighty Voice myth so prevalent in the Indigenous communities of the Northern Plains, the character of the man who is the historical Almighty Voice has been so distorted that he no longer resembles a mortal man. In the realism of Act I, Moses rejects this kind of characterization.

Because Almighty Voice cannot comprehend the implications of the colonial juggernaut, he dies; however, although he finds no relief in death, he is no vanishing Indian. In Act II, Moses abandons reality and creates a world that, at first, seems mad both to Almighty Voice and to the audience. Act II is set in an afterlife that takes the form of a vaudeville minstrel show, and both characters appear masked in white face. Both Almighty Voice and White Girl are transformed: Almighty Voice as Ghost and White Girl as the Interlocutor, Mr. Drum of minstrel show fame, and a Mountie, the symbol of colonial authority and agent of what Louis Althusser has termed the "repressive state apparatus."[37] At first, Ghost is confused. Speaking only Cree, he is unable to defend himself from the incomprehensible Interlocutor, who speaks only English which s/he uses to torment him with racist quips. She mocks his language saying, "Come on, use the Queen's tongue, or I'll sell you to a cigar store" (30). Through his depiction of the Interlocutor, Moses exposes the attitudes of White society of the Victorian era. Masked in white face, White Girl is no longer recognizable as a Cree woman. Her words suggest that she has now become the "white girl" into which the residential school officials attempted to remake her. Furthermore, like many Indigenous people, she has internalized the racist attitudes that overwhelm her. However, rather than taking herself and her society seriously, the Interlocutor exudes sarcasm and self-conscious irony, thereby exposing the cruelty embedded in the attitudes of that time.[38] In minstrel shows, White men appeared in black face paint to parody their own stereotypical depictions of African slaves. Moses mimics the standard minstrel show by presenting "red" Indians in white face paint in a parody of the White colonizers' stereotypical depictions of Indigenous people. Through his mimicry of minstrel show iconography, Moses exposes the egomaniacal attitudes of the colonizers to reveal to his settler audiences how truly sick their predecessors were. Thus, through this parody, Moses exposes the flaws in the foundation of colonialism.

As the play progresses, we discover that Moses also engenders optimism for Indigenous people, albeit in the midst of chaos. At first, the Ghost of Almighty Voice seems doomed to spend eternity once again victimized by the colonizer, this time in the form of the Interlocutor. And, the residential school officials seem to have succeeded, because White Girl appears to be forever lost behind her white mask. However, as Ghost, Almighty Voice, like the First Nations people who follow him, refuses to remain in the role of victim. Indeed, like Indigenous people today, Ghost proves to be surprisingly adaptable and acquires an imposing command of the English language in short order, thereby enabling him to employ puns and rhyme to engage in a witty critique of the public policies that were the cause of his death:

INTER-
LOCUTOR   …Newspapers are our pass to an understanding of
          reserves and the life of its denizens.

GHOST   And we don't have to go to the Indian agent to get
          them. The passes.

INTER-
LOCUTOR   Are you making one at me, sire? (*hitting him*) Did
          you read how we're teaching our primitive friends
          agriculture?

GHOST   That'll bring them down to earth.

INTER-
LOCUTOR   And we're giving them the benefit of our modern
          tongue.

GHOST   They'll need no other one, our kingdom come.

INTER-
LOCUTOR   Did you read how tranquil and subordinate they've
          become under our wise and humane government?

The GHOST claps a "gunshot".

INTER-
LOCUTOR   Was that a gun? A shot?

> GHOST   Likely not. The Indian Agent won't give them any
> more ammunition until they put in a crop.
>
> INTER-
> LOCUTOR   What will they eat in the meantime?
>
> GHOST   (*hitting himself*) Off to the hoose-gow with them!
> Lazy is as lazy does. So it says in the newspaper. Or
> the Bible. (48–9)

In this passage, Moses conflates colonial and Christian propaganda to reveal how the two are inextricably linked to the imperial objective. Ultimately, the Ghost of Almighty Voice seizes control of the show from the Interlocutor, causing her to wipe off the white paint that masks her true identity, and the White attitudes that accompany it, restoring her to her true self, White Girl, the Cree woman who is his wife. In life, Almighty Voice could not cope with the colonial world, but in death, he adjusts and prevails.

It should come as no surprise that the story of Kisê-manitô-wêw has acquired mythic proportions in the Indigenous community. Today we regard Kisê-manitô-wêw as an early resistance fighter, and, as such, an inspiration for Indigenous people today and for future generations. But Moses depicts Kisê-manitô-wêw as a man who did not set out to become a myth and certainly did not set out to die. Like all of us, the historical Almighty Voice only wanted what he considered to be the necessities of life—food, freedom, and love—and was thwarted by the colonial bureaucrats and their oppressive policies. In his depiction of Almighty Voice as Ghost, Moses reminds us of the resilience of Indigenous people and how ordinary people can have extraordinary effects in both their lives and their stories. In the same way that Kisê-manitô-wêw resisted the colonial policies, Daniel David Moses employs the language of the colonizer to remind us of our history and to inspire us to keep resistance alive.

"Strength of Indian Women": Family Stories Reveal Old Wounds

Vera Manuel is also interested in informing history and applying theatre to heal her community from its effects. Although her play "Strength of Indian Women" is fictional, the stories her characters tell belong to Manuel's mother. Many Indigenous people who either attended residential school themselves or are the children and grandchildren of those who did recognize these stories as truth. The cast is comprised of three generations of Indigenous women. The women of the older generation—Sousette, Lucy, Mariah, and

Agnes—are close in age and all attended residential school together. Eva is Sousette's daughter and, although she did not attend a residential school herself, her mother's experience has had a profound effect on her. Jeannette Armstrong describes the effects of residential schools on Indigenous communities and how they caused the "social problems" that Manuel illustrates in this play:

> Arising out of the siege conditions of this nightmare time, what is commonly referred to as the "social problems" of Native peoples emerged. Homes and communities without children had nothing to work for, or live for. Children returned to communities and families as adults, without the necessary skills for parenting, for Native life style, or self-sufficiency on their land base, and deteriorated into despair. With the loss of cohesive cultural relevance with their own peoples and a distorted view of the non-Native culture from the clergy who ran the residential schools, an almost total disorientation and loss of identity occurred. The disintegration of family and community and nation was inevitable, originating with the individual's internalized pain. Increasing death statistics from suicide, violence, alcohol and drug abuse, and other poverty-centred physical diseases, can leave no doubt about the question of totalitarianism and genocide.[39]

Manuel does not merely depict a community in despair, however. Eva's daughter and Sousette's granddaughter, Suzie, represents a new generation and new hope. The ceremony that her grandmother and friends hold to celebrate her entry into womanhood is central to the play. Nevertheless, even though Suzie's childhood is much different from her mother's and grandmother's, the residential schools still affect her.

Manuel introduces the published version of her play with a discussion of the effects of the residential schools and the responsibility of storytellers to help individuals and communities to heal from their wounds. Like the creators of the Power Plays, Manuel begins with the reality of her community. She explains: "I didn't make up the stories told in 'Strength of Indian Women.' They came from pictures my mother painted for me with her words, words that helped me see her as a little girl for the first time."[40] Deeply affected by her mother's stories and her own experiences, Manuel is intensely aware of the Indigenous people who form a portion of her audience and who have suffered similar traumas as she and her family have as a result of the policies that created the residential schools: "Each time we staged a performance of the play, I mourned that little girl who never had a childhood. I mourned the mother missing from my childhood…. The responsibility we hold in passing on these stories is to role model a healthy lifestyle for our children, who are always watching us for direction" (76). Manuel's goal in writing and performing "Strength of Indian Women" is to transform the current reality of Indigenous people by applying theatre to the problem of the intergenerational effects of residential schools. Philip Taylor claims that "applied theatre becomes a medium through which storytellers can step into the perspectives of others and gain entry points to different worldviews—perspectives that might even articulate why the events of that day of barbarity might have occurred."[41] The audience gains perspective on the trauma that the schools caused when they hear Manuel's characters each describe the barbarity of the residential schools and articulate how it continues to affect them.

Characteristic of most Indigenous literature from Canada, rather than an individual, the community in "Strength of Indian Women" is the protagonist. Every community, however, has its organizers, and in this community it is Sousette who organizes the gathering of women. Because of the closeness she feels with her former schoolmates, she takes Lucy, Mariah, and Agnes as her sisters and asks them, as her sisters, to support Suzie during her fast and to stand with her the feast that will follow. The fact that Suzie will be participating in a traditional ceremony to celebrate her transition into womanhood brings back memories for all the women. For Sousette, Lucy, Mariah, and Agnes, the memories are of the barbarity of residential school and the problems it caused them throughout their lives. Not only were they forbidden from participating in traditional ceremonies at residential school, they were taught that these ceremonies were evidence that their cultures were savage, clearly inferior to the colonizers' culture. Throughout their lives, the women were victimized because of their culture and their gender, and that victimization began at residential school. At residential school they became painfully aware that their entry into womanhood was no cause for celebration.

Although each woman experiences residential school in very different ways, the common denominators for Sousette, Agnes, and Lucy are the violence they witnessed there and the sexual abuse they suffered at the hands of the priest. Sousette tells that she was able to evade him for a time, but eventually the priest, whom Manuel fittingly names Father LeBlanc, catches her. Although she is aware that LeBlanc has abused at least one other girl and has heard rumours of others, Sousette's childlike reasoning causes her to believe that she alone was singled out to become his sexual toy, and for this she is ashamed. Feelings of shame cause her to be silent, and Sousette maintains her silence for most of her life. Still, even though Sousette is able to repress the story of her abuse, she is not able to repress the emotions that accompanied the unresolved trauma. Thus, Sousette lives her life with anger overflowing. She is angry with the priest for abusing her, angry with herself for letting him catch her, and angry at the colonial regime for creating the residential schools. Unable to direct this anger at its rightful cause, Sousette takes her anger out on all those around her, especially her daughter. Suzie's ceremony brings up memories of the absence of ceremony and tradition in Eva's childhood because her mother, Sousette, still carried the trauma and shame of residential school with her. Eva confronts her mother, bringing up her treatment of her as a child, and explains how she now treats her daughter, Suzie, in a like manner:

> Do you remember how you used to beat me, Mom? Do you even remember the bruises? Do you remember the ugly things you used to call me, and all those times you left me alone. I wouldn't have cared, if only you would have loved me. Do you even know what that means, love? Every time I go to hug you, you stiffen up. Do you know that you do that, Mom? Do you know how that makes me feel? And now I'm doing the same thing to Suzie. I push her away, Mom. I call her stupid, and I hit her, and I don't want to. (108)

At a subconscious level, Sousette believes that her body has betrayed her because it was her body to which LeBlanc was attracted. The thought of using her body to express her love for her daughter, not in an abusive way but by merely hugging her, is repugnant to her. As a consequence, Sousette "stiffens up" when her young daughter reaches out for her. Furthermore, the young Eva is a daily reminder of Sousette's lost girlhood, which causes her anger to surface again and again. The violence that ensues is followed by shame, not just in the first generation but also in the next.

Through her depiction of this family, Manuel demonstrates the intergenerational effects of residential school and the unresolved trauma that continues to wound our communities. The traumatic memories of LeBlanc's sexual abuse remain inside Sousette and fester there, and so she lashes out at her daughter who reminds her of herself. Unaware of her mother's story, Eva accepts her mother's treatment of her as evidence that her mother does not love her and as proof that she is inherently unlovable. In some ways this is even more damaging than the residential school abuse. None of the Indigenous children who attended residential schools had any cause to expect love from the school staff. The schools were the creation of the colonial regime, and their mandate was to kill the Indian in the child. Eva, on the other hand, certainly had cause to expect love from her mother, the woman who gave her life. Not surprisingly, her mother's betrayal fills her with hurt, and that hurt is expressed in anger, the only form of emotional expression that she has witnessed and learned. It is also not surprising that Eva's daughter becomes a constant physical reminder of her lost girlhood. Filled with anger and unable to express her love for her child, especially physical expressions of love, Eva lashes out with violence towards Suzie. She does not want to treat her child in the same way that she was treated, but she has not learned any other way to express herself as a parent. And so she, too, feels shame. As a result, her daughter Suzie, although two generations removed from the residential school experience, is still a victim of its violence and barbarity. Violence breeds shame, and shame breeds more violence. This is the despicable legacy of the colonial regime's policy of "Indian" residential schools, and without healing that legacy will be passed down from one generation of Indigenous people to the next.

Lucy and Agnes experience the violence of residential school not only as sexual abuse but also as extreme physical abuse. Unable to accept victimization any longer, the young Agnes organizes an escape. Finding Lucy behind the stairs, physically ill following LeBlanc's sexual advances, Agnes invites her to escape with her and the others. Unfortunately, the escape fails. Lucy tells Sousette how they were betrayed: "Our own people brought us back" (92). The nuns and priest begin beating the girls as soon as they are captured and continue until they arrive at the school. At the school, they force the other girls to witness the beatings, and Sousette remembers that the nuns would not permit them to close their eyes or turn away. Lucy remembers:

> They took turns whipping us. When one of them would get tired, another would step in. They were harder on Agnes because they said she was the ringleader, and because she wouldn't cry. I wanted to tell her to cry, so they would stop, but she wouldn't cry.
>
> The priest was yelling at her, "Cry! Cry! Cry!" but she wouldn't. Then I noticed a trickle of blood running down her leg, and when she fell, it smeared on the floor. She had started on her period, started bleeding, and still they wouldn't stop. (93)

Clearly, the onset of Agnes' womanhood was no cause for celebration. This experience causes a rift between Lucy and Agnes because Lucy blames Agnes for her beating. Although their lives take much different paths after residential school, Lucy continues to hold on to this resentment.

When Lucy returns to the reserve, she is pregnant, presumably by Father LeBlanc, and her family arranges a marriage to Joe Sam, a widower with small children. At that time there were no social services, and marriage was the only security available for a young pregnant woman. This is a practical arrangement for both Joe, who needs someone to care for his children, and for Lucy, who needs someone to support her; however, it is not a successful union. Joe, who is also a survivor of residential school, is consumed with jealousy even though Lucy gives him no cause. Although there is no logic to his thinking, given that LeBlanc raped Lucy, Joe cannot forgive her for becoming pregnant by another man. Thus, Joe becomes a violent alcoholic and beats Lucy every time he drinks. Joe, too, has learned violence at the residential school, and Sousette points out that "the way they used to beat those boys in that school, it's a wonder that they didn't all turn out mean" (81). Lucy lives with violence for most her life. Her baby dies, as do the fourteen others that she conceives with Joe, so at the time of Suzie's ceremony, she is alone. Joe has died, and so have his children, all prematurely. Much of Lucy's time is spent visiting her babies in the cemetery and looking after her husband's grave. She will not acknowledge his violence, even though the evidence of it is clear. Her eye is missing and her arm is disfigured. There is no joy in Lucy's life, not as a child or as an elder.

Lucy's emotional development seems to have stopped at the time that she attended residential school, and even as an elder she behaves like a recalcitrant child in her relationships with her former classmates. She never forgives Agnes for the beating that the nuns and priests meted out after catching the runaway girls. She tells Sousette, "It was her [Agnes's] fault that we got caught that day. She was too kind-hearted" (92). To the audience, her logic seems specious: it does not follow that Lucy would blame Agnes for her suffering. Why would she not blame Father LeBlanc, whose sexual abuse prompted her to run away? Why would she not blame the nuns and priest who beat the girls? Why blame Agnes, whose only crime was being "too kind-hearted"? It is important to remember that the nuns and priests at the residential schools presented themselves to the children and their parents as God's helpers.[42] Although she despises them, how can Lucy blame God's agents on earth?

Lucy also harbours resentment for Mariah because she witnesses the nuns and priest singling her out for superior treatment. Because they equate Mariah's light-coloured skin with virtue, she becomes the favourite of the nuns and priest. Lucy blames Mariah for this inequity, and tells Sousette, "You should hear the way she talks about the place sometimes, you'd think it was the Newcastle Hotel and we were royalty, the way she describes it. That's probably the way it was for her, but it sure wasn't the way for us black Indians" (86). In the same way that she blames Agnes for the nuns' and priest's violence, so does she blame Mariah for their cruelty. Clearly, Mariah had no control over whom the nuns and priest selected to favour and whom they chose to spurn. She was a child, as was Lucy. Yet, the elderly Lucy persists in playing childish tricks on Mariah in attempt to punish her for the actions of the nuns and priest. Painful memories of residential school are always with her, and it is easier—and safer—to blame another "Indian" than it would be to blame "God's helpers." And so the residential school policy succeeds in dividing Indigenous people by creating a hierarchy within their ranks based on the colour of their skin. Lucy's relationships reveal how residential schools' conflation of religion with violence becomes a continuing divisive force within Indigenous communities.

Even though her life has been equally difficult, Agnes has confronted her memories and, as a result, has found a degree of peace in her life. When Agnes leaves residential school and returns to the reserve, she discovers that she has no family to care for her. Some have died from smallpox, and the rest are drinking. With no home and no means of support, her only alternative is to move to the city in search of work. She leaves on the bus accompanied by her friend Annie, another former student of the residential school. Having spent their formative years in residential school, they are naive and actually think that the education that they received at school might have made them employable. They are terribly wrong, and soon they discover that their bodies are their only "assets." With no alternatives, they prostitute themselves to stay alive. It is ironic that when Agnes finally escapes the school and Father LeBlanc, she discovers that her survival is now dependent on LeBlanc's "lessons," his teachings of sexual abuse. Agnes and Annie remain prostitutes until a customer murders Annie. Unable to tolerate any more pain, Agnes tells the women, "I stayed drunk after that. I can't remember a time when I ever felt so alone, or so sad as that time" (101). Agnes's and Annie's stories are not uncommon. Looking at a photograph of the children at the school, Sousette remembers the other former students who died violently and prematurely and tells Eva, "You know, out of all these girls there must only be a handful of us still alive. Most of them died, pretty violent too...alcohol, suicide...murder" (82). Agnes is fortunate, however. When her former schoolmates hear about her plight, they gather enough money to pay for her to return home. At the time of Suzie's ceremony, Agnes refuses to feel ashamed of the choices she made as a youth:

LUCY   Agnes, how can you talk about that [her prostitution]? Don't it make you shamed?

AGNES   Ashamed of what, Lucy, that we made the best use out of the only assets that we had? Annie and me, we didn't know any better and we were just trying to survive. We left here with that little bit of money in our pockets. (99)

Manuel gives us no explanation for how Agnes heals. We only learn that in the now of the story she spends her life actively working to save other young women from Annie's fate. To that end, she travels across the country sharing her story with others. She understands that the words that comprise her story are sacred, and she uses them in a sacred, a healing manner.

It is not only the women who experienced physical and sexual abuse who bear the scars of residential school, however. Although Mariah was the favourite of the nuns and priest, she, too, is troubled by her memories. The guilt that Mariah suffers is for people who, by chance, survive in violent situations while others around them do not, causing her to wonder "why [she] should still be livin' and all those other women are dead" (104). She feels guilt because she is alive and physically healthy, having eluded sexual and physical abuse. As a witness to the victimization of the other girls from her community, she comprehends that she has done nothing to merit her favoured position and that the only difference between her and the other girls is the colour of their skin. When she leaves residential school, she continues to be burdened by survivor's guilt. In an effort to escape her memories, she moves to the city where she lives for most of her adult life. Thus, the nuns' and priest's favouritism succeed in disconnecting her from her community. Still, Mariah cannot forget about her people, and haunted by memories, she returns later in life. When she returns to the reserve, Mariah finds no respite. Paralyzed by fear, she avoids most of the other women, especially Lucy, whose mean-spirited and childish pranks she dreads. She is close to Sousette, however, and it is Sousette's Indian medicine that relieves Mariah's suffering, albeit temporarily. Sousette recommends taking Mariah to a medicine person, but this is problematic for Mariah.

Mariah is a devout Christian, having accepted Christianity at the residential school; however, she did not live in a Christian environment before she was taken away to school. When she was small she lived with her grandmother, who taught her the traditional ceremonies of her people and loved her unconditionally. For her grandmother, Mariah's light skin was not a problem, and because of her grandmother's love, she came to know serenity:

> I knew who I was when she would light the juniper and guide my
> tiny hands over the smoke, puling it up over my hair, across my
> heart, and down the rest of my body. She would turn me in a circle,
> always to the right, and she would tell me that the Creator gave me
> as a special gift to her, to watch over for a time. That, at that time,
> I was the most perfect, and precious being, there was no doubt.
> I believed that with all my heart. What I seen [sic] in that school
> shocked me into silence, and disbelief in everything that was good.
> (105)

Mariah quickly learns that if she follows the ways of her grandmother at
residential school, she will put her life in danger.

Ostracized because of the nuns' and priests' preferential treatment of
her, Mariah has but one friend at residential school, a girl named Theresa.
Not only is Theresa proud of her culture, which she persists in practising,
she is "always encouragin' others not to forget they were Indian" (105). Her
resistance arouses the ire of the nuns, and Mariah witnesses Sister Luke
throw Theresa down two flights of stairs for refusing "to stop speakin' Indian,
refuse to quit prayin' to Napika" (105). After witnessing Sister Luke murder
her friend, Mariah's world is turned upside down, and all those things that
were once a source of comfort and love are now a source of fear. She comes to
believe that her very survival depends upon her remaining silent. Terrified,
she does not resist when the nuns and priest single her out for special treatment. And so she survives to become a silent witness to their malevolent
conduct. As she grows older, she finds it more and more difficult to repress
the memories of what she has witnessed, and as a consequence she has difficulty sleeping. Although Sousette's medicine provides temporary relief, it
cannot heal Mariah from the trauma that she carries within her. It is not until
she breaks the silence and tells the women her story that Mariah finds relief,
and she is comforted in the camaraderie of the women who understand.
After she tells her story, Agnes observes, "And you are [perfect], Mariah,
you're magnificent" (107).

By dramatizing her mother's stories of residential school, Manuel breaks
the silence of shame and fear. Although this is not participatory theatre in
a physical sense, her audience is engaged at the level of emotions. For other
Indigenous people whose stories resemble those of Sousette, Lucy, Agnes,
and Mariah, Manuel's characters validate their experiences, which they are
able to examine from a safe distance. The play also provides explanations for
the children and grandchildren of residential school survivors who might

not understand how their loved ones' experiences at school could continue to affect them. And, the play reveals to non-Indigenous audiences a hidden segment of Canadian history and illustrates the continuing effects of the policies of their government. Learning of the abominable behaviour of the school officials would be difficult for many non-Indigenous people and not congruent with their experience, especially with the clergy. In her study of the intergenerational effects of residential school, Rosalyn Ing draws on social psychology theories of cognitive dissonance to explain how people who perceive themselves to be good are able to rationalize their evil behaviour. Manuel illustrates how the nuns and priests justified their violence by convincing themselves that the children, because of their Indigeneity, are "unworthy, subhuman, stupid, [and especially] immoral."[43] Thus, because Mariah's friend Theresa is an affront to the Christian god in that she refuses to cease her "pagan" ways, Sister Luke flies into a fit of rage and executes her as if she were battling the Devil. This kind of revelation is especially difficult for a non-Indigenous audience to believe, especially those audience members who are Christians. This might explain why "Strength of Indian Women" has played almost exclusively in Indigenous communities, for whom the play ends with optimism. Suzie represents hope for the next generation. Although she is still touched by trauma, she is fortunate to live in a time of healing through cultural reclamation and regeneration. Agnes articulates that hope saying, "Suzie will turn the world right side up again, the way it was meant to be, and we will all celebrate" (113).

Say *fareWEL* to Easy Answers, or, the Challenges of Indigenous "Self-Governance"

The purpose of Ian Ross's play *fareWel* is not so much to engender hope as to challenge Indigenous people to examine the roles that we play in perpetuating our own victimization and subsequent oppression. In *fareWel*, Ross illustrates the byzantine relationship between contemporary Indigenous people and the colonial regime: "You don't come with guns anymore; you don't have to. You come with briefcases and we kill ourselves."[44] The play is set in the present day on a fictional reserve, which Ross names Partridge Crop, situated in the Interlake area of southern Manitoba, part of the area covered by Treaty Four. The population of Partridge Crop is comprised of Nakawe (Saulteaux), the most western of the Anishinaubae. Life on Partridge Crop is bleak, and the issues that Ross brings to light are common to many

Canadian "Indian" reserves. As author of *fareWel*, Ross assumes the role of translator as Mojica and Knowles define it:

> One of the tasks of First Nations theatre artists…*is* translation, broadly understood: translation between cultures and world views; translation between the unseen and the material worlds; translation between interior and exterior realities; translation between languages and discourses, including the values and ideologies they embody; and translation of the ways in which First Nations people navigate identity. Because most Native peoples in the contemporary world *live* in translation, and theatre can provide the opportunity to envision and embody…the interior experience of Native peoples. It allows First Nations artists to examine, show, and validate their experience of living in a hostile environment. It allows them to take the risk of turning that experience inside out—a kind of voluntary disembowelling—so that people can see what it feels like on the inside, and so that the healing can begin.[45]

Without question, *fareWel* is "a kind of voluntary disembowelling," and although the setting of the play is specific to Status Indian people living on reserves, the "hostile environment" that Ross turns inside out is one that is familiar to the Métis and Inuit as well. By exposing the problems that are common to Indigenous communities and governments, Ross challenges us to critically examine the course of action that Indigenous politicians have advanced as the solution to all the problems that their communities are experiencing.

From its inception, the colonial regime set out to destroy Indigenous governance systems and replace them with ones that the regime itself created, ones that would be its subordinates. As a result, colonial bureaucrats, not Indian people, designed the chief-and-council system that is the governance model that most reserves employ today. Although women played important roles in the governance of most Indigenous nations, the colonial regime banished them from its system, which in turn destroyed the gender balance that existed for millennia in many Indigenous nations. Until very recently the Indian agent presided over council meetings, and the men elected as chief and council were mere figureheads without power or responsibility. Although the Indian agent is a thing of the past and the regime now permits women to run for political office, colonial officials continue to define the powers and limitations of the chief and council. Furthermore, colonial bureaucrats monitor their actions to ensure that they adhere to the policies and restrictions that the regime imposes. To that end, the Department of Indian Affairs has grown into an enormous arm of the federal government and employs thousands of people across the country.

Indian leaders would like to eliminate the Department of Indian Affairs and contend that Indigenous self-government cannot possibly harm their people any more than the government of the colonial regime has. They claim that even the most cursory review of the harm that colonization has caused would suggest that they are most likely correct. These politicians have been particularly vocal in demanding the right to govern their own people independently from the colonial regime. Although the *Indian Act* permits Indian bands[46] to pass band council resolutions to reinstate forms of traditional governance based on band custom, most still operate under the system imposed by the colonial regime. As a result, individual reserve governments and the larger Status Indian political organizations still lack gender balance because they are still male-dominated. Thus, the speed with which they want the transition from colonial to Indigenous governance is a concern for Ross, who is also a Status Indian and has witnessed the growing pains of the self-governance movement. In *fareWel*, Ross illustrates the downside of Indigenous self-government if Status Indian people enter into it in haste and without adequate forethought and preparation.

The colonial regime has been surprisingly, and some might say suspiciously, responsive to Indian politicians' demands for the right to govern their people. To that end, the regime has transferred the responsibility to administer many programs to Indian bands, programs that the regime's bureaucrats once administered, such as education and social welfare. Thus, rather than granting Indian people the right to self-determination, the colonial regime has merely devolved the responsibility for administering pre-existing programs. Worse yet, the regime expects Indian governments to deliver these programs with little or no infrastructure, no training, and with smaller budgets than its Indian Affairs bureaucracy itself has received to deliver the same services. Thus, the colonial bureaucrats have set the stage for Indian governments to fail. In *fareWel*, Ross illustrates this scenario and its consequences: "The story, fareWel's story, isn't a rejection of self-government but a subtle demonstration through a difference in action of how we should go about achieving it."[47]

At the beginning of the play, we learn that the colonial regime has transferred to the Partridge Crop chief and council full responsibility for delivering services such as health, education, and social welfare to their band members. Along with transferring responsibility for delivering these services, the colonial regime has also handed over responsibility for managing the band's finances, which would vary depending on the population but would typically amount to millions of dollars. The regime's decision to transfer these responsibilities in their entirety to Partridge Crop is beyond belief, given that there are only two band members who have managed businesses and neither of them is on the council. However astonishing this action might be, it is not unusual. What happened on the fictional Partridge Crop reserve is happening on reserves across the country. Politicians and their bureaucrats claim that they are merely responding to Indigenous people's desire for self-determination; however, their claims of altruism are highly questionable. Turning over control of multi-million dollar budgets to people who lack education and training and who have lived their lives in poverty is tantamount to setting the stage for administrative failure. Administrative failure is not the worst possible consequence. Having easy access to enormous amounts of money is tempting to most people, and irresistible for some, especially people who have spent their entire lives in poverty and comprise a social underclass. And power is particularly seductive for people who have spent their lives being powerless. Not surprisingly, then, the chief and council of Partridge Crop have mismanaged the band's funds. As a result, although the residents of the reserve continue to live in poverty and almost all are dependent on social welfare, the chief drives a luxury car.

Through his depiction of the Partridge Crop chief and council, Ross holds up for critical examination what some Indian people now term the "New Wîhtikowak."[48] The *Wîhtikow*, in Cree tradition, like the *Windigo* of the Anishinaubae, is a giant insatiable cannibal spirit who eats everything and everyone in its path; it is the personification of greed. In traditional stories, the *Wîhtikow* embodies that quality that communal people could not tolerate—greed—because in communal societies survival was dependent on mutual support and sharing. Cree poet Neal Mcleod has employed the *Wîhtikow* as a metaphor for the sickness of colonial greed.[49] Anishinaubae poet and playwright Armand Ruffo has used the term "Windigoness" to describe aberrant behaviour, especially incestuous behaviour. Ruffo writes: "In his text *The Manitous*, Ojibway educator Basil Johnston refers to what he calls 'Modern Weendigoes.' 'Actually the Weendigoes did not die out or disappear,' he says; 'they have only been assimilated and reincarnated.'"[50] Not surprisingly, some Indigenous people use this same metaphor to represent the greed that has insidiously infiltrated some segments of our own political leadership. That greed has infiltrated the ranks of our leadership is not difficult to understand since for too many years the colonial bureaucrats have been their only role models. Moreover, on many Indian reserves, the only employment options available are chief, councillor, and band office employee. The remainder of the population have no options but to depend on social welfare or to seek work away from the reserve. Ross dares us to examine this system and the social sicknesses that it elicits.

At the beginning of the play, we learn that the regime has reacted to the chief and council's financial mismanagement by partially taking back control of the Partridge Crop finances. Robert Traverse, one of the two band members to own his own business, understands that the chief and council have mismanaged the finances and the consequences of their actions. He tells his fellow band members that "this band is in a co-manager's agreement with Indian Affairs. It's been in receivership. That's like being bankrupt."[51] Having neither education nor training, and lacking access to a skilled workforce, the chief and council are clearly not capable of properly managing the band's finances. Consequently, they address the band's financial crisis in a bizarre fashion. Presumably in an effort to generate revenues, the chief has taken the little money remaining and has gone to Las Vegas, leaving his people to cope as best they can with no money and no leadership. At the beginning of the play, the characters are not aware that their leadership has abandoned them. It is not until the social-welfare cheques fail to arrive that they realize that something is amiss.

Social welfare is the way of life for most members of the Partridge Crop band, and the characters refer to their social-welfare payments as their "fareWel." It is ironic that the colonial regime's policy of providing meagre social-welfare payments to Indigenous people—yet another policy whose purpose was ostensibly to help—has had insidious consequences for Indigenous communities. The regime's educational policies, especially those that created the residential schools, deprived people of the traditional teachings that Indigenous people needed to live off the land but did not provide sufficient training for people to succeed in colonial society. Social welfare was the solution, a solution that resulted in people bidding "farewell" to their independence. Thus, with unemployment almost universal on Partridge Crop—the exception being the elected chief and council—the band members are not able to "fare well" without government handouts. *fareWel* is the story of six Partridge Crop band members who attempt to take control of their own welfare and, in the process, learn that self-determination means finding a way to unite their impoverished and divided community, thereby restoring the community to balance and health.

When the band members discover that the chief has absconded with their money and that their fareWel is not forthcoming, Teddy Sinclair takes charge. An entrepreneur of sorts, Teddy subsidizes his fareWel by running a pawnshop out of his house. When the fareWel cheques do not arrive, Teddy organizes a band meeting to discuss self-government. Like many Status Indian people, Teddy believes that self-government will be the panacea for all that ails his community and that the revenues derived from the slot machines he proposes to purchase will fund their government. Independence in Teddy's mind means not only from the colonial regime but also from the duly elected chief and council, who are incompetent and corrupt. We learn that they buy their votes by plying Sheldon Traverse, an alcoholic with the controversial nickname "Nigger," with cases of beer, and Melvin McKay, who is addicted to sniffing gasoline, with gas vouchers. With the chief and council in Las Vegas, Teddy plots a *coup d'état* and plans to take over as chief himself. To that end, he will tolerate no opposition, no discussion, and no delays.

Unfortunately, although determined, Teddy has no more qualifications than does the current chief, and the defects in his leadership abilities become rapidly apparent during the course of the meeting. He refuses to discuss the ramifications of assuming control of the reserve and tells the other band members, "I'm doing it. No more talking. There's been too much of that already.... No more tomorrow. No more waiting. It's time we took control of our own money. No more fuckin' fareWel" (47). Clearly, Teddy recognizes the problems that colonial control and the soul-destroying dependence on social welfare have caused; however, he understands nothing about governing. When Robert suggests that an election must follow due process, Teddy replies "that's white man's ways." Yet, when Robert mentions that he should consult Indian elders, Teddy opposes that idea as well and retorts, "Consult. Talk. We do it. Now" (45). That Teddy cannot tolerate questions is indicative of his feelings of insecurity, and those feelings are justified. Questions require answers, answers that Teddy is incapable of providing.

Taking back the right to govern one's community after being denied that right for more than a century is complex and Partridge Crop, like almost all Status Indian communities, has no band members remaining who would have witnessed their traditional government in operation. Any traditional leaders died in the early reserve period, and the only resource that today's leaders can draw upon are stories of traditional leaders that have been passed down through the oral tradition or, more often, historical records that describe those leaders. It is ironic that the only living role models of leadership that most contemporary Indigenous people have witnessed in operation are the colonial bureaucrats and the residential school officials. Ross makes it clear that Indigenous self-government demands leaders who possess not only determination, like Teddy, but also emotional and spiritual health, and a strong knowledge of their traditions coupled with imagination and wisdom. These requirements are daunting, yet these are the qualities required to reinvent a governance system that is based on traditional values but is also able to function in our current environment. Unfortunately for Partridge Crop, the chief and council do not possess these qualities and their current alternative, Teddy, possesses only determination. Rachel and Robert, both of whom comprehend some of the complexity of the situation, thwart Teddy's aspirations by calling the process he advances into question and challenging his claim to leadership.

Rachel Traverse has seen Teddy at his weakest moment, and he despises her for it. Believing that life on the reserve was hopeless, Rachel left and moved to the city, where she worked as a prostitute for an escort service. During the course of her work she encounters Teddy. She explains to her friend Phyllis Bruce that the escort agency sent her to provide services for a customer at a downtown hotel, but when she arrived she discovered that the customer was Teddy. Until that time, the world of prostitution was Rachel's fantasy world where she could hide from herself, from her identity as an Indian woman, and forget who she was and where she came from. She explains to Phyllis that as an Indian woman she grew up with no hope of a future: "When I was small I didn't even want to be anything. Nobody said to me you can be this or you can be that, and when I left here I saw what I was…A woman. A Native woman. With no education. No money. No future" (88). Prostitution was the best option that she could envision. To transform herself, Rachel adopted a new identity, renaming herself Simone, because that name sounded French and, therefore, exotic. To Rachel, it was better to identify as a French prostitute than an Indian woman. To survive the shame of prostitution, she numbs her emotions and eventually ceases feeling. Face-to-face with Teddy, however, Rachel is reminded of who she truly is and what she has become and, at that moment, she realizes that she can no longer live with the choices that she has made. Although Teddy wants her to stay and have sex with him, she refuses and returns home to the reserve and to her people.

Rachel's rejection of Teddy explains, in part, his animosity towards her, but does not explain his hostility towards Indigenous women in general. Teddy has never told anyone on the reserve that he hires prostitutes during his travels to the city. Like Rachel, Teddy discovers that the city is a place to escape from the hopelessness of life on the reserve; it is a place where he can become someone other than himself. Teddy discovers that money provides him with power in the city, and with that power he can purchase another human being who will obey him and help him to live out his escapist fantasies. Again, social psychology's theories of cognitive dissonance are useful in that they explain how Teddy is able to rationalize his feelings of superiority to the prostitutes whom he hires, even though he is clearly a partner in this same commercial transaction. Furthermore, to an impoverished man living under colonial oppression, the ability to purchase another human is particularly seductive in that it enables the oppressed to become the oppressor. However, when the human he purchases is not only an Indigenous woman but one with whom he has grown up, Teddy can no longer rationalize his behaviour and is ashamed.

Not surprisingly, Teddy has told no one on the reserve about his encounter with Rachel. Still, at every opportunity Teddy surreptitiously abuses her. In an effort to eliminate his feelings of shame, Teddy assigns the shame to Rachel. He labels her "whore" and "akitten"[52] and when she challenges his attempted *coup d'état*, he threatens to expose her as a prostitute: "Rachel, you owe me to keep quiet and keep my mouth shut" (57). Teddy knows, however, that by exposing Rachel, he would also expose himself as a man who must pay for sex. Worse yet, such revelations would inevitably include the information that even a prostitute has rejected him. His only solution is to get rid of the source of his shame. Teddy attempts to banish Rachel from the reserve and, in an effort to garner support, he asks the people, "What kind of reserve would I be running here if I let hookers live here?" (59). Rachel holds her ground, however, refusing to accept the blame and the shame that Teddy endeavours to heap on her, and continues to challenge him until he explodes. Unable to answer her questions and unable to face her accusations, Teddy becomes violent. Not only does he assault Rachel by pulling her by the hair, he also kicks her friend Phyllis, who has had no part in the discussion.

Duran and Duran's analysis of the function of violence in Indigenous communities is particularly germane to this incident: "This aggression [of Native Americans against their own people] serves a dual purpose. The perpetrator of the violence can achieve momentary catharsis and relief while at the same time destroying the part of him/herself that reminds him/her of that helplessness and lack of hope. In essence, the individual attacks his or her own projection in a person close by. Meanwhile, the person inflicting the violence may or may not be aware that he/she really would like to vent this rage on the oppressor."[53] Teddy's attempt to take control of the Partridge Crop governance is fantasy, but it is a fantasy grounded in hope. That Teddy is unable to answer Rachel's questions shatters that hope and returns him to the feeling of helplessness that is his norm and the norm for most band members. It is significant to note that when Robert challenges him, Teddy resists but does not erupt into violence. Through his characterization of Teddy, Ross explores the complex and ambivalent relationship between many Indigenous men and women living under colonial oppression.

Teddy identifies with the men he perceives to be his oppressors—not only the colonial bureaucrats but also the Partridge Crop chief and council—and aspires to seize their power. He perceives that a *coup d'état* under the guise of self-governance would provide a means to this end. He also perceives that Rachel could thwart his desire. Duran and Duran examine the deep psychological loss of identity that occurs when Indigenous men, equating their identity with the warrior tradition, discover that they cannot achieve that identity while living under colonial oppression. Unable to lash out at their oppressors, having learned that retribution would be speedy and harsh, Indigenous men lash out at the very people whom a warrior would be charged to protect, the women and children. Indigenous women, in particular, as life-givers and eternal reminders of Indigenous identity, then become prime targets of this violence. Duran and Duran postulate that Indigenous "women and children have been sacrificing themselves [by allowing themselves to be the objects of violence] in order to preserve the tattered remains of the warrior tradition."[54] Phyllis is willing to continue making this sacrifice. When Rachel confronts her for her passivity, reminding her that Teddy kicked her, Phyllis replies: "I know. But I've had lots worse things done to me than get kicked in the ass. You just have to be careful Rachel. Wait till the fareWel comes back and everything goes back to normal" (66). It is important to note that for Phyllis social welfare has become normalized, so she attributes to its absence the cause of the discord. Although Phyllis believes that the restoration of "fareWel" will return the reserve to a state of equanimity, Rachel does not. Rachel understands that their dependence on "fareWel" robs her people of their dignity. Having sacrificed her dignity as a prostitute, Rachel is no longer willing to sacrifice herself for any cause.

Rachel's refusal to accept victimization takes a startling form. She takes possession of Angus's dancing regalia, which Bertha, presumably a member of Angus's family, has gifted to Phyllis at Angus's wake. Phyllis, however, is a fundamentalist Christian, and, therefore, throws the regalia into the garbage, explaining, "It's heathen this thing" (17). Rachel, in an attempt to follow her Anishinaubaek[55] traditions, recovers the outfit from the garbage and accuses Phyllis of disrespecting Angus's memory. Determined to remain on the reserve and equally determined to put a stop to Teddy's ambitions, Rachel refuses to help Phyllis make pies for yet another wake of another band member who has died prematurely, and sets out to take action. She tells Phyllis, "I've got something to do.... Women's work" (65). Rachel takes Angus's regalia to her cousin "Nigger" and offers him tobacco to bless the regalia. Rachel refuses to address Sheldon as "Nigger" and treats him with the respect typically accorded a traditional elder, even though he is an alcoholic and a derelict. Sheldon is shocked by her respect but agrees.

Donning Angus's newly blessed regalia, Rachel sets out, bare-breasted, to face Teddy. Rachel's actions would be considered shocking in any Indian community because, for most Indigenous people, traditional forms of modesty have become conflated with memories of residential school where staff and clergy taught Indigenous children to be ashamed of their bodies. Rachel, however, refuses to accept any more shame. Having abused her life-giving qualities when she turned to prostitution, Rachel reclaims her pride in herself as an Indigenous woman by displaying her breasts as sustainers of life. That she does this while dressed in a man's traditional dance regalia is significant. Prostitution has taught her about men and by donning a man's clothes and dancing his dance, she demonstrates that knowledge. She confronts Teddy, telling him, "And I see. A man. A Native man. A strong man, but one who's afraid. Afraid because I know you. I know you men, and what you want. When you'd go in me, I could feel your heart. Beating. And when you were finished, laying on top of me I could still feel your life beating faster. What you were. What you are. But it's time to make things right. To say goodbye to the things that keep us down. Our peoples' future comes from the past. Not male or female. Pure or mixed. Christian or Traditional. Together. Respected" (88). Although Rachel's speech is clearly optimistic, her line of reasoning is problematic in a number of ways.

Steeped in the liberal humanism that is the dominant ideology of contemporary Canada, Rachel believes that divisions can be healed and that antithetical belief systems can coexist if the Partridge Crop band members cultivate a climate of tolerance. Unfortunately, the fundamentalist Christianity that Phyllis and Robert practice is not tolerant: witness Phyllis throwing Angus's dancing regalia in the garbage because she believes that it is a "heathen" thing. Robert also demonstrates his intolerance when he quarrels with Teddy. When tempers flare, he labels Teddy a "Fuckin' heathen" (85).

Apparently Robert is able to reconcile his form of Christianity with profanity but not with his Anishinaubae traditions. Teddy is no different. Although he purports to be an Anishinaubae traditionalist, Teddy, too, is intolerant. The objects of his scorn are those Indigenous people who regained their status when Bill C-31 amended the *Indian Act* in 1985 and those band members who adhere to Christian beliefs. In his "campaign" speech to the people, he explains: "we'll decide who's an Indian. No more of this blond-haired blue-eyed Bill C-31ers, coming on our reserve and taking our money. And the Indian religion. The true religion will be what we practice. No more of this whiteman's church" (57). Teddy's intention to reclaim the right for the band to identify its membership and to support traditional spiritual practices is commendable. Nevertheless, the way that he plans to carry out his intention distorts the Anishinaubae belief system by dictating that it become fundamentalist. One of Indigenous peoples' core values is respect, including respect for a person's right to choose her own form of spiritual expression. Furthermore, the Anishinaubae, like most Indigenous peoples, value family above all else, including those family members who might have blond hair or blue eyes. Despite Teddy's abhorrence of mixed-blood people, his surname is Scottish, and presumably his ancestors were Scots as well.

Ross advances the idea that these two antithetical positions can and must be reconciled if Indian communities are to heal the social rift that exists within them. To that end, Melvin McKay, who is one of Teddy's despised "Bill C-31ers," has a revelation. As a Bill C-31er, Melvin has Indian status granted by the colonial regime; however, this does not guarantee him membership into the Partridge Crop band. Clearly, the Partridge Crop band has accepted him as a member—witness the fact that he is on their "fareWel" roll—however, Teddy continually treats him as if he were a second-class citizen and threatens to revoke his membership if he becomes chief. This uncertainty, coupled with Melvin's confusion about his mixed heritage, causes him to question who he is and where he belongs. In the end, however, he realizes that he is the only one who has the right to determine his identity: "I figured out that I'm an Indian from these two parts on my Treaty card. My face is on one half and my number is on the other half. The picture is what people see. The number is what the government sees. And the card's like me. In two parts. Part white. Part Indian. And you put them together. And you get an Indian. Me. But not 'cause the government says so. 'Cause I say so. I had to get mad to find that out. That's good, eh?" (54). Self-government, for Melvin, is an individual act in which he reclaims his right to determine his identity.

Ross also advances the notion that the religious differences that divide the Partridge Crop band members must end and religious tolerance and even synthesis must occur. To that end, the Partridge Crop Pentecostal Church, like Melvin, undergoes a significant transformation. Under Teddy's short reign as self-appointed chief, Christianity is outlawed. Teddy forces the Pentecostal Church to convert into the Creator's Church, a church of his own creation, and that church will presumably follow Teddy's interpretation of Anishinaubaek spiritualism, that is, spirituality that is intolerant and fundamentalist. In the end the two versions of the church are synthesized into the Partridge Crop Pentecostal Church of the Creator. Although this appears to be Ross's attempt at optimism, this transformation is suspect. It is highly unlikely that Christian fundamentalist Pentecostalism can unite in a respectful way with Anishinaubaek traditional spirituality, given that the first commandment forbids the worship of any god other than the Christian god. Furthermore, competing and oppositional belief systems are always competitive because each calls into question the validity of the other.

Robert Traverse's decision to leave the reserve is also cause for pessimism because the reserve needs people like him. Robert is a tradesperson who owns a small plumbing and septic service business and sincerely wants to help his community. He offers his people much-needed employment but becomes discouraged because no one seems interested in working. It is significant to note that not only is Robert unable to recruit band members to work for him, and the council will not contract his company to do work for the Partridge Crop band. In an effort to persuade Robert to lend him money to buy slot machines for his economic development scheme, Teddy promises that, as chief, he will contract Robert to take care of the reserve's plumbing requirements. He reminds Robert that, "Everybody knows that the old chief and council hired a white guy in Ashern before they would hire you. You and I know they're jealous" (63). Robert declines because, as a Christian, he cannot support gambling, which he believes is morally wrong. When Teddy manipulates Melvin to steal Robert's new truck to haul in the new slot machines, Robert can tolerate Partridge Crop life no longer: "I'm sick of this place. I'm sick of no one respecting me. I'm the only one around here besides Walter who owns a business. I'm the only one around here who works. I'm the only one around here who cares about this community. But not no more. That's it. I've had enough" (83). Disgusted with the antics of the corrupt chief and council and appalled by Teddy's alternative, Robert can tolerate no more of what he believes to be a hopeless situation. He decides to leave the reserve and move to Winnipeg. Living with the settlers seems preferable to living with his people. Educated to believe the rhetoric of the settler culture—the rhetoric that purports to be inclusive, multicultural, and superior, especially in its government—and witnessing the weaknesses of his own community, Robert concludes that life in the city will be better for his family. Robert represents many of the young educated Indigenous people who leave their communities in dismay. Thus, the colonizers win and assimilation is well on its way to becoming a *fait accompli*.

When Ross toured *fareWel* to eight Indian communities, he observed that there was "no recognition of make believe."[56] Audience members recognized the characters and knew them intimately, and although *fareWel* was not meant to be participatory theatre, Indian audiences participated nonetheless. Indeed, "in virtually every instance in the north the audience spoke directly to the actors throughout the performance, asking questions and vocalizing comments on, or objections to, what the characters were doing. Also, there were moments when the audience watched in an ineffable silence."[57] Although fictitious, *fareWel* reveals many truths. Thus, through his "voluntary disembowelling" of lives and systems that are all too common in many Indigenous communities, Ross issues a challenge to Indigenous people. Although he does not blame us for inflicting the wounds that have caused the problems facing our communities, he still challenges us to take responsibility for our healing.

chapter 6

Final thoughts, future directions

Throughout this book, I have argued that contemporary Indigenous literature cannot be divorced from its contextual framework. Not only do history, politics, and public policy shape Indigenous literature, but by documenting Indigenous people's reality in way that promotes empathy and understanding, Indigenous literature also has the ability to shape history, politics, and public policy. Not so long ago—certainly in my lifetime—the Canadian news media, and by extension the Canadian public, had little interest in Indigenous peoples' stories. Indeed, Indigenous people appeared only in the court briefs if we were mentioned at all. Today, however, the stories that are the foundation of Indigenous literature have become newsworthy. Not only do Indigenous people's stories repeatedly dominate the news, they also belie the popular mythology of the Canadian settler-state.

When I began this project, the media were preoccupied with stories of Indigenous people suffering and even dying at the hands of police. Susanne Reber and Rob Renaud had just launched their work of investigative journalism, *Starlight Tour: The Last, Lonely Night of Neil Stonechild*, and Tasha Hubbard's film *Two Worlds Colliding* had been awarded a prestigious Gemini. Both works describe how members of the Saskatoon Police Service had allegedly driven drunken Indigenous men to the city limits and abandoned them there in temperatures lower than –20° C. Both document how the bodies of Rodney Naistus, Lawrence Wegner, and seventeen-year-old Neil Stonechild were all found frozen to death in a secluded field on the edge of the city. In the Indigenous community, where black humour abounds, these excursions became known as "Starlight Tours."[1] Although stories such as this were familiar to Saskatchewan's Indigenous people, the settlers had been oblivious and were shocked when these stories became public.

Then there was the testimony of Charles Harnick, the former Attorney General of Ontario, at the Ipperwash Inquiry. The Inquiry was established to investigate the conduct of the Ontario Provincial Police who shot and killed Dudley George, an Anishinaubae man who was protesting at Ipperwash Provincial Park in 1995. On 28 November 2005, the Honourable Sidney B. Linden heard the testimony of the former Attorney General who stated that on 6 September 1995, at a meeting called to determine how to end the protest, then Premier Mike Harris gave a brief and very blunt order to his staff. He said, "I want those fucking Indians out of the park."[2] A short eleven hours later, the Ontario Provincial Police shot and killed Dudley George and ended the protest. Is this how the premier envisioned his officials acting in their efforts to follow orders and to get "those fucking Indians out of the park"? In his report, Commissioner Linden found that "taken together, the interaction between police and government at Ipperwash created the appearance of inappropriate interference in police operations."[3] The commissioner also made note of the blatant racism and cultural insensitivity among members of the Ontario Provincial Police.[4] This news, along with stories of Saskatoon's Starlight Tours, residential school abuse, and the Amnesty International report of 500 missing or murdered Indigenous women[5] combined to shake the settler population's faith in the myth of the fundamental goodness of the nation and its institutions.

Despite such bleak headlines, this project began in a time of real optimism. The Government of Canada, under the leadership of then Prime Minister Paul Martin, had entered into a series of consultations with First Nations, Métis, and Inuit leaders along with the provincial premiers. This was a first. The result was a working document titled "First Ministers and National Aboriginal Leaders Strengthening Relationships and Closing the Gap,"[6] fondly remembered as the Kelowna Accord. Prime Minister Paul Martin's Liberal government announced a plan to set aside $5 billion dollars to improve the lot of Indigenous people. The money was intended to fund advancements in health, education, and housing as well as compensating former residential school students, and "closing the gap" became the buzzwords of the day. That optimism was short-lived, however. A few short months later, Stephen Harper's Conservatives ousted the Liberals and promptly cancelled the agreement. Disappointment reigned as Indigenous people witnessed once again the tenuous and fragile nature of Canada's promises.

Today, however, I find myself feeling optimistic once again, albeit cautiously. On 11 June 2008, the world changed for Indigenous people living within the boundaries of Canada when the Honourable Stephen Harper, the prime minister of Canada, stood before the House of Commons and, on behalf of the people of Canada, apologized to former students of Indian residential schools. Not only did he apologize for the emotional, physical, and sexual abuse that some students suffered, he also apologized for the assimilationist policy that caused them so much pain. The prime minister also acknowledged that the negative consequences of Canada's residential school policy were not limited to former students, and that the children and grandchildren of former students also continue to be affected negatively.[7] Following the prime minister, the leaders of each opposition party also apologized, while a small group of former students, now called "the survivors," and First Nations, Métis, and Inuit leaders witnessed. Across the country, Indigenous people gathered to watch and to support one another on this emotional day.

Like many Indigenous people, I wonder what this will mean. How much will these words change the daily lives of Indigenous people? Was the prime minister sincere or was this merely a performance? Although Prime Minister Harper's apology for the residential schools is positive and, as many Indigenous political leaders mentioned, long overdue, there is still much to concern us.

The apology is part of a larger settlement for former students. A significant component of the settlement agreement is a Truth and Reconciliation Commission (TRC), which is just beginning its work. Unfortunately, the TRC's work has been stalled with the chair, Justice Harry LaForme, having resigned because of committee infighting before the commission's work began. LaForme spoke publicly stating that the TRC "was on the verge of paralysis and doomed to failure."[8]

A second component to the residential settlement is the "common experience payments." Each former student is to receive $10,000 for the first year that they attended residential school and $3000 for each subsequent year.[9] Unfortunately, processing of the common experience claims has taken longer than anticipated, and consequently, many former students died before receiving compensation. Other former students who did receive their compensation report that they received less than what is owed them because of inaccurate and incomplete government records. Forced to either give up or go through a complicated appeal process, these former students complain of being "revictimized."[10] Likewise, many Métis students who attended residential schools continue to be marginalized. Because the residential schools they attended did not receive federal government funding, Canada has not included them on the list of schools eligible for compensation.[11] Thus, many former Métis and non-Status students have been denied the compensation granted First Nations and Inuit even though they suffered the same abuses.[12] The Métis continue to be caught in the midst of jurisdictional disputes between federal and provincial governments.

But residential schools were only one component of Canada's assimilationist "Indian" policies, and the consequences of those policies are all around us. Poverty and its corollaries abound, and Indigenous people still count as the poorest of the poor in Canada, particularly in my home province of Saskatchewan.[13] Indigenous people lag behind other Canadians in education, income, and life expectancy.[14] The 1998 Canadian Incidence Study on Reported Abuse and Neglect suggests that, in contrast to middle- and upper-class Canadians, poor Indigenous people live under the gaze of child-welfare officials. Consequently, Indigenous people are "drastically overrepresented in the child welfare system at every point of intervention *despite the fact that they [are] not overly represented for reports of sexual abuse, physical abuse, emotional abuse, and exposure to domestic violence.*"[15] And it should come as no surprise that, following childhoods in the child-welfare system, Indigenous people are over-represented in the justice system and are 8.5 times more likely to be incarcerated than non-Aboriginal Canadians.[16]

The physical environment of Indigenous people does not fare much better than do the legal and social ones. Indigenous people living on reserve or in isolated communities often live in over-crowded, substandard housing in communities without basic functioning infrastructure. Although Canada is a First World country, ninety-five of the First Nations communities within its boundaries currently make do with unsafe drinking water.[17]

Inequities breed despair so that the prospects for Indigenous youth, who are our hope for the future, continue to be bleak. Gang involvement and crime are increasing rapidly not only in urban areas but also in rural and northern communities. Taiaiake Alfred links these problems to the continuing oppression of Indigenous people: "Young people, those who have not yet learned to accommodate to the fact that they are expected to accept their lesser status quietly, are especially hard hit by defeatism and alienation. Youth in our communities and in urban centres are suffering. Suicide, alcohol and drug abuse, cultural confusion, sexual violence, obesity: they suffer these scourges worse than anyone else."[18] By only apologizing for one element of its genocidal policies—the residential schools—Canada implicitly refuses to take responsibility for the trauma that the remainder of its policies continue to cause.

I fear that, since Canada has closed the residential schools, is paying compensation, and has apologized, the onus is now on Indigenous people to pull up our collective socks and heal ourselves, our families, and our communities. The question that I anticipate hearing is, "What else can Canada do?" As I have mentioned before, one benefit of White privilege in this country is the right to a guilt-free existence, and Canada's apology has done much to free even the most liberal Canadians from guilt for the sins of the past. Yet, the low self-esteem, poverty, poor educational outcomes, reduced life expectancy, involvement in the child-welfare system, violence, and addictions that define "normal" for far too many Aboriginal people cannot be healed so easily.

Indigenous Literatures Changing the World

Although the modern Canadian settler-state purports to be multicultural and inclusive, there is, in effect, an invisible boundary between settler and Indigenous society, which creates what John Stackhouse has dubbed a "quiet apartheid": "Economically, socially, politically, culturally, we have come to accept a quiet apartheid that segregates, and thus weakens, native and non-native society."[19] Indigenous literature exposes its settler readers to another side of Canada thereby providing them with an opportunity to break through the walls of Canada's "quiet apartheid" and to learn about Indigenous people through narratives, poetry, and theatre. Indigenous literature examines many of the "social problems" that Indigenous communities experience today—"the disunity of our people, the alienation of our youth, our men disrespecting our women, the deculturing of our societies, epidemic mental and physical sicknesses, the lack of employment in meaningful and self-determining indigenous ways of working…and the exploitation of our lands and peoples"[20]—and reveals how these problems are linked to the policies of the colonial regime.

Most of contemporary Indigenous literature written in English can fall under Thomas King's category of "associational literature" and, as such, provides settler readers with a window into the daily life of Indigenous people, including the challenges and disappointments along with hopes and dreams.[21] Indigenous literature, therefore, enables settler readers to relate to Indigenous peoples on an emotional level thereby generating empathy. By reading Indigenous literature, settlers come to understand Indigenous people as fellow human beings. Empathy, in turn, has the potential to create a groundswell of support for social-justice initiatives to improve the lot of Indigenous people. Social-justice initiatives have included positive changes to public policy, which for the first time have had input from Indigenous people. Indigenous literature also changes the world by helping Indigenous people heal from the trauma that colonial policies have caused and by educating settler society and its governments.

Public response to Indigenous literature has resulted in Indigenous writers becoming important advocates for Indigenous people. Many Indigenous writers have received honours from their own communities and the settler communities. The National Aboriginal Achievement Awards were created to recognize the contributions of Indigenous people, including writers and filmmakers such as Alanis Obomsawin (1994), Maria Campbell (1996), Rita Joe and Gil Cardinal (1997), Tantoo Cardinal (1998), Tomson Highway (2001), Thomas King (2003), Basil Johnston (2004), and Emma LaRocque (2005). Alanis Obomsawin, Rita Joe, and Thomas King are also Members of the Order of Canada, and Basil Johnston received the Order of Ontario in 1989. This is only a small sample of the honours given Indigenous writers for their contributions. The minister of First Nations and Métis relations for the Province of Saskatchewan, for example, appointed Métis author and playwright Maria Campbell to chair a commission established to hold public consultations and make recommendations regarding the problematic 2004 elections of the Métis Nation of Saskatchewan. The Province of Saskatchewan also named Cree poet Louise Halfe poet laureate in its centennial year. Halfe used this opportunity to bring attention to the contributions of Indigenous people as well as the community's challenges. Marilyn Dumont used her poetry to educate the community about the historical contributions of Indigenous women in the fur trade when, as part of the Province of Alberta's centennial celebrations, the City of Edmonton displayed as public art her poem "This Is For the Wives" on city buses. Describing himself as "outspoken on issues of social justice, and advocating for fairness in our society," Thomas King entered national politics as the New Democratic Party candidate for the riding of Guelph, Ontario, in the 2008 federal election. Indigenous writers are moving out of the margins of Canadian literature into the forefront of Canadian society as advocates for Indigenous people. Indigenous writers and their literary output might very well surpass governments in bringing about social change and healing for Indigenous people.

Many of today's Indigenous writers and artists embrace as their motto words attributed to Métis leader Louis Riel: "My people will sleep for one hundred years, but when they awake, it will be the artists who give them their spirit back."[22] Although I have heard this quotation on many occasions and have seen it in popular writing, I cannot find a written source. Nevertheless, these are words that many Indigenous artists live by. Maria Campbell tells me that she first heard this quotation in the mid-sixties when she interviewed Métis leader Jim Brady. Brady was delighted to learn that she was writing for radio and radio drama, and emphasized the importance of Indigenous people writing both non-fiction and fiction. Brady predicted that one day Canada would be full of brown artists, literary and otherwise, because of Riel's prophecy. Maria said that Jim Brady often spoke about the role of artists, especially writers, in creating change. He was also the first person whom she had heard call Riel an artist poet, explaining that this was why Gabriel Dumont listened to him. Brady told her that in the old days the people loved and respected artists, particularly poets, because their poetry mirrored the soul of the people. Maria has heard many people, both old and young, quote these words attributed to Riel and assumes that they might have come from the Métis oral tradition since Jim Brady and Joe Dion, both early leaders of the Métis and non-Status Indians, collected many oral stories from elders.

This quotation has become so popularized that whether the words are actually Louis Riel's or not has become irrelevant. The words have taken on a life of their own and created their own reality for Indigenous artists. Riel's words suggest that, with a future fraught with both optimism and apprehension, Indigenous writers will have no choice but to continue to apply their art to the service of Indigenous people.

Indigenous Literatures are Applied Literatures

In traditional Indigenous societies, the arts were valued equally for their aesthetic beauty and for their functionality. The visual arts, for instance, served multiple functions. As decorative arts they adorned homes and clothing, but they also served a spiritual function when used to express individual and community beliefs. Likewise, while stories, dance, and song were considered beautiful in their own right, they served educational, spiritual, and healing functions. This multiple functionality has not been lost in contemporary Indigenous literature.

Today's Indigenous people create literature—not only autobiography, fiction, and drama, but also film scripts, screenplays, and song lyrics—with a goal of creating aesthetically beautiful and compelling works that depict Indigenous reality. Because this literature is beautiful and compelling, it has ability to draw attention to the Indigenous experience and ultimately improve the lot of Indigenous people. Like the stories of the oral tradition, contemporary Indigenous literature serves a socio-pedagogical function as well as an aesthetic one. By challenging the prevailing mythology about the formation of the settler state, it teaches both settlers and Indigenous people, who too often blame themselves for the problems that plague our communities, about the damaging effects of colonization. Based on the premise that an enlightened population will demand equitable and effective public policy, this socio-pedagogical function of Indigenous literature promotes social justice for Indigenous people, perhaps more effectively than political rhetoric. Indigenous literature also serves a therapeutic function by using story to help Indigenous people heal from the trauma of colonization.

Contemporary Indigenous storytellers continue to utilize the colonizer's language and literary forms to actively apply their art in projects whose focus is health and/or social justice, albeit in an aesthetic framework. Performance artists in groups, for example, Toronto's Native Earth and Turtle Gals, Manitoulin Island's De-Ba-Jeh-Mu-Jig, Saskatoon's Saskatchewan Native Theatre, and Regina's Thinking Out Loud, create theatrical productions that heal by acknowledging and validating Indigenous realities and by promoting social justice among the larger society. Likewise, writers' groups, such as the Aboriginal Writers' Collective of Winnipeg, work within the Indigenous community to create poetry and stories that mirror Indigenous peoples' truths. Indigenous storytellers are active in their communities, using their art to nurture young people to learn to use story to examine their world and to express that world in language. Groups of artists from multiple disciplines, such as Regina's Crow Hope Café, take their art into the community, where they engage community members, especially the youth. Indigenous filmmakers, such as Big Soul Productions, work in the inner city, where they engage young Indigenous people to shadow professional film company staff to teach Indigenous youth how to use film to tell the stories of contemporary Indigenous people. Anecdotal evidence suggests that youth who become involved in literary arts or theatre go on to better things.[23] Indigenous writers and theatre artists are well aware of the need for healing and hope within our communities and, despite a lack of financial resources, continue to use their art to meet those needs.

As I work on this project, I continue to observe the applications of Indigenous literature as it moves outside the boundaries of the text to affect the material world. Just recently, I spoke to a young researcher working in an Indigenous political organization who asked, when I told him about this project, that I make sure to include the story of the "Sixties Scoop" children, of whom he was one. He felt as if Indigenous adoptees and foster children have been forgotten with all the attention given to the residential schools and explained how the suffering that he experienced was very similar to that of the former students of residential schools. His story of his childhood and his feelings were startlingly similar to what I'd read in Richard Wagamese's *Keeper 'n Me* and *For Joshua*, and I found myself "prescribing" these works for him. Shortly afterward, I heard a radio program that drew attention to Cheryl L'Hirondelle, a Métis singer and songwriter, who was working with Indigenous women in the Pine Grove Provincial Correctional Centre to create songs based on Indigenous traditional music. The goal of the project was to help inmates overcome the low self-esteem and shame that contributed to their lives as petty thieves, drug addicts, and prostitutes. L'Hirondelle challenged the women to identify and recognize that they, too, have beauty. The outcome of the project was a healing song called "The Beauty Within," which is a collaborative venture in which each woman has contributed one line to articulate her experience and aspirations. One of the inmates, Tracey Gamble, explained how this song has become so important because it has helped her identify and articulate what she needs to do to heal: "I need courage to trust again, to respect, to love, and to forgive." Members of the correctional centre staff have noticed how working on the song has helped the women open up and express their feelings, ultimately improving their self-esteem.[24] Indigenous literature's applications are present throughout our communities. We just have to look for them.

Indigenous views on health are holistic in that they do not separate body from mind, emotions, and spirit. Holism also defines Indigenous communities in which a person is never a singular, isolated individual. Instead, Indigenous people are part of a complex network of relationships that, when healthy, respect the autonomy of the individual within the supportive environment of the group. As Daniel David Moses points out, the first questions that Indigenous people ask upon meeting are, Where are you from? Who are your relatives?[25] Indigenous literature, as a healing implement, is holistic and relationship-oriented in that it "treats" the minds, bodies, spirits, and hearts of individuals and repairs the rifts in communities. Indigenous literature is inclusive as well; it does not limit its healing properties to Indigenous people. Indigenous literature reaches out to settler communities to advance social justice, to heal the wounds of oppression, and to reconcile our communities. Indigenous literature is, indeed, powerful medicine with which contemporary Indigenous writers are taking back our spirits. The prophecy is being fulfilled. Uncle Louis would be proud.

Notes

Chapter 1

1   Apologies to my colleagues, who have listened to me tell this story ad nauseam.

2   Hilde Lindemann Nelson, *Damaged Identities: Narrative Repair* (Ithaca and London: Cornell University Press, 2001), 6.

3   Ibid.

4   Thomas King, *The Truth About Stories: A Native Narrative* (Toronto: House of Anansi Press, 2003), 10.

5   Ibid, 9.

6   Ronald Wright, *A Short History of Progress* (Toronto: House of Anansi Press, 2004), 112 (emphasis in the original).

7   King, *The Truth*, 12.

8   Thanks to Dr. Linda Goulet of the Department of Indian Education at the First Nations University of Canada who, over kitchen-table scholarly discussions, explained to me the concept of land-based literacy that enables Indigenous people to "read" the land.

9   Joseph Gold, *The Story Species: Our Life-Literature Connection* (Markham: Fitzhenry and Whiteside, 2002), 104.

10 Ibid., 32.

11 Rudyard Kipling, "The White Man's Burden," *McClure's Magazine,* 12 February 1988, http://wwwf.countryday.net/facstf/us/hammondk/MEH/White%20Mans%20Burde n%20and%20Criticism.doc.

12 Wright, *A Short History*, 4.

13 See Stephanie M. McKenzie, "Canada's Day of Atonement: The Contemporary Native Literary Renaissance, The Native Cultural Renaissance And Postcentenary Canadian Mythology" (PhD diss., University of Toronto, 2001), http://www.collectionscanada. ca/obj/s4/f2/dsk3/ftp04/NQ58966.pdf.

14 Dara Culhane, *The Pleasure of the Crown: Anthropology, Law and First Nations* (Vancouver: Talonbooks, 1998), 49.

15 McKenzie, "Canada's Day of Atonement," iii.

16 Clifford Krauss, "Capone May Have Slept Here, Too, Canada Town Says," *New York Times*, 16 November 2004, http://www.nytimes.com/2004/11/16/international/americas/16moosejaw.html?oref=regi.

17 Culhane, *Pleasure of the Crown*, 49.

18 Ward Churchill, "Kizhiibaabinesik: A Bright Star, Burning Briefly," preface to *In My Own Voice: Explorations in the Sociopolitical Context of Art and Cinema*, by Leah Renae Kelly (Winnipeg: Arbeiter Ring, 2001), 14.

19 In Culhane, *Pleasure of the Crown*, 45.

20 Kendall Clark, "Defining 'White Privilege,'" http://whiteprivilege.com/definition/ (accessed 6 September 2005). Clark defines "White privilege" as *"a social relation" that confers White-skinned people with unearned advantages over darker-skinned people, for example:*

1. **a.** A right, advantage, or immunity granted to or enjoyed by white persons beyond the common advantage of all others; an exemption in many particular cases from certain burdens or liabilities.
    b. A special advantage or benefit of white persons; with reference to divine dispensations, natural advantages, gifts of fortune, genetic endowments, social relations, etc.

2. A privileged position; the possession of an advantage white persons enjoy over non–white persons.

3. **a.** The special right or immunity attaching to white persons as a social relation; prerogative.
    b. *display of white privilege*, a social expression of a white person or persons demanding to be treated as a member or members of the socially privileged class.

4. **a.** To invest white persons with a privilege or privileges; to grant to white persons a particular right or immunity; to benefit or favor specially white persons; to invest white persons with special honorable distinctions.
    b. To avail oneself of a privilege owing to one as a white person.

5. To authorize or license of [?] white person or persons what is forbidden or wrong for non–whites; to justify, excuse.

6. To give to white persons special freedom or immunity *from* some liability or burden to which non–white persons are subject; to exempt.

21 Peggy McIntosh, "White Privilege: Unpacking the Invisible Knapsack," *Independent School*, Winter 1990, http://www.case.edu/president/aaction/UnpackingTheKnapsack.pdf.

22 Jeannette Armstrong, "The Disempowerment of First North American Native Peoples and Empowerment Through Their Writing," in *An Anthology of Canadian Native Literature in English*, eds. Daniel David Moses and Terry Goldie, 3rd ed. (Toronto: Oxford University Press, 2005), 245.

23 Dean Neu and Richard Therrien, *Accounting for Genocide: Canada's Bureaucratic Assault on Aboriginal People* (Black Point: Fernwood, 2003), 4.

24 Eduardo Duran and Bonnie Duran, *Native American Postcolonial Psychology,* (Albany: State University of New York Press, 1995), 45.

25 In Penny Petrone, *First People, First Voices* (Toronto: University of Toronto Press, 1983), 152.

26 Duran and Duran, *Postcolonial Psychology*, 32.

27 James W. Pennebaker, *Opening Up: The Healing Power of Confiding in Others,* 2nd ed. (New York: Guilford, 1997), 176.

28 Duran and Duran, *Postcolonial Psychology*, 95.

29 Ibid. Duran and Duran refer specifically to the US government; however, there is no doubt that their words apply equally to the policies of the Government of Canada.

30 Gerald Vizenor, "Native American Indian Literatures: Narratives of Survivance," in *Native North America: Critical and Cultural Perspectives*, ed. Rene Hulan (Toronto: ECW Press, 1999), 57–8.

31 Terry L. Mitchell and Dawn T. Maracle, "Post-Traumatic Stress and the Health Status of Aboriginal Populations in Canada," *Journal of Aboriginal Health* 2, 1 (2005): 14–25.

32 Ibid., 17.

33 Monique Mojica, "Postcolonial Traumatic Stress Syndrome: Ethno Stress," address to the annual conference of the Association of Canadian College and University Teachers of English at the Congress of Humanities of Social Sciences, University of Ottawa, Ottawa, May 1998.

34 Manitoba, *The Report of the Aboriginal Justice Inquiry of Manitoba*, Paul L.A.H. Chartrand, Wendy Whitecloud, Eva McKay, and Doris Young, November 1999, http://www.ajic.mb.ca/volumel/chapter4.html#5.

35 CBC Manitoba, "J.J. Harper: 15 Years Later," 7 March 2003, http://www.winnipeg.cbc.ca/indepth/20030304harper.html.

36 The Catholic and Anglican churches operated the majority of the residential schools with the United and Presbyterian churches operating the remainder.

37 Canada, Indian Residential Schools Resolution Canada, "Key Events," http://www.irsr-rqpi.gc.ca/english/key_events.html.

38 Churchill, "Kizhiibaabinesik," 56.

39 McIntosh, "Unpacking."

40 Gold, *Read*, 104.

41 Armstrong, "Disempowerment," 244.

42 Jace Weaver, *That the People Might Live: Native American Literatures and Native American Community* (New York: Oxford University Press, 1997), xii.

43 Joy Harjo and Gloria Bird, introduction to *Reinventing the Enemy's Language: Contemporary Native Women's Writings of North America*, eds. Joy Harjo and Gloria Bird (New York: Norton, 1997), 22 and 24.

44 This irony has not escaped Indigenous writers. See Armand Ruffo, "Why Native Literature?" in *Native North America: Critical and Cultural Perspectives*, ed. Renee Hulan (Toronto: ECW Press, 1999), 120.

45 Louis Owens, *Other Destinies: Understanding the American Indian Novel* (Norman: University of Oklahoma Press, 1992), 14.

46 Joseph Gold, *Read for Your Life: Literature as a Life Support System* (Markham: Fitzhenry and Whiteside, 2001), ix–x.

47 Terry Tafoya, "Teams, Networks and Clans: The Circle of Support," address at Epidemics in Our Communities 2005, Regina, SK, 3 February 2005.

48 Basil Johnston, "One Generation from Extinction," in *An Anthology*, eds. Moses and Goldie, 101.

49 Harjo and Bird, *Reinventing*, 21–2.

50 Ruffo, "Why Native Literature?" 119.

51 Oskiniko Larry Loyie, "Ora Pro Nobis (Pray for Us)," in *Two Plays About Residential School* (Vancouver: Living Traditions, 1998), 8.

52   Christine Watson, "Autobiographical Writing as a Healing Process: Interview with Alice Masak French," *Canadian Literature* 167 (Winter 2000): 38–9.

53   Vera Manuel, "Strength of Indian Women," in *Two Plays About Residential School* (Vancouver: Living Traditions, 1998), 76.

54   In Beatrice Culleton, *In Search of April Raintree* (1983; repr. Winnipeg: Peguis Publishers, 1992), 7 (emphasis added).

55   In Susan Egan, "Telling Trauma: Generic Dissonance in the Production of *Stolen Life*," *Canadian Literature* 167 (2000): 11.

56   Charlotte Linde, in Linda C. Garro and Cheryl Mattingly, "Narrative as Construct and as Construction," *Narrative and Cultural Construction of Illness and Healing*, eds. Cheryl Mattingly and Linda C. Garro (Berkeley: University of California Press, 2000), 11.

57   Willie Ermine, personal conversation with the author, Waskesiu, SK, 27 January 2005.

58   Garro and Mattingly, "Narrative as Construct," 7.

59   Dan P. McAdams, *The Stories We Live By: Personal Myths and the Making of the Self* (New York: Guilford, 1993), 12.

60   Ibid.

61   See Pennebaker, *Opening Up*. Pennebaker explains that psychologists recognize that writing can be a powerful healing tool when used to create narratives that describe traumatic events that the author has experienced and to examine and describe their resultant feelings. Pennebaker and his graduate student Sandra Beall compared the physiological effects of writing on two groups of research subjects. One group wrote about trauma while the other wrote about trivial topics. The result of their research is significant: "People who wrote about their deepest thoughts and feelings surrounding traumatic experiences evidenced heightened immune function compared to those who wrote about superficial topics. Although this effect was more pronounced after the last day of writing, it tended to persist six weeks after the study. In addition, health-center visits dropped for those who wrote about traumas compared to those who wrote on the trivial topics" (48).

62   Gold, *Read*, xii.

63   Ibid., 45 (emphasis in the original).

64   Tafoya, "Teams."

65   Gold, *Read*, 48.

66   Egan, "Telling Trauma," 14.

67   Weaver, *That the People Might Live*, x.

Chapter 2

1   Canada, Indian and Northern Affairs, *Gathering Strength: Canada's Aboriginal Action Plan*, http://dsp-psd.pwgsc.gc.ca/Collection/R32-192-2000E.pdf.

2   Ibid.

3   Terry Wotherspoon and Vic Satzewich, *First Nations: Race, Class, and Gender Relations* (Regina: Canadian Plains Research Center, 2000), 43–5.

4   Arthur J. Ray, *I Have Lived Here Since The World Began* (Toronto: Lester, 1996), 177.

5   Neu and Therrien, *Accounting for Genocide*. Neu and Therrien contend that settlement was a common imperial strategy for land acquisition: "Using settlers to crowd out the Indigenous people and gaining control by importing an elite to

oversee the territorial operations are commonly used strategies. The Indigenous inhabitants are targeted subjects of social control so concentrated its outcomes can be indistinguishable from genocide" (18).

6   See R. Bruce Shepherd, *Deemed Unsuitable: Blacks from Oklahoma move to the Canadian Prairies in Search of Equality in the Early 20th Century only to find Racism in their new Home* (Toronto: Umbrella Press, 1997) for a thorough study of Black immigrants to Canada post-Confederation.

7   For a thorough discussion of this conflict, see Sam McKegney's *Magic Weapons: Aboriginal Writers Rebuilding Community after Residential School* (Winnipeg: University of Manitoba Press, 2007).

8   Only after the violence suitably pacified people, did the colonial officials begin to create policies to maintain the oppression. Bonita Lawrence, *"Real" Indians and Others: Mixed-Blood Urban Native Peoples and Indigenous Nationhood* (Vancouver: University of British Columbia Press, 2004), 30.

9   Ibid.

10 Neu and Therrien, *Accounting for Genocide*, 4.

11 It is ironic that the same colonial officials had no appreciation for the Métis free traders.

12 Bruce K. Alexander, *The Roots of Addiction in Free Market Society* (Ottawa: Canadian Centre for Policy Alternatives, April 2001), http://www.policyalternatives.ca/bc/rootsofaddiction.html.

13 Michael White and David Epston, *Narrative Means to Therapeutic Ends* (New York: Norton, 1990), 24.

14 John S. Milloy, *A National Crime: The Canadian Government and the Residential School System—1879 to 1986* (Winnipeg: University of Manitoba Press, 1999), 32.

15 Neu and Therrien, *Accounting for Genocide*, 3.

16 Wotherspoon and Satzewich, *First Nations*, 119.

17 Neu and Therrien, *Accounting for Genocide*, 9.

18 Even though one cannot be directly denied employment, housing, or services because of culture in Canada, there are many subtle ways to exclude and deprive non-Whites.

19 Ward Churchill, "Kizhiibaabinesik," 20.

20 See Niel Bissoondath, *Selling Illusions: The Cult of Multiculturalism in Canada* (Toronto: Penguin 1994).

21 Alexander, *Roots of Addiction*, 14.

22 In Patrick Johnston, *Native Children and the Child Welfare System* (Toronto: Canadian Council on Social Development and Lorimer, 1983), 79.

23 See Dan Beavon and Martin Cooke, "An Application of the United Nations Human Development Index to Registered Indians in Canada, 1966," in *Aboriginal Conditions: Research as a Foundation for Public Policy*, eds. Jerry P. White, Paul S. Maxim, and Dan Beavon (Vancouver: University of British Columbia Press, 2003), 201–221. Beavon and Cook apply the United Nation's Human Development Index, revealing that the situation of Registered ("Status") Indians has improved only marginally between 1981 and 2001. Status Indians still lag behind the remainder of the population in education, income, and life expectancy. Indian and Northern Affairs Canada databases provided the data necessary to do this analysis. There are no comparable studies of Métis people.

24 Neu and Therrien, *Accounting for Genocide*, 13.

25   Lawrence, *"Real" Indians*, 5.

26   Paragraph 4 of the pre-confederation *Act for the gradual enfranchisement of Indians, the better management of Indian affairs, and to extend the provisions of the Act 31st Victoria, Chapter 42*, which was passed in 1869, states that any Indigenous person with less than one-fourth Indian blood was not entitled to share in any property or profit of his band. Although the Act refers to "person," it is clear that this does not include female persons.

27   Ken S. Coates and W.R. Morrison, "More Than a Matter of Blood: The Federal Government, the Churches and the Mixed Blood Populations of the Yukon and the Mackenzie River Valley, 1890–1950," in *1885 and After: Native Society in Transition*, proceedings of Canadian Plains Conference, May 1985, eds. F. Laurie Barron and James B. Waldram (Regina: Canadian Plains Research Center, 1986), 261.

28   Lawrence, *"Real" Indians*, 89.

29   Coates and Morrison, "Matter of Blood," 262.

30   The imposition of patriarchal determiners of identity had begun before Confederation with the 1869 Act for the gradual enfranchisement of Indians noted above. Paragraph 6 of that Act attaches children's identity to their father and women's identity to their husband.

31   In 1939, the Supreme Court of Canada ruled that, for the purposes of the *British North America Act* of 1867, Inuit were legally "Indian" and, as such, were the responsibility of the federal government.

32   In David M. Quiring, *CCF Colonialism in Northern Saskatchewan: Battling Parish Priests, Bootleggers, and Fur Sharks* (Vancouver: University of British Columbia Press, 2004), 64.

33   Neu and Therrien, *Accounting for Genocide*, 26.

34   Lawrence, *"Real" Indians*, 31.

35   In Ray, *I Have Lived Here*, 229.

36   Lawrence, *"Real" Indians*, 31.

37   CBC Saskatchewan, "FSIN Apologizes For Comments About Métis People," http://sask.cbc.ca/regional/servlet/View?filename=comments062404.

38   Eric Guimond, "Fuzzy Definitions and Population Explosion: Changing Identities of Aboriginal Groups in Canada," in *Not Strangers in These Parts: Urban Aboriginal Peoples*, proceedings of Aboriginal Policy Research Conference, November 2002, University of Western Ontario, eds. David Newhouse and Evelyn Peters (Ottawa: Government of Canada, 2004).

39   Eric Guimond, "Changing Ethnicity: The Concept of Ethnic Drifters," in *Aboriginal Conditions: Research as a Foundation for Public Policy*, eds. Jerry P. White, Paul S. Maxim, and Dan Beavon (Vancouver: University of British Columbia Press, 2003), 91–107.

40   Wotherspoon and Satzewich, *First Nations*, 32

41   Lee Maracle, "Dear Daddy," in *Sojourner's Truth and Other Stories* (Vancouver: Press Gang, 1990), 77

42   *Indian Act*, R.S. 1985, c. 1–5, http://laws.justice.gc.ca/en/I-5/.

43   C.L. Higham, *Noble, Wretched, and Redeemable: Protestant Missionaries to the Indians in Canada and the United States, 1820–1900* (Calgary: University of Calgary Press, 2000), 10.

44   Helen Buckley, *From Wooden Ploughs to Welfare: Why Indian Policy Failed in the Prairie Provinces* (Montreal and Kingston: McGill-Queen's University Press, 1992), 40.

45   Brett Christophers, *Positioning the Missionary: John Booth Good and the Confluence of Cultures in Nineteenth-Century British Columbia* (Vancouver: University of British Columbia Press, 1998), 88.

46   Although all treaty Indians have status under the *Indian Act*, not all Status Indians are treaty Indians.

47   Buckley, *Wooden Ploughs*, 5.

48   See Peter Douglas Elias, *The Dakota of the Canadian Northwest* (Regina: Canadian Plains Research Center, 2002). Elias argues that the Dakota who lived in this area were not subject to these policies because they did not sign treaties with the British Crown; however, they were able to take advantage of the benefits that these policies provided.

49   Sarah Carter, *Aboriginal People and Colonizers of Western Canada to 1900* (Toronto: University of Toronto Press, 1999), 117. The *Indian Act* of 1876 "consigned Aboriginal people to the status of minors; they were British subjects but not citizens, sharing the status of children, felons, and the insane, and it established the federal government as their guardians."

50   Ray, *I Have Lived Here*, 244–5.

51   Sarah Carter, *Lost Harvests: Prairie Indian Reserve Farmers and Government Policy* (Montreal: McGill-Queen's University Press, 1990), 41–2.

52   Ibid., 50.

53   Ray, *I Have Lived Here*, 249.

54   Carter, *Lost Harvests*, 51.

55   Ray, *I Have Lived Here*, 254; Carter, *Lost Harvests*, 64.

56   Carter, *Lost Harvests*, 142.

57   Ibid., 142, 147–9.

58   Ray, *I Have Lived Here*, 251; Carter, *Lost Harvests*, 64.

59   Ray, *I Have Lived Here*, 252.

60   Ibid., 253–4.

61   In Carter, *Lost Harvests*, 70.

62   Ray, *I Have Lived Here*, 254; Carter, *Lost Harvests*, 85.

63   Carter, *Lost Harvests*, 85. Treaties One and Two were signed in 1872; Three in 1873; Four in 1874; Six in 1876; and Seven 1877.

64   Alvina Dreaver, "Why My Dad Went To Jail," in *". . . And They Told Us Their Stories,"* eds. Jack Funk and Gordon Lobe (Saskatoon: Saskatoon District Tribal Council, 1991), 22.

65   Carter, *Lost Harvest*, 87.

66   In Carter, *Lost Harvests*, 213.

67   Carter, *Aboriginal People*, 168–70.

68   Ibid., 162.

69   Ibid., 162–3

70   Ibid., 117.

71   Personal communication, 27 January 2004.

72   Ray, *I Have Lived Here*, 315.

73   John Hamer and Jack Steinberg, *Alcohol and Native Peoples of the North* (Washington: University Press of America, 1980), 6–9.

74   Ibid., 5.

75   Ibid., 4.

76   Ibid., 16–18.

77   Ray, *I Have Lived Here*, 89.

78   Alexander, *Roots of Addiction*, 14.

79   Ibid., 15.

80   The words "Indian" could easily be substituted for "the Irish," in Jonathan Swift's famous essay "A Modest Proposal."

81   Treaty 7 Elders and Tribal Council, Walter Hildebrandt, Sarah Carter, and Dorothy First Rider, *The True Spirit and Original Intent of Treaty 7* (Montreal and Kingston: McGill-Queen's University Press, 1996), 263–4.

82   Canada, Indian and Northern Affairs, Report of the Royal Commission on Aboriginal Peoples, *Volume One: Looking Forward Looking Back*, by René Dussault, George Erasmus, Paul L.A.H. Chartrand, J. Peter Meekison, Viola Robinson, Mary Sillett, and Bertha Wilson, October 1996, http://www.aincinac.gc.ca/ch/rcap/sg/sg25_e.html (accessed 24 December 2003).

83   The Roman Catholic Church and Anglican Church of Canada operated the majority of the schools. The United Church of Canada and the Presbyterian Church operated the remainder.

84   John S. Milloy, *National Crime*, 302. Milloy's book is based on his research report, "Suffer the Little Children," that the Government of Canada's Royal Commission on Aboriginal Peoples commissioned him to write.

85   James Iron Eagle, who is now deceased, was an elder at the Saskatchewan Indian Federated College for many years. When he talked to Indigenous students about education, he emphasized that it was crucial that they learn "the cunning of the Whiteman" to enable them to survive in today's world; however, he also emphasized that Indigenous people must know and preserve our cultures.

86   Milloy, *National Crime*, 26.

87   Buckley, *Wooden Ploughs*, 47.

88   In Milloy, *National Crime*, 7.

89   Buckley, *Wooden Ploughs*, 47.

90   In Milloy, *National Crime*, 44.

91   Ibid., 70–1.

92   Ibid., 31.

93   Ibid., 33.

94   Agnes Grant, *No End of Grief: Indian Residential Schools in Canada* (Winnipeg: Pemmican Publications, 1996), 17–20.

95   Ibid., 189.

96   Jeannette Armstrong, a speaker of "high" Okanagan, the language of ceremony, reports that, as a result of attending residential schools, few Okanagan are able to speak even the day-to-day language and even fewer have retained the ability to speak the language of ceremony.

97   Kim Anderson, *A Recognition of Being: Reconstructing Native Womanhood* (Toronto: Second Story, 2000), 61–2.

98   Roland Chrisjohn, Sherri Young, Agnes Grant, J.R. Miller, and John S. Milloy, to name but a few, have done exhaustive studies on the conditions at the residential schools and are unanimous in their agreement that the schools were chronically underfunded and that students' physical needs, that is diet, clothing, and health care, were sorely neglected.

99 G. Manuel and M. Posluns, *The Fourth World: An Indian Reality* (Don Mills: Collier Macmillan Canada, 1974), 67.

100 Milloy, *National Crime*, 131.

101 Grant, *No End of Grief*, 145.

102 Christophers, *Positioning the Missionary*, 103.

103 In Louise Halfe, *Bear Bones and Feathers* (Regina: Coteau, 1994), 105.

104 Linda Jaine, ed., *Residential Schools: The Stolen Years* (Saskatoon: University of Saskatchewan Extension Press, 1993); Suzanne Fournier and Ernie Crey, *Stolen From Our Embrace: The Abduction of First Nations Children and the Restoration of Aboriginal Communities* (Vancouver: Douglas and McIntyre, 1997).

105 I would like to acknowledge Cree elder Beatrice Lavallee (1929–2003) of the Piapot First Nation, whose teachings contributed to my discussion of the shame-based curriculum of residential schools. Ms. Lavallee revealed how this practice profoundly damaged her sense of self and identity as a child when she spoke to many classes at the First Nations University of Canada and the University of Regina.

106 Beatrice Lavallee, personal conversations and public presentations at the Saskatchewan Indian Federated College and University of Regina, 1998–2003.

107 Milloy, *National Crime*, 179.

108 Basil H. Johnston, *Indian School Days* (Norman, OK: University of Oklahoma Press, 1988).

109 Halfe, *Bear Bones*.

110 Milloy, *National Crime*, 290.

111 In Milloy, *National Crime*, 299.

112 Manuel, "Strength of Indian Women," 75–119.

113 Robert Arthur Alexie, *Porcupines and China Dolls* (Toronto: Stoddart, 2002).

114 Milloy, *National Crime*, 190.

115 Churchill, "Kizhiibaabinesik," 18.

116 Milloy, *National Crime*, 9.

117 Buckley, *Wooden Ploughs*, 51.

118 The Métis took up arms in resistance in 1869, 1870, and 1885.

119 Jacqueline Peterson, "Many Roads to Red River: Métis Genesis in the Great Lakes Region, 1680–1815," in *The New People: Being and Becoming Métis in North America*, eds. Jacqueline Peterson and Jennifer S.H. Brown (Winnipeg: University of Manitoba Press, 1985), 39.

120 St-Onge, Nicole J.M., *Race, Class and Marginality: A Métis Settlement in the Manitoba Interlake, 1850–1914* (PhD diss., University of Manitoba, 1990), 8.

121 Murray Dobbin, *The One-And-A-Half Men* (Vancouver: New Star, 1981).

122 John S. Long, "Treaty No. 9 and fur trade company families: Northeastern Ontario's halfbreeds, Indians, petitioners and métis," in *The New People*, eds. Peterson and Brown, 140.

123 Higham, *Noble, Wretched, and Redeemable*, 122.

124 Diane Payment, "Batoche After 1885: A Society in Transition," in eds. Barron and Waldram, 179–80.

125 Ray, *I Have Lived Here*, 201.

126 St-Onge, *Race, Class and Marginality*, 100.

127 Ray, *I Have Lived Here*, 217.

128 St-Onge, *Race, Class and Marginality*, 102.

129 Payment, "Batoche After 1885," 183.

130 St-Onge, *Race, Class and Marginality*, iii.

131 Ibid., 182–3.

132 Lawrence, *"Real" Indians*, 7.

133 Andrew J. Siggner, "Urban Aboriginal Populations: An Update Using 2001 Census Results," in *Not Strangers*, eds. Newhouse and Peters.

134 Tricia Logan, "A Métis Perspective on Truth and Reconciliation," in *From Truth to Reconciliation: Transforming the Legacy of Residential Schools*, eds. Marlene Brant Castellano, Linda Archibald, and Mike DeGagné (Ottawa: Aboriginal Healing Foundation, 2008), 78.

135 There may have been similar schools in other provinces but finding records of them is difficult because of the dearth of information available on the Métis.

136 Clement Chartier, "Address By President Chartier To The Senate In Response To The Apology For Residential Schools," http://www.metisnation.ca/press/08-june11C.html.

137 Milloy, *National Crime*, 62.

138 Ibid., 67–8.

139 Logan, "Métis Perspective," 76.

140 My now-deceased mother-in-law, Mathilda Bunnie, attended the Marieval Residential School in the Qu'Appelle Valley in 1920 for grade one and part of grade two. Because she did not have Indian status, she was required to discontinue part way through grade two. She received no further formal education and remained barely literate for the remainder of her life.

141 Tantoo Cardinal, "There Is A Place," in *Our Story: Aboriginal Voices on Canada's Past* (Toronto: Anchor Canada, 2005).

142 Logan, "Métis Perspective," 76.

143 Chartier, "Address."

144 Quiring, *CCF Colonialism*, 246.

145 I use the term "racial" deliberately because it was those families who were visibly Indigenous who suffered the most. Many Métis who were able, that is to say those with light skin, went underground.

146 Lawrence, *"Real" Indians*, 35.

147 Quiring, *CCF Colonialism*, 240.

148 In Quiring, *CCF Colonialism*, 65.

149 The Supreme Court of Canada only recognized Métis hunting rights in 2003 but limits that recognition to those Métis people living and hunting in historical Métis communities.

150 P. Johnston, *Native Children*, 2.

151 H. Philip Hepworth, *Foster Care and Adoption in Canada* (Ottawa: Canadian Council on Social Development, 1980), 112.

152 P. Johnston, *Native Children*, 2–3.

153 "In 1951, major revisions to the Indian Act were introduced, including a clause that seemed to allow for the extension of provincial child welfare services. The changes, however, did not authorize additional funding to defray the cost of newly provided services, so over the ensuing years only some provincial child welfare programs were extended to residents of some reserves in some provinces.

"The resulting confusion and disparity was acknowledged in H.B. Hawthorn's classic study of Indians published in 1966. In describing child welfare services available to Indians in most of Canada, Hawthorn said that 'the situation varies from unsatisfactory to appalling.'" P. Johnston, *Native Children,* 3. Johnston comments that, by 1982, little had changed. In 2004, the situation still remains bleak. Now social-service agencies are reluctantly to permit non-Indigenous families to adopt Indigenous children. As a result, most Indigenous children in care of the child-welfare agencies live for many years in what are supposed to be temporary foster homes. And, most of those foster families are still White and working-class.

154 Milloy, *National Crime,* 302.

155 P. Johnston, *Native Children,* xx.

156 P. Johnston, *Native Children,* 23.

157 As part of its comprehensive survey of Aboriginal child-welfare policies and procedures, in 1983 the Canadian Council on Social Development compiled a statistical overview of Aboriginal children in the care of child-welfare authorities across Canada. The director of the project, Patrick Johnston, found that Aboriginal children were highly over-represented in the child-welfare system. They represented 40 to 50 percent of children in care in the province of Alberta, 60 to 70 percent of children in care in Saskatchewan, and some 50 to 60 percent of children in care in Manitoba. Johnston estimated that, across Canada, Aboriginal children were 4.5 times more likely than non-Aboriginal children to be in the care of child-welfare authorities. Other experts have made similar findings. What began in the 1960s, with very few exceptions, carried on through the 1970s and 1980s. Manitoba, *Report of the Aboriginal Justice Inquiry of Manitoba.* In western Canada, it continues to this day. To remedy the effects of its genocidal policy, the Government of Saskatchewan implemented a policy whereby only Indigenous families would be allowed to adopt Indigenous children. On 10 December 2004, Madam Justice Jacelyn Ann Ryan-Froslie of the Saskatchewan Court of Queen's Bench struck down that policy and once again permitted White adoptions of Indigenous children.

158 Edwin C. Kimelman, et al., *No Quiet Place: Review Committee on Indian and Metis Adoptions and Placements* (Winnipeg: Manitoba Department of Community Services, 1985), 276.

159 P. Johnston, *Native Children,* 23.

160 Ibid., 23.

161 Hepworth, *Foster Care,* 96.

162 Fournier and Crey, *Stolen From Our Embrace,* 86.

163 Ibid., 83.

164 P. Johnston, *Native Children,* 24.

165 United Nations Office of the High Commissioner for Human Rights, *Convention on the Prevention and Punishment of the Crime of Genocide,* approved and proposed for signature and ratification or accession by the General Assembly Resolution 260 A (III) 9 December 1948 *entry into force* 12 January 1951 in accordance with article XIII, http://www.hrweb.org/legal/genocide.html.

Chapter 3

1 McAdams, *Stories We Live By,* 12.

2 Ibid., 34.

3 Ibid., 12 (emphasis added).

4   Edward M. Bruner, "Experience and Its Expressions," in *The Anthropology of Experience*, eds. V.W. Turner and E.M. Bruner (Urbana: University of Illinois Press, 1986), 6.

5   McAdams, *Stories We Live By*, 31.

6   Garro and Mattingly, "Narrative as Construct and Construction," 15.

7   McAdams, *Stories We Live By*, 12.

8   Canada, Office of the Privy Council, "Canada's Ranking on the Human Development Index (HDI)," in the *Former Prime Minister's Archives (1995–2003)*, http://www.pcobcp.gc.ca/default.asp?Language=E&Page=pmarchive&Sub=FactSheets&Doc=canada_hdi_2001_e.htm.

9   Beavon and Cooke, "An Application," 207.

10   Armstrong, "Disempowerment," 240.

11   In McAdams, *Stories We Live By*, 32.

12   Churchill, "Kizhiibaabinesik," 10.

13   Harjo and Bird, introduction to *Reinventing the Enemy's Language*, 22.

14   Churchill, "Kizhiibaabinesik," 57 (emphasis in the original).

15   Gold, *Read* , 53.

16   In Egan, "Telling Trauma," 15.

17   Garro and Mattingly, "Narrative as Construct," 18.

18   McAdams, *Stories We Live By*, 12.

19   Paolo Freire, *Pedagogy of the Oppressed*, 1970, trans. Myra Bergman Ramos (New York: Continuum, 1981).

20   Maria Campbell, *Halfbreed* (Halifax: Goodread, 1973). Further references to this text appear as page numbers in parentheses.

21   Gold, *Read*, 45.

22   Maria Campbell, telephone conversation, 25 March 1998.

23   Hartmut Lutz, ed., *Contemporary Challenges: Conversations with Canadian Native Authors* (Saskatoon: Fifth House, 1991), 53.

24   Egan, "Telling Trauma," 15.

25   Joseph Gold, "Biography as Fiction: The Art of Invisible Authorship," in *Reflections: Autobiography and Canadian Literature*, ed. K.P. Stich (Ottawa: University of Ottawa Press, 1988), 132.

26   Susan Sniader Lanser, *Fictions of Authority: Women Writers and Narrative Voice* (Ithaca: Cornell University Press, 1992), 21.

27   Alexander, *Roots of Addiction*, 2.

28   Significantly, another word for the Métis in Nêhiyawêwin is *otipêyimisowak*, which literally translated means "they own themselves."

29   Many Status Indians at the time would not have considered themselves fortunate since they were overwhelmed by the colonial regime's legislated oppression. Many Indians considered the Métis the fortunate ones because they did not live under the daily scrutiny of the agents of the colonial regime, the Indian agent and farm instructor, and were not compelled to send their children to residential schools.

30   Ironically, the Canadian nation-state welcomes immigrants from all over the world as new citizens, but forbids the First Nations to allow immigrants into their midst.

31   Maria Campbell, personal conversation, 18 September 2003.

32   Hillary Harper, speech to *Community Based Research and Aboriginal Women's Health and Healing*, Saskatoon, Saskatchewan, 29 November 2004.

33 Alexander, *Roots of Addiction*, 2.

34 Freire, *Pedagogy of the Oppressed*, 44 (emphasis in the original).

35 St. Peter Claver's became the Garnier Residential School in 1945, and Loyola College merged with St. George William's University to become Concordia University in 1974.

36 I have used Basil Johnston's spelling for references to the *Anishinaubaemowin* (Ojibway language). Thanks to Margaret Cote from the Department of Indigenous Languages, Literatures, and Lingustics for help with grammar.

37 David Newhouse, "A Tale Twice Told: Academic Freedom and Responsibility and Aboriginal Governments," First Nations Higher Education and The First Nations University of Canada: A Symposium, Regina, SK, 10 November 2005.

38 Johnston, *Indian School Days*, 11. Further references to this text appear as page numbers in parentheses.

39 King, *Truth About Stories*, 68.

40 Basil Johnston, preface to McKegney, *Magic Weapons*, ix.

41 Milloy, *National Crime*, 33.

42 Ibid., 185.

43 Kristina Fagan provides a comprehensive study of the function of humour in *Laughing to Survive: Humour in Contemporary Canadian Native Literature*.

44 Gold, "Biography," 131.

Chapter 4

1 McAdams, *Stories We Live By*, 12.

2 Ronald Wright, *Stolen Continents: The "New World" Through Indian Eyes* (1992, Toronto: Penguin, 1993), 5.

3 Gold, *Read*, 53.

4 In 1984, at the request of the Province of Manitoba Department of Education Beatrice Culleton published April Raintree as a sanitized version of the original novel *In Search of April Raintree* (1983) that would be suitable for children. Helen Hoy's "'Nothing but the Truth': Discursive Transparency in Beatrice Culleton" and Peter Cumming's "'The Only Dirty Book': The Rape of April Raintree" both examine the implications of *April Raintree*. Both essays appear in *In Search of April Raintree: Critical Edition*, ed. Cheryl Suzack (Winnipeg: Peguis Publishers, 1999). Hoy argues that the revised narrative constitutes a new text. Cummings contends that it "is a travesty, a depoliticized echo of *Search*" (307).

5 Gary D. Fireman, Ted E. McVay, Jr., and Owen J. Flanagan, introduction to *Narrative and Consciousness: Literature, Psychology, and the Brain*, eds. Gary D. Fireman, Ted E. McVay, Jr., and Owen J. Flanagan (Oxford: Oxford University Press, 2003), 5–6.

6 Helen Hoy, *How Should I Read These? Native Women Writers in Canada* (Toronto: University of Toronto Press, 2001), 288.

7 Deanna Reder, "Stories of Destruction and Renewal: Images of Fireweed," in *Creating Community: A Roundtable on Aboriginal Literatures*, eds. Renate Eigenbrod and Jo-Ann Episkenew (Penticton: Theytus, 2001), 278.

8 Beatrice Culleton Mosionier, "The Special Time," in *In Search of April Raintree: Critical Edition*, 248.

9 Beatrice Culleton Mosionier, *In Search of April Raintree: Critical Edition*, 9. Further references to this text (Peguis edition) will appear as page numbers in parentheses.

10 James S. Frideres, *Aboriginal Peoples in Canada: Contemporary Conflicts*, 5th ed. (Scarborough: Prentice Hall, 1998), 8.

11 Alexander, *Roots of Addiction*.

12 Ibid.

13 Fournier and Crey, *Stolen From Our Embrace*, 87.

14 Johnston, *Native Children*, 68.

15 Ibid., 69.

16 Ibld., 74.

17 Ibid., 77.

18 Fournier and Crey, *Stolen From Our Embrace*, 84.

19 Ibid., 87.

20 Freire, *Pedagogy of the Oppressed*, 45.

21 Fournier and Crey, *Stolen From Our Embrace*, 85.

22 Daniel Francis, *The Imaginary Indian: The Image of the Indian in Canadian Culture* (Vancouver: Arsenal, 1992).

23 Culleton Mosionier, "The Special Time," 248–9.

24 The "Friendship Centre" is the Indian and Métis Friendship Centre. The Friendship Centre movement began in the 1960s, when friendship centres were created to help Indian and Métis people make the transition to life in the city. Today, friendship centres exist in most major cities in Canada.

25 For similar accounts of Indigenous people who suffered despair in transcultural adoptions see Shandra Spears's story in Anderson and Lawrence, *Strong Women Stories*, 81–94, and Joyce McBryde's story in Fournier and Crey, *Stolen From Our Embrace*, 95–99.

26 Reder, "Stories of Destruction and Renewal," 279.

27 Ibid.

28 Shirley Sterling, *My Name Is Seepeetza* (Toronto: Groundwood Books, 1992), 7. Further references to this text will appear as page numbers in parentheses.

29 Although I could find no official sources regarding coyotes in my own city, Regina, I have witnessed them. Given the large number of white-tailed jack rabbits (*Lepus townsendii*) that now live in Regina, it should come as no surprise that coyotes have followed their prey.

30 Granted, Canada was not comprised of only Whites and Status Indians in 1958; there were African and Asian Canadians as well as Métis. Still, these other racial minorities faced discrimination both in the education system and elsewhere.

31 Culhane, *Pleasure of the Crown*, 40.

32 Since 1991, many Indigenous people have attempted to impose legal penalties in the form of criminal charges and civil law suits on those residential school employees who assaulted them; however, some former students did not live to be able to seek legal redress, many having died prematurely from violence, suicide, and addictions.

33 Pennebaker, *Opening Up*, 153.

34 Ibid., 154.

35 Although Status Indians were not Canadian citizens, they still enlisted in the military in large numbers and fought in both world wars and the Korean War.

36 Ken Goodwill, an elder from the Standing Buffalo First Nation, tells me that he was one of three Indigenous students at the University of Saskatchewan in Saskatoon in 1958. None graduated.

37 Reder, "Stories of Destruction and Renewal," 282.

38 Jan Van Eijk, e-mail to the author, 7 November 2005.

39 Laurence Thompson and Terry Thompson, *Dictionary of N'laka'pamux (Thompson) Language* (Billings: University of Montana Occasional Papers in Linguistics, 1996), 327

40 Brent Galloway, e-mail to the author, 7 November 2005.

41 Personal conversation, Saskatoon, SK, 15 November 2005.

42 My father was a World War II veteran. As a member of the Winnipeg Grenadiers, he was captured by the Japanese on Christmas Day 1941 and was incarcerated in a prisoner-of-war camp in Hong Kong until the end of the war. My mother tells me that there was a powerful stigma attached to asking for mental health services. Veterans were encouraged to get married, have children, and forget the whole thing. For many years, the bars in the local branches of the Royal Canadian Legion were filled with veterans who drank to forget.

43 Wagamese also uses the term "Ojibway." Wagamese translates Anishinaubae as meaning "the good people."

44 Richard Wagamese, *Keeper 'n Me* (Toronto: Doubleday, 1994), 11. Further references to this text will appear as page numbers in parentheses.

45 Richard Wagamese, *For Joshua: An Ojibway Father Teaches His Son* (Toronto: Doubleday, 2002), 40–1. Further references to this text will appear as page numbers in parentheses.

46 Duran and Duran, *Postcolonial Psychology*, 24.

47 This is not as illogical as it might sound. In many countries, such as Mexico, "Indian" identity is not racialized; it is a lowly social class from which one can escape by elevating one's status by way of education and employment.

48 Tafoya, "Teams, Networks and Clans."

Chapter 5

1 Monique Mojica and Ric Knowles, introduction to *Staging Coyote's Dream: An Anthology of First Nations Drama in English*, eds. M. Mojica and R. Knowles (Toronto: Playwrights Canada Press, 2003), v.

2 Lauri Shannon Seidlitz, *Native Theatre for the Seventh Generation: On the Path to Cultural Healing* (MA thesis, Dalhousie University, 1994), 8–9.

3 Geraldine Manossa, "The Beginning of Cree Performance Culture," in *(Ad)dressing Our Words: Aboriginal Perspectives on Aboriginal Literatures*, ed. Armand Garnet Ruffo (Penticton: Theytus, 2001), 180.

4 Floyd Favel Starr, "The Artificial Tree: Native Performance Culture Research 1991–1996," *Canadian Theatre Review* 90 (1997): 83.

5 Mojica and Knowles, *Staging Coyote's Dream*, v.

6 Philip Taylor, *Applied Theatre: Creating Transformative Encounters in the Community* (Portsmouth: Heinemann, 2003), 1.

7 Ibid., xviii.

8 Monique Mojica, "Theatrical Diversity on Turtle Island: A tool towards the healing," *Canadian Theatre Review* 68 (1991): 3.

9 David Diamond, "*Out of the Silence*: Headlines Theatre and Power Plays," in *Playing Boal: Theatre, Therapy, Activism*, eds. Mady Schutzman and Jan Cohen-Cruz (London and New York: Routledge, 1994), 37.

10   Ibid., 37.

11   Mady Schutzman and Jan Cohen-Cruz, introduction to *Playing Boal: Theatre, Therapy, Activism*, eds. Mady Schutzman and Jan Cohen-Cruz (London and New York: Routledge, 1994), 1.

12   Taylor, *Applied Theatre*, 5.

13   Diamond, "*Out of the Silence*," 36.

14   Ibid., 35.

15   Common Weal, "About," http://www.commonweal-arts/about (accessed 29 April 2005)

16   Ibid.

17   "Indian reserve" is the legal designation of the small parcels of land "reserved" for people with status under the *Indian Act*.

18   Rachel Van Fossen, "Writing for the Community Play Form," *Canadian Theatre Review* 90 (1997): 10.

19   Aboriginal Healing Foundation, "Mission, Vision, and Values," http://www.ahf.ca/about-us/mission.

20   Aboriginal Healing Foundation, "Funded Projects: Saskatchewan Native Theatre Company Inc., Grant I.D. 3490.00, Title: Circle of Voices, 1999–2004, http://www.ahf.ca/newsite/english/funded_projects/pull_project.php?id=3490.00.

21   Daniel David Moses and Terry Goldie, preface to first edition in *An Anthology of Canadian Native Literature in English*, 3rd ed. (Toronto: Oxford University Press, 2005), xxiv.

22   Seidlitz, *Native Theatre*, 7–8.

23   In Jordan Wheeler, "A Revolution in Aboriginal Theatre: Our Own Stories," *Canadian Theatre Review* 66 (1991): 12.

24   The term "First Nations" is used to refer to those people designated as having Indian status under the *Indian Act*. The term "Indigenous" is used as an inclusive term to include First Nations, Métis, and Inuit.

25   Carter, *Aboriginal People*, 161.

26   S.D. Hanson, "Kitchi-Manito-Waya," in Canada, National Archives of Canada and National Library of Canada, *Dictionary of Canadian Biography Online*, http://www.biographi.ca/EN/ShowBio.asp?BioId=40324.

27   Ibid.

28   Carter, *Aboriginal People*, 174.

29   Daniel David Moses, "How My Ghosts Got Pale Faces," in *Speaking for the Generations: Native Writers on Writing*, ed. Simon J. Ortiz (Tucson: University of Arizona Press, 1998), 135.

30   Robert Appleford, "The Desire to Crunch Bone: Daniel David Moses and the 'True Real Indian,'" *Canadian Theatre Review* 77 (1993): 22.

31   Ibid.

32   Hanson, "Kitchi-Manito-Waya."

33   Daniel David Moses, *Almighty Voice and His Wife* (Toronto: Playwrights Canada Press, 1991), 20. Further references to this text appear as page numbers in parentheses.

34   Louise Bernice Halfe, "Returning," in *Bear Bones and Feathers*, 105.

35   Appleford, "The Desire to Crunch Bone," 24.

36   Ibid.

37   Louis Althusser, "Ideology and Ideological State Apparatuses," in *Lenin and Philosophy and Other Essays*, trans. Ben Brewster (New York: New Left Books, 1971), 60–102.

38   CBC, "Racist Comments by Ontario Police caught on Videotape," 20 January 2004, http://www.cbc.ca/stories/2004/01/20/ipperwash040120 (accessed 25 February 2004). Unfortunately, little has changed in modern-day Canada as evidenced by the attitudes of members of the Ontario Provincial Police that were revealed on a video-tape that was recently disclosed and that the media made public. Police were filmed discussing First Nations protestors, one of whom they later shot, in a demeaning and stereotypical manner:

   "Is there still a lot of press down there," one officer is says [sic]. "No, there's no one down there. Just a great big fat fuck Indian," replies another. "The camera's rolling, eh?" "Yeah."

   "We had this planned, you know. We thought if we could get five or six cases of Labatts 50, we could bait them." "Yeah." "Then we'd have this big net at a pit." "Creative thinking." "Works in the [US] South with watermelon."

39   Armstrong, "Disempowerment", 243.

40   Manuel, "Strength of Indian Women," 76. Further references to this text appear as page numbers in parentheses.

41   Taylor, *Applied Theatre*, xviii.

42   My husband, Clayton Episkenew, attended the Catholic Residential School at Lebret, Saskatchewan, in the 1950s and remembers the school staff emphasizing their role as "God's helpers." The children understood this to mean that God appointed them and that God authorized their actions.

43   N. Rosalyn Ing, *Dealing with Shame and Unresolved Trauma: Residential School and Its Impact on the 2nd and 3rd Generation Adults* (PhD diss., University of British Columbia, 2000), 33.

44   These words are attributed to a young Aboriginal man quoted in Mitchell and Maracle, "Post-Traumatic Stress," 16.

45   Mojica and Knowles, introduction to *Staging Coyote's Dream*, v–vii (emphasis in the original).

46   I deliberately use the term "band" rather than "First Nation," which has become the more commonly used term. When the treaties were negotiated, the signatories were the headmen of individual bands, which were small groups of families who happened to be camped together at the time. I would argue that a "nation" would be comprised of many bands or communities and that the fact that the colonial regime supports the notion of referring to individual communities are nations is suspect and suggests another way of dividing and conquering. Small communities have little political power and the regime's past practices clearly indicate that it would prefer to negotiate with a small powerless community than a large and unified nation. Furthermore, it is important to note that the original band membership lists were random because membership was fluid. Today, any discussion regarding band membership lists suggests that people believe that the same families have lived together since time immemorial, but this is false.

47   Christine Lenze, "'The Whole Thing You're Doing Is White Man's Ways': *fareWel's* Northern Tour," *Canadian Theatre Review* 108 (2001), http://www.utpjournals.com/product/ctr/108/108/Lenze.html.

48   Jack D. Forbes, *A World Ruled by Cannibals: The Wetiko Disease of Asggression, Violence and Imperialism* (Davis, CA: D-Q University Press, 1979).

49   Neal McLeod, *Songs to Kill a Wîhtikow* (Regina: Hagios, 2007).

50   Armand Ruffo, "A Windigo Tale: Contemporizing and Mythologizing the Residential School Experience," in *Aboriginal Drama and Theatre: Critical Perspectives on Canadian Theatre in English, Volume One*, ed. Robert Appleford (Toronto: Playwrights Canada Press, 2005), 167–8.

51   Ian Ross, *fareWel* (Toronto: Scirocco Drama, 1998), 24. Further references to this text appear as page numbers in parentheses.

52   This is a derogatory word for a woman in Nahkawêwin (Plains Anishinaubaemowin). Like all derogatory words for women, it has explicit sexual connotations.

53   Duran and Duran, *Postcolonial Psychology*, 30.

54   Ibid., 37.

55   I am being consistent with Ross's spelling.

56   Lenze, "'The Whole Thing You're Doing.'"

57   Ibid.

Chapter 6

1   After Darrell Night, a Cree man, survived and formally complained to the police, the Saskatoon Police Service's Starlight Tours became public knowledge. The discovery of the deaths made front-page headlines and forced an investigation and a public inquiry. As a result, four police officers lost their jobs, and two were charged with unlawful confinement, found guilty, and sentenced to eight months in jail. To date, no one has been charged with more serious crimes, such as criminal negligence causing death.

2   CBC, "Ipperwash Inquiry told of profane Harris directive to end standoff," 28 November 2005, http://www.cbc.ca/ottawa/story/ot-ipperwash20051128.html.

3   Ontario, *The Honourable Sidney B. Linden's Report of The Ipperwash Inquiry*, 30 May 2007, http://www.attorneygeneral.jus.gov.on.ca/inquiries/ipperwash/report/vol_1/pdf/E_Vol_1_Conclusion.pdf, 677.

4   Ibid., 642.

5   Amnesty International, *Stolen Sisters: A Human Rights Response to Discrimination and Violence Against Indigenous Women in Canada*, AI Index: AMR 20/003/2004, http://www.amnesty.ca/stolensisters/amr2000304.pdf.

6   "First Ministers and National Aboriginal Leaders Strengthening Relationships and Closing the Gap," Kelowna, BC, 24–25 November 2005, http://www.scics.gc.ca/cinfo05/800044004_e.pdf.

7   Canada, Office of the Prime Minister, "Prime Minister Harper offers full apology on behalf of Canadians for Residential Schools system," (Ottawa: Canada, Office of the Prime Minister, 2008), http://www.pm.gc.ca/eng/media.asp?id=2149.

8   CBC, "'Moral code' was behind resignation from schools commission: LaForme," 13 November 2008, http://www.cbc.ca/canada/edmonton/story/2008/11/13/laforme-resignation.html.

9   Canada as represented by the Honourable Frank Iacobucci, and plaintiffs as represented by the National Consortium and the Merchant Law Group, and the Assembly of First Nations and Inuit Representatives, and Independent Council, and the General Synod of the Anglican Church of Canada, the Presbyterian Church of Canada, the United Church of Canada and Roman Catholic Entities, *Indian Residential Schools Settlement Agreement*, 8 May 2006, 22, http://www.residentialschool settlement.ca/settlement.pdf.

10   CBC, "Former Students being revictimized: First Nations Group," 22 January 2008, http://www.cbc.ca/canada/saskatchewan/story/2008/01/22/residential-schools. html.

11   Canada et al., Schedule E of the *Indian Residential Schools Settlement Agreement*, 8 May 2006, http://www.residentialschoolsettlement.ca/Schedule_E-ResidentialSchools. PDF.

12   Chartier, "Address."

13   John Richards, "Closing the Aboriginal—Non-Aboriginal Education Gap: A S.I.P.P. Armchair Discussion" (presentation, Saskatchewan Institute of Public Policy, Regina, SK, 4 March 2008).

14   Dan Beavon and Martin Cooke, "An Application of the United Nations Human Development Index to Registered Indians in Canada, 1966," in *Aboriginal Conditions: Research as a Foundation for Public Policy*, eds. Jerry P. White, Paul S. Maxim, and Dan Beavon (Vancouver: University of British Columbia Press, 2003), 201–221.

15   From the 1998 Canadian Incidence Study on Reported Child Abuse and Neglect in Cindy Blackstock, "Reconciliation Means Not Saying Sorry Twice: Lessons from Child Welfare in Canada," in *From Truth to Reconciliation: Transforming the Legacy of Residential Schools*, eds. Marlene Brant Castellano, Linda Archibald, and Mike DeGagné (Ottawa: Aboriginal Healing Foundation, 2008), 166–7. Emphasis in the original.

16   Canada, Department of Justice, Aboriginal Justice Strategy, Fact Sheet, 9 April 2008, http://www.justice.gc.ca/eng/pi/ajs-sja/pub/fs-fi.html (accessed 16 June 2008).

17   Canada, Health Canada, First Nations, Inuit and Aboriginal Health, "Drinking Water Advisories," 11 June 2008, http://www.hc-sc.gc.ca/fniah-spnia/promotion/water-eau/advis-avis_concern-eng.php (accessed 16 June 2008).

18   Taiaiake Alfred, *Wasa'se: Indigenous Pathways of Action and Freedom* (Peterborough: Broadview, 2005), 37.

19   John Stackhouse, "Canada's Apartheid," *Globe and Mail*, http://www.theglobeandmail. com/series/apartheid/stories/introduction.html.

20   Alfred, *Wasa'se*, 44–5.

21   Thomas King, "Godzilla vs. Post-Colonial," *World Literature Written in English* 30, 2 (1990): 12.

22   Maria Campbell, e-mail message to author, 6 January 2006.

23   I have had numerous informal discussions with literary and theatre artists who are involved in community outreach as well as the youth who are part of these projects. All commented on how these projects improved the lives of the community. These effects need to be documented.

24   CBC, "Women at the Pine Grove Correctional Centre are using music to confront their inner demons," 18 June 2008, http://www.cbc.ca/morningedition/topstory. html#Wednesday.

25   Daniel David Moses, "The Trickster's Laugh: My Meeting with Tomson and Lenore," *American Indian Quarterly* 28, 1/2 (2004): 110–1.

Bibliography

Abel, Lisa. "Mental Health and the Medicine Wheel." *RedwireMag.Com* 7, 1. http://redwiremag.com/mentalhealth.htm (accessed 2 May 2005).

Aboriginal Healing Foundation. "Funded Projects." Saskatchewan Native Theatre Company Inc. Grant ID 3490.00. Title: Circle of Voices. 1999–2004. http://www.ahf.ca/newsite/english/funded_projects/pull_project.php?id=3490.00 (accessed 26 April 2005).

_____. "Mission, Vision, and Values." http://www.ahf.ca/about-us/mission (accessed 26 April 2005).

Achebe, Chinua. "Colonialist Criticism." In *The Post-Colonial Studies Reader*, ed. Bill Ashcroft, Garreth Griffiths, and Helen Tiffin. London and New York: Routledge, 1995.

Acoose, Janice. "A Vanishing Indian? Or Acoose: Woman Standing Above Ground?" In *(Ad)dressing Our Words: Aboriginal Perspectives on Aboriginal Literatures*, ed. Armand Garnet Ruffo. Penticton: Theytus, 2001.

_____. "*Halfbreed*: A Revisiting of Maria Campbell's Text from an Indigenous Perspective." In *Looking at the Words of our People: First Nations Analysis of Literature*, ed. Jeannette C. Armstrong. Penticton: Theytus, 1993.

_____. *Iskwewak—kah ki yaw ni wahkomakanak: Neither Indian Princesses Nor Easy Squaws*. Toronto: Women's Press, 1995.

_____. "Post Halfbreed: Indigenous Writers as Authors of Their Own Realities." In *Looking at the Words of our People: First Nations Analysis of Literature*, ed. Jeannette C. Armstrong. Penticton: Theytus, 1993.

_____. "The Problem of 'Searching' For April Raintree." In *In Search of April Raintree: Critical Edition*, by Beatrice Culleton Mosionier. Ed. Cheryl Suzack. Winnipeg: Peguis, 1999.

Adams, Howard. *Howard Adams: Otapawy!* ed. Hartmut Lutz, Murray Hamilton, and Donna Heimbecker. Saskatoon: Gabriel Dumont Institute, 2005.

_____. *Prison of Grass: Canada from a Native Point of View*. 1975. Revised and Updated. Saskatoon: Fifth House, 1989.

_____. *The Outsiders: An Educational Survey of Metis and Non-Treaty Indians of Saskatchewan*. Saskatoon: Metis Society of Saskatchewan, 1972.

_____. *A Tortured People: The Politics of Colonization*. Penticton: Theytus, 1999.

Akiwenzie-Damm, Kateri, and Jeannette C. Armstrong, eds. *Standing Ground: Strength and Solidarity Amidst Dissolving Boundaries*. Penticton: Theytus, 1996.

Alexander, Bruce K. *The Roots of Addiction in Free Market Society*. Canadian Centre for Policy Alternatives. April 2001. http://www.policyalternatives.ca/bc/rootsofaddiction.html (accessed 24 November 2004).

Alexie, Robert Arthur. *Porcupines and China Dolls*. Toronto: Stoddart, 2002.

———. *The Pale Indian*. Toronto: Penguin, 2005.

Alfred, Taiaiake. *Wasa'se: Indigenous Pathways of Action and Freedom*. Peterborough: Broadview, 2005.

Altbach, Philip G. "Education and Neocolonialism." In *The Post-Colonial Studies Reader*, eds. Bill Ashcroft, Garreth Griffiths, and Helen Tiffin. London and New York: Routledge, 1995.

Althusser, Louis. "Ideology and Ideological State Apparatuses." In *Lenin and Philosophy and Other Essays*. Trans. Ben Brewster. New York: New Left Books, 1971.

Amnesty International. *Stolen Sisters: A Human Rights Response to Discrimination and Violence Against Indigenous Women in Canada*. 4 October 2004. http://www.amnesty.ca/stolensisters/amr2000304.pdf (accessed 26 November 2005).

Amuta, Chindi. "Fanon, Cabral and Ngugi on National Liberation." In *The Post-Colonial Studies Reader*, eds. Bill Ashcroft, Garreth Griffiths, and Helen Tiffin. London and New York: Routledge, 1995.

Anderson, Kim. *A Recognition of Being: Reconstructing Native Womanhood*. Toronto: Second Story, 2000.

Anderson, Kim, and Bonita Lawrence, eds. *Strong Women Stories: Native Vision and Community Stories*. Toronto: Summach, 2003.

Anzaldúa, Gloria. *Borderlands La Frontera: The New Mestiza*. San Francisco: Aunt Lute Books, 1987.

Appleford, Robert. "Daniel David Moses: Ghostwriter With A Vengeance." In *Aboriginal Drama and Theatre: Critical Perspectives on Canadian Theatre in English, Volume One*, ed. Robert Appleford. Toronto: Playwrights Canada Press, 2005.

———. "Seeing the Full Frame." Introduction. In *Aboriginal Drama and Theatre: Critical Perspectives on Canadian Theatre in English, Volume One*, ed. Robert Appleford. Toronto: Playwrights Canada Press, 2005.

———. "The Desire to Crunch Bone: Daniel David Moses and the 'True Real Indian.'" *Canadian Theatre Review* 77 (Winter 1993): 21–26.

———. *The Indian "Act": Postmodern Perspectives on Native Canadian Theatre*. PhD diss., University of Toronto, 1999. http://www.collectionscanada.ca/obj/s4/f2/dsk3/ftp04/nq41007.pdf (accessed 28 July 2008).

Armstrong, Jeanette C. *Breath Tracks*. Stratford: William-Wallace, 1991.

———. "The Disempowerment of First North American Native Peoples and Empowerment Through Their Writing." In *An Anthology of Canadian Native Literature in English*, eds. Daniel David Moses and Terry Goldie. 3rd ed. Toronto: Oxford University Press, 2005.

Ashcroft, Bill, Gareth Griffiths, and Helen Tiffin. *The Empire Writes Back: Theory and Practice in Post-Colonial Literatures*. London and New York: Routledge, 1989.

Assembly of First Nations. "Assembly of First Nations National Chief Applauds Historic Reconciliation and Compensation Agreement as a Major Victory For Residential School Survivors." 23 November 2005. http://www.afn.ca/article.asp?id=1935 (accessed 24 November 2005).

———. *Breaking the Silence: An Interpretive Study of Residential School Impact and Healing as Illustrated by the Stories of First Nations Individuals*. Ottawa: Assembly of First Nations, 1994.

Atwood, Margaret. "A Double-Bladed Knife: Subversive Laughter in Two Stories by Thomas King." In *Native Writers and Canadian Writing*, ed. W.H. New. Vancouver: University of British Columbia Press, 1990.

_____. *Survival: A Thematic Guide to Canadian Literature*. Toronto: Anasi, 1972.

Backhouse, Constance. *Colour-Coded: A Legal History of Racism in Canada, 1900–1950*. Toronto: University of Toronto Press, 1999.

Baird, Robert M., and Stuart E. Rosenbaum, eds. *Bigotry, Prejudice and Hatred: Definitions, Causes and Solutions*. New York: Prometheus Books, 1992.

Baker, Marie Anneharte. "Angry Enough To Spit But With *Dry Lips* It Hurts More Than You Know." *Canadian Theatre Review* 68 (Fall 1991): 88–9.

_____. "An Old Indian Trick is to Laugh." *Canadian Theatre Review* 68 (Fall 1991): 48–53.

_____. "Medicine Lines: The Doctoring of Story and Self." *Canadian Woman Studies* 14, 2 (Spring 1994): 114.

Barkwell, Laurence J., Leah Dorion, Darren R. Préfontaine. *Resources for Métis Researchers*. Winnipeg and Saskatoon: Louis Riel Institute and Gabriel Dumont Institute, 1999.

Barkwell, Laurence J., Lyle N. Longclaws, and David N. Chartrand. "Status of Métis Children Within the Child Welfare System." Brandon: Brandon University, n.d. http://www.brandonu. ca/Library/CJNS/9.1/metis.pdf (accessed 28 July 2008).

Barron, F. Laurie. "Indian Agents and the North-West Rebellion." In *1885 and After: Native Society in Transition*, eds. Laurie F. Barron and James Waldram. Proceedings of the Canadian Plains Conference, University of Saskatchewan, Saskatoon, SK, May 1985. Regina: Canadian Plains Research Center, 1986.

Bear, Lena. "My Cow Will Not Be Branded I.D." In *"… And They Told Us Their Stories,"* eds. Jack Funk and Gordon Lobe. Saskatoon: Saskatoon District Tribal Council, 1991.

Beavon, Dan, and Martin Cooke. "An Application of the United Nations Human Development Index to Registered Indians in Canada, 1966." In *Aboriginal Conditions: Research as a Foundation for Public Policy*, eds. Jerry P. White, Paul S. Maxim, and Dan Beavon. Vancouver: University of British Columbia Press, 2003.

Bhabha, Homi K. "Signs Taken for Wonders." In *The Post-Colonial Studies Reader*, eds. Bill Ashcroft, Garreth Griffiths, and Helen Tiffin. London and New York: Routledge, 1995.

_____. "Cultural Diversity and Cultural Differences." In *The Post-Colonial Studies Reader*, eds. Bill Ashcroft, Garreth Griffiths, and Helen Tiffin. London and New York: Routledge, 1995.

Bissoondath, Niel. *Selling Illusions: The Cult of Multiculturalism in Canada*. Toronto: Penguin 1994.

Blackstock, Cindy. "Reconciliation Means Not Saying Sorry Twice: Lessons from Child Welfare in Canada." In *From Truth to Reconciliation: Transforming the Legacy of Residential Schools*, eds. Marlene Brant Castellano, Linda Archibald, and Mike DeGagné. Ottawa: Aboriginal Healing Foundation, 2008.

Blaeser, Kimberly M. "Native Literatures: Seeking a Critical Center." In *Looking at the Words of our People: First Nations Analysis of Literature*, ed. Jeannette C. Armstrong. Penticton: Theytus, 1993.

Boal, Augusto. *Legislative Theatre: Using Performance to Make Politics*. Trans. Adrian Jackson. London and New York: Routledge, 1998.

_____. *Theatre of the Oppressed: New Edition*. 1974. Trans. C.A. McBride, M.L. McBride, and E. Fryer. London: Pluto, 2000.

Bonnycastle, Stephen. *In Search of Authority: An Introductory Guide to Literary Theory*. 2nd ed. Peterborough: Broadview, 1996.

Borgerson, Lon. "Ile-á-la-Crosse Upisasik Theatre in Our Schools." *Canadian Theatre Review* 65 (Winter 1990): 48–51.

Brant, Beth. *Food and Spirits*. Vancouver: Press Gang, 1991.

_____. *Mohawk Trail*. Toronto: Women's Press, 1985.

_____. *Writing As Witness: Essay and Talk*. Toronto: Women's Press, 1994.

Brundage, David. "Confluence: Confessions of a White Writer Who Reads Native Lit." In *Creating Community: A Roundtable on Aboriginal Literatures*, eds. Renate Eigenbrod and Jo-Ann Episkenew. Penticton: Theytus, 2001.

Bruner, Edward M. "Experience and Its Expressions." In *The Anthropology of Experience*, eds. V.W. Turner and E.M. Bruner. Urbana: University of Illinois Press, 1986.

Bryde, John F. *Modern Indian Psychology*. Vermillion: University of South Dakota, 1971.

Buckley, Helen. *From Wooden Ploughs to Welfare: Why Indian Policy Failed in the Prairie Provinces*. Montreal and Kingston: McGill-Queen's University Press, 1992.

Bull, L.R. *Indian Residential Schooling: The Native Perspective*. MA thesis, University of Alberta, 1991.

Campbell, Maria, ed. *Achimoona*. Saskatoon: Fifth House, 1985.

_____. Address. Community-Based Research and Aboriginal Women's Health and Healing Colloquium. University of Saskatchewan, Saskatoon, SK, 29 November 2004.

_____. *Halfbreed*. Halifax: Goodread, 1973.

_____. *Stories of the Road Allowance People*. Penticton: Theytus, 1995.

Canada as represented by the Honourable Frank Iacobucci, and Plaintiffs as represented by the National Consortium and the Merchant Law Group, and the Assembly of First Nations and Inuit Representatives, and Independent Council, and the General Synod of the Anglican Church of Canada, the Presbyterian Church of Canada, the United Church of Canada and Roman Catholic Entities. *Indian Residential Schools Settlement Agreement*. 8 May 2006. http://www.residentialschoolsettlement.ca/Settlement.pdf (accessed 16 June 2008).

Canada. Health Canada. First Nations and Inuit Health Branch. *First Nations Comparable Health Indicators*. January 2005. http://www.hc-sc.gc.ca/fnih-spni/pubs/gen/2005-01_health-sante_indicat/index_e.html (accessed 24 January 2006).

Canada. Health Canada. First Nations, Inuit and Aboriginal Health. "Drinking Water Advisories." 11 June 2008. http://www.hc-sc.gc.ca/fniah-spnia/promotion/water-eau/advis-avis_concern-eng.php (accessed 16 June 2008).

Canada. Indian and Northern Affairs. "Amended Indian Band Election Regulations & Indian Referendum Regulations: Chronology of Events." 23 April 2004. http://www.ainc-inac.gc.ca/nr/prs/s-d2000/00168bka_e.html (accessed 25 November 2005).

_____. *Gathering Strength: Canada's Aboriginal Action Plan*. http://dsp-psd.pwgsc.gc.ca/Collection/R32-192-2000E.pdf (16 May 2008).

_____. "Health and Social Indicators." *Social Development*. 3 April 2004. http://www.ainc-inac.gc.ca/gs/soci_e.html (accessed 24 January 2006).

_____. *Report of the Royal Commission on Aboriginal Peoples, Volume One: Looking Forward Looking Back*. By René Dussault, George Erasmus, Paul L.A.H. Chartrand, J. Peter Meekison, Viola Robinson, Mary Sillett, and Bertha Wilson. October 1996. http://www.aincinac.gc.ca/ch/rcap/sg/sg25_e.html (accessed 24 December 2003).

_____. "Statement of Reconciliation: Learning from the Past." 23 April 2004. http://www.ainc-inac.gc.ca/gs/rec_e.html (accessed 9 November 2006).

Canada. Indian Residential Schools Resolution Canada. "Key Events." http://www.irsr-rqpi.gc.ca/english/key_events.html (accessed 23 August 2004).

_____. "The Residential School System Historical Overview." http://www.irsr-rqpi.gc.ca/english/history.html (accessed 23 August 2004).

_____. "Indian Residential Schools in Canada—Historical Chronology." http://www.irsr-qpi.gc.ca/english/historical_events.html (accessed 23 August 2004).

Canada. Justice. Aboriginal Justice Strategy. Fact sheet. 9 April 2008. http://www.justice.gc.ca/eng/pi/ajs-sja/pub/fs-fi.html (accessed 16 June 2008).

_____. *Indian Act (R.S. 1985, c. 1–5)*. 30 April 2004. http://laws.justice.gc.ca/en/I-5/ (accessed 13 July 2004).

Canada. National Archives of Canada and National Library of Canada. *Dictionary of Canadian Biography Online*. "Kitchi-Manito-Waya." By S.D. Hanson, 2000. http://www.biographi.ca/EN/ShowBio.asp?BioId=40324 (accessed 24 October 2003).

Canada. Natural Resources Canada. "Historical Indian Treaties Time Line." *Atlas of Canada*. 26 February 2004. http://atlas.gc.ca/site/english/maps/historical/indiantreaties/historical-treaties/8 (accessed 26 January 2006).

Canada. Office of the Prime Minister. "Prime Minister Harper offers full apology on behalf of Canadians for Residential Schools system." 11 June 2008. http://www.pm.gc.ca/eng/media.asp?id=2149 (accessed 12 June 2008).

Canada. Office of the Privy Council. "Canada's Ranking on the Human Development Index (HDI)." *Former Prime Minister's Archives (1995–2003)*. 28 January 2006. http://www.pcobcp.gc.ca/default.asp?Language=E&Page=pmarchive&Sub=FactSheets&Doc=canada_hdi_2001_e.htm (accessed 28 January 2006).

Canada. Statistics Canada. "Aboriginal Peoples of Canada." 16 April 2003. http://www12.statcan.ca/english/census01/Products/Analytic/companion/abor/canada.cfm (accessed 10 January 2006).

_____. "Community Highlights for Prince Albert," 15 January 2008. http://www12.statcan.ca/english/census06/data/profiles/aboriginal/Details/Page.cfm?Lang=E&Geo1=CSD&Code1=4715066&Geo2=PR&Code2=47&Data=Count&SearchText=prince%20albert&SearchType=Begins&SearchPR=47&B1=All&Custom= (accessed 12 June 2008).

"Canadian Government's Apology to Aboriginal People." ABC Newslink. 8 January 1998. http://sisis.nativeweb.org/clark/jan0898cli.html (accessed 11 January 2006).

Cardinal, Douglas, and Jeannette Armstrong. *The Native Creative Process*. Penticton: Theytus, 1991.

Cardinal, Tantoo et al. *Our Story: Aboriginal Voices on Canada's Past*. Toronto: Anchor Canada, 2005.

Cariou, Warren. "The Racialized Subject in James Tyman's *Inside Out*." *Canadian Literature* 167 (Winter 2000): 68–84.

Carr, Daniel B., John D. Loeser, and David B. Morris. "Why Narrative?" *Narrative, Pain, and Suffering*. Vol. 34 of *Progress in Pain Research and Management*. Seattle: IASP Press, 2005.

Carter, Sarah. *Aboriginal People and Colonizers of Western Canada to 1900*. Toronto: University of Toronto Press, 1999.

_____. *Lost Harvests: Prairie Indian Reserve Farmers and Government Policy*. Montreal: McGill-Queen's University Press, 1990.

Canadian Broadcasting Corporation (CBC). "Women at the Pine Grove Correctional Centre are using music to confront their inner demons." 18 June 2008. http://www.cbc.ca/morningedition/topstory.html#Wednesday (accessed 24 June 2008).

_____. "Former Students being revictimized: First Nations Group." 22 January 2008. http://www.cbc.ca/canada/saskatchewan/story/2008/01/22/residential-schools.html (accessed 17 June 2008).

_____. "Ipperwash Inquiry told of profane Harris directive to end standoff." 28 November 2005. http://www.cbc.ca/ottawa/story/ot-ipperwash20051128.html (accessed 7 December 2005).

_____. "'Moral code' was behind resignation from schools commission: LaForme." 13 November 2008. http://www.cbc.ca/canada/edmonton/story/2008/11/13/laforme-resignation.html (accessed 20 November 2008).

_____. "Racist Comments by Ontario Police caught on Videotape." 20 January 2004. http://www.cbc.ca/stories/2004/01/20/ipperwash040120 (accessed 25 February 2004).

CBC Manitoba."J.J. Harper: 15 Years Later." 7 March 2003. http://www.winnipeg.cbc.ca/indepth/20030304harper.html.

CBC Saskatchewan. "FSIN Apologizes For Comments About Métis People." 25 June 2004. http://sask.cbc.ca/regional/servlet/View?filename=comments062404 (accessed 25 June 2004).

_____. "First Nations respond to aboriginal justice report." 22 June 2004. http://sask.cbc.ca/regional/servlet/View?filename=sk_report20040622 (accessed 22 June 2004).

Chamberlin, J. Edward. *If This is Your Land, Where are Your Stories? Finding Common Ground.* Toronto: Vintage, 2004.

Chartier, Clement. "Address by President Clement Chartier in Response to the Residential School Apology." Metis National Council. http://www.metisnation.ca/press/08-june11B.html (accessed 12 June 2008).

_____. "Address By President Chartier To The Senate In Response To The Apology For Residential Schools." http://www.metisnation.ca/press/08-june11C.html (accessed 16 June 2008).

Chartrand, Paul L.A.H. *Manitoba's Métis Settlement Scheme of 1870.* Saskatoon: Native Law Center, 1991.

Chatman, Seymour. *Story and Discourse: Narrative Structure in Fiction and Film.* Ithaca: Cornell University Press, 1978.

"Child Welfare Report Sites Need for Change." *Saskatchewan Indian,* April 1983, 5. http://www.sicc.sk.ca/saskindian/a83apr05.htm (accessed 5 February 2004).

Chrisjohn, Roland, and Sherri Young, with Michael Maraun. *The Circle Game: Shadows and Substance in the Indian Residential School Experience in Canada.* Penticton: Theytus, 1997.

Christophers, Brett. *Positioning the Missionary: John Booth Good and the Confluence of Cultures in Nineteenth-Century British Columbia.* Vancouver: University of British Columbia Press, 1998.

Churchill, Ward. "Kizhiibaabinesik: A Bright Star, Burning Briefly." Preface. *In My Own Voice: Explorations in the Sociopolitical Context of Art and Cinema,* by Leah Renae Kelly. Winnipeg: Arbeiter Ring, 2001.

Clark, Kendall. "Defining 'White Privilege.'" *WhitePrivilege.com.* Ed. Kendall Clark. 6 September 2005. WordPress Entries (RSS). http://whiteprivilege.com/definition/ (accessed 7 October 2005).

Clatworthy, Stewart. "Impacts of the 1985 Amendments to the Indian Act on First Nations Populations." In *Aboriginal Conditions: Research as a Foundation for Public Policy,* eds. Jerry P. White, Paul S. Maxim, and Dan Beavon. Vancouver: University of British Columbia Press, 2003.

Coates, K.S., and W.R. Morrison. "More Than a Matter of Blood: The Federal Government, the Churches and the Mixed Blood Populations of the Yukon and the Mackenzie River Valley, 1890–1950." In *1885 and After: Native Society in Transition,* eds. Laurie F. Barron and James Waldram. Proceedings of the Canadian Plains Conference, University of Saskatchewan, Saskatoon, SK, May 1985. Regina: Canadian Plains Research Center, 1986.

Common Weal. "About." http://www.commonweal-arts/about (accessed 29 April 2005).

CTV News. "Aboriginals promised $5 billion to solve poverty." 26 November 2005. http://www.ctv.ca/servlet/ArticleNews/story/CTVNews/20051125/native_summit_051125?s_name=election2006&no_ads= (accessed 13 January 2006).

Culhane, Dara. *The Pleasure of the Crown: Anthropology, Law and First Nations.* Vancouver: Talonbooks, 1998.

Culleton, Beatrice. *In Search of April Raintree.* Winnipeg: Peguis, 1992. First published in 1983 by Pemmican Publications.

Culleton Mosionier, Beatrice. *In Search of April Raintree: Critical Edition.* Ed. Cheryl Suzack. Winnipeg: Peguis, 1999.

_____. "The Special Time." In *In Search of April Raintree: Critical Edition*, by Beatrice Culleton Mosionier. Ed. Cheryl Suzack. Winnipeg: Peguis, 1999.

Cumming, Peter. "'The Only Dirty Book': The Rape of *April Raintree*." In *In Search of April Raintree: Critical Edition*, by Beatrice Culleton Mosionier. Ed. Cheryl Suzack. Winnipeg: Peguis, 1999.

Damm, Kateri. "Says Who: Colonialism, Identity and Defining Indigenous Literature." In *Looking at the Words of our People: First Nations Analysis of Literature*, ed. Jeannette C. Armstrong. Penticton: Theytus, 1993.

Daniels, Harry W. *We Are the New Nation: Nous Sommes La Nouvelle Nation.* Ottawa: Native Council of Canada, 1979.

David, Jennifer. *Story Keepers: Conversations with Aboriginal Writers.* Owen Sound, ON: Ningwakwe Learning Press, 2004.

De Santos, Solange. "Court Rules Churches Still Liable for Abuse." *Anglican Journal*, December 2005. http://anglicanjournal.com/131/10/canada05.html (accessed 20 January 2006).

Devine, Heather. *The People Who Own Themselves: Aboriginal Ethnogenesis in a Canadian Family, 1660–1900.* Calgary: University of Calgary Press, 2004.

Diamond, David. Concluding remarks. *Gimme the Keys.* Dir. David Diamond, assisted by Lori Whiteman and Kevin Parisien. Scott Collegiate Auditorium, Regina, SK, 6 February 2005.

_____. "*Out of the Silence*: Headlines Theatre and Power Plays." In *Playing Boal: Theatre, Therapy, Activism*, eds. Mady Schutzman and Jan Cohen-Cruz. London and New York: Routledge, 1994.

Dickason, Olive Patricia. *Canada's First Nations: A History of Founding Peoples from Earliest Times.* 2nd ed. Don Mills: Oxford University Press, 1997.

Dobbin, Murray. *The One-And-A-Half Men.* Vancouver: New Star, 1981.

Dreaver, Alvina. "Why My Dad Went To Jail." In *"… And They Told Us Their Stories,"* eds. Jack Funk and Gordon Lobe. Saskatoon: Saskatoon District Tribal Council, 1991.

Dreaver, Chief Joseph. "Far Short of Expectations." In *"… And They Told Us Their Stories,"* eds. Jack Funk and Gordon Lobe. Saskatoon: Saskatoon District Tribal Council, 1991.

Dudek, Debra. "Begin With the Text: Aboriginal Literatures and Postcolonial Theories." In *Creating Community: A Roundtable on Aboriginal Literatures*, eds. Renate Eigenbrod and Jo-Ann Episkenew. Penticton: Theytus, 2001.

Dumont, Marilyn. *A Really Good Brown Girl.* London: Brick, 1996.

_____. "Popular Images of Nativeness." In *Looking at the Words of our People: First Nations Analysis of Literature*, ed. Jeannette C. Armstrong. Penticton: Theytus, 1993.

Duran, Eduardo, and Bonnie Duran. *Native American Postcolonial Psychology.* Albany: State University of New York Press, 1995.

Dusenberry, Verne. "Waiting for a day that never comes: The disposed métis of Montana." In *The New Peoples: Being and Becoming Métis in North America*, eds. Jacqueline Peterson and Jennifer H. Brown. Lincoln: University of Nebraska Press, 1985.

Edwards, Peter. *One Dead Indian: The Premier, the Police and the Ipperwash Crisis*. Toronto: McLelland and Stewart, 2003.

Egan, Susan. "Telling Trauma: Generic Dissonance in the Production of *Stolen Life*." *Canadian Literature* 167 (Winter 2000): 10–29.

Eigenbrod, Renate. "'Don't Fence Me In': Insider-Outsider Boundaries In and Around Indigenous Literatures." In *Connections: Non-Native Responses to Native Canadian Literature*, eds. Harmut Lutz and Coomi S. Vevaina. New Dehli: Creative Books, 2003.

_____. "Not Just a Text: 'Indigenizing' the Study of Indigenous Literatures." In *Creating Community: A Roundtable on Aboriginal Literatures*, eds. Renate Eigenbrod and Jo-Ann Episkenew, 69–88. Penticton: Theytus, 2001.

_____. *Travelling Knowledges: Positioning the Im/Migrant Reader of Aboriginal Literatures in Canada*. Winnipeg: University of Manitoba Press, 2005.

Elias, Peter Douglas. *The Dakota of the Canadian Northwest*. Regina: Canadian Plains Research Center, 2002.

Emberley, Julia V. *Defamiliarizing the Aboriginal: Cultural Practices and Decolonization in Canada*. Toronto: University of Toronto Press, 2007.

_____. *Thresholds of Difference: Feminist Critique, Native Women's Writings, Postcolonial Theory*. Toronto: University of Toronto Press, 1993.

Ens, Gerhard J. *Homeland to Hinterland: The Changing Worlds of the Red River Metis in the Nineteenth Century*. Toronto: University of Toronto Press, 1996.

Episkenew, Jo-Ann. "Aboriginal policy through literary eyes." *Inroads: A Journal of Opinion* 10 (2001): 123–136.

_____. "Living and Dying with the Madness of Colonial Policies: The Aesthetics of Resistance in Daniel David Moses' *Almighty Voice and His Wife*." In *What is Your Place? Indigeneity and Immigration in Canada*, ed. Harmut Lutz with Thomas Rafico Ruiz. Beiträge zur Kanadistik, Band 14. Shriftenreihe der Gesselschaft für Kanada-Studien. Augsburg: Wißner-Verlag, 2007.

_____. "Socially Responsible Criticism: Aboriginal Literature, Ideology, and the Literary Canon." In *Creating Community: A Roundtable on Aboriginal Literatures*, eds. Renate Eigenbrod and Jo-Ann Episkenew. Penticton: Theytus, 2001.

Erikson, Kai. "Notes on Trauma and Community." In *Trauma: Explorations in Memory*, ed. Cathy Caruth. Baltimore and London: John Hopkins University Press, 1995.

Ermine, Willie. Address. Indigenous Peoples' Health Research Centre Advance. Waskesiu, SK, 26 January 2005.

Fagan, Kristina. *Laughing to Survive: Humour in Contemporary Canadian Native Literature*. PhD diss., University of Toronto, 2001.

_____. "'What about you?' Approaching the Study of 'Native Literature.'" In *Creating Community: A Roundtable on Aboriginal Literatures*, eds. Renate Eigenbrod and Jo-Ann Episkenew. Penticton: Theytus, 2001.

Fanon, Frantz. "On National Culture." In *Colonial Discourse and Post-colonial Theory: A Reader*, eds. Patrick Williams and Laura Chrisman. New York: Columbia University Press, 1994.

Farrell Racette, Sherry. *Sewing Ourselves Together: Clothing, Decorative Arts and the Expression of Metis and Halfbreed Identity*. PhD diss., University of Manitoba, 2004.

_____. "The Problematization of Metis Identity: Theoretical/Historical Questions and Personal Reflections." Unpublished Essay. 1999.

Favel Starr, Floyd. "The Artificial Tree: Native Performance Culture Research 1991–1996." *Canadian Theatre Review* 90 (Spring 1997): 83–85.

Fee, Margery. "Aboriginal Writing in Canada and the Anthology of Commodity." In *Native North America: Critical and Cultural Perspectives*, ed. Renee Hulan, 135–155. Toronto: ECW, 1999.

_____. "Deploying Identity in the Face of Racism." In *In Search of April Raintree: Critical Edition*, by Beatrice Culleton Mosionier. Ed. Cheryl Suzack. Winnipeg: Peguis, 1999.

_____. Introduction. *Canadian Literature* 161/162 (Summer/Autumn 1999): 9–11.

_____. "Reading Aboriginal Lives." *Canadian Literature* 167 (Winter 2000): 5–7.

_____. "Upsetting Fake Ideas: Jeannette Armonstrong's *Slash* and Beatrice Culleton's *In Search of April Raintree*." *Canadian Literature* 124–5 (Spring Summer 1990): 168–80.

_____. "Who Can Write as Other?" In *The Post-Colonial Studies Reader*, eds. Bill Ashcroft, Garreth Griffiths, and Helen Tiffin. London and New York: Routledge, 1995.

Finlay, Len. "Always Indigenize! The Radical Humanities in the Postcolonial Canadian University." *ARIEL* 31: 1–2 (2000): 307–26.

_____. "Intend for a Nation." *English Studies in Canada* 30, 2 (June 2004): 39–48.

Fireman, Gary D., Ted E. McVay, Jr., and Owen J. Flanagan, eds. Introduction. *Narrative and Consciousness: Literature, Psychology, and the Brain*. Oxford: Oxford University Press, 2003.

"First Ministers and National Aboriginal Leaders Strengthening Relationships and Closing the Gap." 24–25 November 2005. http://www.scics.gc.ca/cinfo05/800044004_e.pdf (accessed 17 June 2008).

Forbes, Jack D. *A World Ruled by Cannibals: The Wetiko Disease of Aggression, Violence and Imperialism*. Davis, CA: D-Q University Press, 1979.

Fortier, Mary. *Behind Closed Doors: A Survivor's Story of the Boarding School Syndrome*. Belleville: Epic Press, 2002.

Foucault, Michel. *Power/Knowledge: Selected Interviews and Other Writings*. New York: Pantheon, 1980.

_____. "The Body of the Condemned." In *The Foucault Reader*, ed. Paul Rabinow. New York: Pantheon, 1984.

_____. "Docile Bodies." In *The Foucault Reader*, ed. Paul Rabinow. New York: Pantheon, 1984.

_____. "The Means of Correct Training." In *The Foucault Reader*, ed. Paul Rabinow. New York: Pantheon, 1984.

Fournier, Suzanne, and Ernie Crey. *Stolen From Our Embrace: The Abduction of First Nations Children and the Restoration of Aboriginal Communities*. Vancouver: Douglas and McIntyre, 1997.

Francis, Daniel. *The Imaginary Indian: The Image of the Indian in Canadian Culture*. Vancouver: Arsenal Pulp Press, 1992.

Freedman, Jill, and Gene Combs. *Narrative Therapy: The Social Construction of Preferred Realities*. New York: Norton, 1996.

Freeman, Mark. "Rethinking the Fictive, Reclaiming the Real: Autobiography, Narrative Time, and the Burden of Truth." In *Narrative and Consciousness: Literature, Psychology, and the Brain*, eds. Gary D. Fireman, Ted E. McVay, Jr., and Owen J. Flanagan. Oxford: Oxford University Press, 2003.

Freire, Paolo. *Pedagogy of the Oppressed*. 1970. Trans. Myra Bergman Ramos. New York: Continuum, 1981.

Frideres, James S. *Aboriginal Peoples in Canada: Contemporary Conflicts*. 5th ed. Scarborough: Prentice Hall, 1998.

Friesen, John W. *The Riel/Real Story*. Ottawa: Borealis, 1994.

Friesen, John W., and Virginia Lyons Friesen. *We Are Included: The Métis People of Canada Realize Riel's Vision*. Calgary: Detselig Enterprises, 2004.

Frink, Lisa, Rita S. Shepard, and Gregory A. Reinhardt, eds. *Many Faces of Gender: Roles and Relationships Through Time in Indigenous Communities*. Calgary: University of Calgary Press, 2002.

Frum, David. "Natives Should Do the Thanking: The European Settlement Of North America Aided Their Lifestyle." *Financial Post*, 13 January 1998. http://sisis.nativeweb.org/clark/jan0898cli.html (accessed 11 January 2006).

Garro, Linda C., and Cheryl Mattingly. "Narrative as Construct and Construction." In *Narrative and Cultural Construction of Illness and Healing*, eds. Cheryl Mattingly and Linda C. Garro. Berkeley: University of California Press, 2000.

Gergen, Kenneth J., and Mary M. Gergen. *Social Psychology*. New York: Harcourt Brace Jovanovich, 1981.

Giraud, Marcel. *The Métis of the Canadian West*. 2 vols. Trans. George Woodcock. Edmonton: University of Alberta Press, 1986.

Goble, Deborah. "Healing Through Theatre." CBC Archives. 26 March 1999. http://archives.cbc.ca/IDC-1-70-692-4010/disasters_tragedies/residential_schools/clip8 (accessed 26 April 2006).

Godard, Barbara. "The Politics of Representation: Some Native Candian Women Writers." *Canadian Literature* 124–5 (Spring–Summer 1990): 183–225.

_____. *Talking About Ourselves: The Literary Productions of the Native Women of Canada*. Ottawa: Canadian Research Institute for the Advancement of Women, 1985.

Gold, Joseph. "Biography as Fiction: The Art of Invisible Authorship." In *Reflections: Autobiography and Canadian Literature*. Ed. K.P. Stich. Ottawa: University of Ottawa Press, 1988.

_____. *Read For Your Life: Literature as a Life Support System*. Markham: Fitzhenry and Whiteside, 2001.

_____. "The Function of Fiction: A Biological Model." In *Why the Novel Matters: A Postmodern Perplex*, eds. Mark Spilka and Caroline McCracken-Flesher. Bloomington: Indiana University Press, 1990.

_____. *The Story Species: Our Life-Literature Connection*. Markham: Fitzhenry and Whiteside, 2002.

Goldie, Terry. *Fear and Temptation: The Image of the Indigene in Canadian, Australian, and New Zealand Literatures*. Montreal and Kingston: McGill-Queen's University Press, 1989.

Goodwill, Ken. "Overview of Indigenous Higher Education." Lecture, University 100-S01, First Nations University of Canada, Regina, SK, 27 January 2004.

Gopalan, Kamala. "Writing the Coloured Body and Ambivalent Identity in Beatrice Culleton's *In Search of April Raintree*." In *Connections: Non-Native Responses to Native Canadian Literature*, eds. Hartmut Lutz and Coomi S. Vevaina. New Dehli: Creative Books, 2003.

Gosselin, Mike. "Sask Native Theatre production reveals housing scandals." *Eagle Feather News*, November 2005, p. 11.

Goulet, Linda. *Creating Culturally Meaningful Learning Environments: Teacher Actions to Engage Aboriginal Students*. PhD diss., University of Regina, 2005.

Graham, Elizabeth, comp. *The Mush Hole: Life at Two Indian Residential Schools*. Waterloo, ON: Heffle Publishing, 1997.

Grant, Agnes. "Abuse and Violence: April Raintree's Human Rights (if she had any)." In *In Search of April Raintree: Critical Edition*, by Beatrice Culleton Mosionier. Ed. Cheryl Suzack. Winnipeg: Peguis, 1999.

_____. "Contemporary Native Women's Voices in Literature." *Canadian Literature* 124–5 (Spring–Summer 1990): 124–32.

_____. "'Great Stories Are Told': Canadian Native Novelists." In *Native North America: Critical and Cultural Perspectives*, ed. Renee Hulan. Toronto: ECW Press, 1999.

_____. *No End of Grief: Indian Residential Schools in Canada*. Winnipeg: Pemmican Publications, 1996.

Graveline, Fyre Jean. *Healing Wounded Hearts*. Halifax: Fernwood Publishing, 2003.

Guelph NDP, *Tom King: Guelph's National Voice*, http://www.tomking.ca (accessed 10 June 2008).

Guimond, Eric. "Changing Ethnicity: The Concept of Ethnic Drifters." In *Aboriginal Conditions: Research as a Foundation for Public Policy*, eds. Jerry P. White, Paul S. Maxim, and Dan Beavon. Vancouver: University of British Columbia Press, 2003.

_____. "Fuzzy Definitions and Population Explosion: Changing Identities of Aboriginal Groups in Canada." In *Not Strangers in These Parts. Urban Aboriginal Peoples*, eds. David Newhouse and Evelyn Peters. Proceedings of the Aboriginal Policy Research Conference, November 2002, University of Western Ontario. Ottawa: Government of Canada, 2004.

Halfe, Louise Bernice. *Bear Bones and Feathers*. Regina: Coteau Books, 1994.

_____. *Blue Marrow*. Regina: Coteau Books, 2004.

Hamer, John, and Jack Steinberg. *Alcohol and Native Peoples of the North*. Washington: University Press of America, 1980.

Hampton, Eber. Address. Indigenous Peoples' Health Research Centre Advance, Waskesiu, SK, 26 January 2005.

_____. Address. Indigenous Peoples' Health Research Centre Advance, Watrous, SK, 26 September 2005.

Harding, Jim, Yussuf Kly, and Dianne MacDonald. *Overcoming Systemic Discrimination Against Aboriginal People in Saskatchewan: Brief to the Indian Justice Review Committee and the Metis Justice Review Committee*. November 1991. Regina: Prairie Justice Research, 1992.

Harjo, Joy, and Gloria Bird. Introduction. *Reinventing the Enemy's Language: Contemporary Native Women's Writings of North America*, eds. Joy Harjo and Gloria Bird. New York: Norton, 1997.

Harishankar, V. Bharanthi. "Motherhood as Counter Discourse in Beatrice Culleton's *In Search of April Raintree*." In *Connections: Non-Native Responses to Native Canadian Literature*, eds. Hartmut Lutz and Coomi S. Vevaina. New Dehli: Creative Books, 2003.

Harper, Hillary. Remarks. Community Based Research and Aboriginal Women's Health and Healing, University of Saskatchewan, Saskatoon, SK, 29 November 2004.

Harris, Judith. *Signifying Pain: Constructing and Healing The Self through Writing*. Albany: State University of New York Press, 2003.

Hart, Michael. "An Ethnographic Study of Sharing Circles." In *Aboriginal Health, Identity and Resources*, eds. Jill Oakes, Rick Riewe, Skip Koolage, Leanne Simpson, and Nancy Schuster. Winnipeg: Native Studies Press, University of Manitoba, 2000.

Hatt, Ken. "The North-West Rebellion Scrip Commissions, 1885–1889." In *1885 and After: Native Society in Transition*, ed. Laurie F. Barron and James Waldram. Proceedings of the Canadian Plains Conference, University of Saskatchewan, Saskatoon, SK, May 1985. Regina: Canadian Plains Research Center, 1986.

Headlines Theatre for Living. "History of Headlines Theatre." http://www.headlinestheatre.com/history1.htm; http://www.headlinestheatre.com/history2.htm (accessed 7 April 2005).

Heillig Morris, Roma. "The Whole Story: Nature, Healing, and Narrative in the Native American Wisdom Tradition." *Literature and Medicine* 15, 1 (1996): 94–111.

Heiss, Anita. "Aboriginal Identity and Its Effects on Writing." In *(Ad)dressing Our Words: Aboriginal Perspectives on Aboriginal Literatures*, ed. Armand Garnet Ruffo. Penticton: Theytus, 2001.

Hepworth, H. Philip. *Foster Care and Adoption in Canada*. Ottawa: Canadian Council on Social Development, 1980.

Higham, C.L. *Noble, Wretched, and Redeemable: Protestant Missionaries to the Indians in Canada and the United States, 1820–1900.* Calgary: University of Calgary Press, 2000.

Hill, Barbara Helen. *Shaking the Rattle: Healing the Trauma of Colonization.* Penticton: Theytus, 1995.

hooks, bell. *Yearning: Race, Gender, and Cultural Politics.* Boston: South End, 1990.

Hoy, Helen. *How Should I Read These? Native Women Writers in Canada.* Toronto: University of Toronto Press, 2001.

———. "'Nothing But the Truth': Discursive Transparency in Beatrice Culleton." In *In Search of April Raintree: Critical Edition,* by Beatrice Culleton Mosionier. Ed. Cheryl Suzack. Winnipeg: Peguis, 1999.

———. "'When You Admit You're a Thief, Then You Can Be Honourable': Native/Non-Native Collaboration in *The Book of Jessica.*" *Canadian Literature* 136 (Spring 1993): 24–39.

Hudson, Peter, and Brad McKenzie. "Child Welfare and Native People: The Extension of Colonialism." *Social Worker* 49, 2 (1981).

Ing, N. Rosalyn. *Dealing with Shame and Unresolved Trauma: Residential School and Its Impact on the 2ⁿᵈ and 3ʳᵈ Generation Adults.* PhD diss., University of British Columbia, 2000.

Isernhagen, Hartwig. *Momaday, Vizenor, Armstrong: Conversations on American Indian Writing.* Norman: University of Oklahoma Press, 1999.

Jaimes-Guerrero, Marianette. "Savage Erotica Exotica: Media Imagery of Native Women in North America." In *Native North America: Critical and Cultural Perspectives,* ed. Renee Hulan. Toronto: ECW Press, 1999.

Jaine, Linda, ed. *Residential Schools: The Stolen Years.* Saskatoon: University of Saskatchewan Extension Press, 1993.

Jaine, Linda, and Drew Taylor, eds. *Voices: Being Native in Canada.* Saskatoon: University of Saskatchewan Extension Press, 1992.

Jennings, John. "The North West Mounted Police and Indian Policy After the 1885 Rebellion." In *1885 and After: Native Society in Transition,* eds. Laurie F. Barron and James Waldram. Proceedings of the Canadian Plains Conference, University of Saskatchewan, Saskatoon, SK, May 1985. Regina: Canadian Plains Research Center, 1986.

Johnston, Basil H. *Indian School Days.* Norman: University of Oklahoma Press, 1988.

———. "One Generation from Extinction." In *An Anthology of Canadian Native Literature in English,* eds. Daniel David Moses and Terry Goldie. 3ʳᵈ ed. Toronto: Oxford University Press, 2005.

———. Preface. *Magic Weapons: Aboriginal Writers Remaking Community After Residential School,* by Sam McKegney. Winnipeg: University of Manitoba Press, 2007.

Johnston, Patrick. *Native Children and the Child Welfare System.* Toronto: Canadian Council on Social Development and Lorimer, 1983.

Kelly, Jennifer. "'You Can't Get Angry with a Person's Life': Negotiating Aboriginal Women's Writing, Whiteness, and Multicultural Nationalism in a University Classroom." In *Creating Community: A Roundtable on Aboriginal Literatures,* eds. Renate Eigenbrod and Jo-Ann Episkenew. Penticton: Theytus, 2001.

Kimelman, Edwin C., et al. *No Quiet Place: Review Committee on Indian and Metis Adoptions and Placements.* Winnipeg: Manitoba Department of Community Services, 1985.

King, Thomas. "Godzilla vs. Post-Colonial." *World Literature Written in English* 30, 2 (1990): 10–16.

———. Introduction. *All My Relations: An Anthology of Canadian Native Fiction,* ed. Thomas King. Toronto: McLelland and Stewart, 1990.

———. *The Truth About Stories: A Native Narrative.* Toronto: Anansi, 2003.

King, Thomas, Cheryl Calver, and Helen Hoy, eds. *The Native in Literature: Canadian and Comparative Perspectives.* Toronto: ECW Press, 1987.

Kimpson, Sally A. "Stepping Off the Road: A Narrative (of) Inquiry." In *Research As Resistance: Critical, Indigenous, and Anti-Oppressive Practices*, eds. Leslie Brown and Susan Strega. Toronto: Canadian Scholars Press, 2005.

Kipling, Rudyard. "The White Man's Burden." *McClure's Magazine*, 12 February 1899, http://wwwf. countryday.net/facstf/us/hammondk/MEH/White% 20Mans%20Burden%20and%20Criticism.doc (accessed 15 April 2008).

Krauss, Clifford. "Capone May Have slept Here, Too, Canada Town Says." *New York Times*, 16 November 2004, http://www.nytimes.com/2004/11/16/ international/americas/16moosejaw. html?oref=regi (accessed 20 November 2004).

Lanser, Susan Sniader. *Fictions of Authority: Women Writers and Narrative Voice.* Ithaca: Cornell University Press, 1992.

LaRocque, Emma. "Aboriginal Literatures: Aesthetics of Resistance." Keynote address. Canadian Association of Commonwealth Literatures and Language Studies at the Congress of Humanities and Social Sciences, University of Manitoba, 30 May 2004.

_____. *Defeathering the Indian.* Agincourt: Book Society of Canada, 1975.

_____. "Teaching Aboriginal Literature: The Discourse of Margins and Mainstreams." In *Creating Community: A Roundtable on Aboriginal Literatures*, eds. Renate Eigenbrod and Jo-Ann Episkenew. Penticton: Theytus, 2001.

_____. "The Metis in English Canadian Literature." *Canadian Journal of Native Studies* 3, 1 (1983): 85–94. http://www.brandonu.ca/Library/CJNS/3.1/laroque.pdf (accessed 14 January 2006).

Lavoie, André. "Native Theatre: Affirmation and Creation." Trans. Andrée McNamara Tait. *National Theatre School of Canada Journal* 24 (2004). http://www.ent-nts.qc.ca/journal/j24p08_theatre-society.htm (accessed 26 April 2005).

Lawrence, Bonita. *"Real" Indians and Others: Mixed-Blood Urban Native Peoples and Indigenous Nationhood.* Vancouver: University of British Columbia Press, 2004.

Legacy of Hope Foundation. *Where Are the Children? Healing the Legacy of the Residential Schools.* http://www.wherearethechildren.ca (accessed 27 April 2005).

Lenze, Christine. "'The Whole Thing You're Doing Is White Man's Ways': fareWel's Northern Tour." *Canadian Theatre Review* 108 (2001). http://www.utpjournals.com/product/ctr/108/108_ Lenze.html (accessed 10 June 2005).

Logan, Tricia. "A Métis Perspective on Truth and Reconciliation." In *From Truth to Reconciliation: Transforming the Legacy of Residential Schools*, eds. Marlene Brant Castellano, Linda Archibald, and Mike DeGagné. Ottawa: Aboriginal Healing Foundation, 2008.

Long, David Alan, and Olive Patricia Dickason, eds. *Visions of the Heart: Canadian Aboriginal Issues.* Toronto: Harcourt Brace, 1996.

Long, John S. "Treaty No. 9 and fur trade company families: Northeastern Ontario's halfbreeds, Indians, petitioners and métis." In *The New Peoples: Being and Becoming Métis in North America*, eds. Jacqueline Peterson and Jennifer H. Brown. Lincoln: University of Nebraska Press, 1985.

Loyie, Oskiniko Larry. "Ora Pro Nobis (Pray for Us)." In *Two Plays About Residential School.* Vancouver: Living Traditions, 1998.

Lundgren, Jodi. "'Being a Half-breed': Discourses of Race and Cultural Syncreticity in the Works of Metis Women Writers." *Canadian Literature* 144 (Spring 1995): 62–77.

Lussier, Antoine S., and D. Bruce Sealey, eds. *The Other Natives: the-les Métis.* Vol. 2. Winnipeg: Manitoba Métis Federation Press, 1978.

Lutz, Hartmut. *Approaches: Essays in Native North American Studies and Literatures.* Augsburg: Wißner-Verlag, 2002.

_____. "Canadian Multicultural Literatures: Ethnic Minorities and 'alterNatives,'" in *Contemporary Challenges: Conversations with Canadian Native Authors*, ed. Hartmut Lutz. Saskatoon: Fifth House, 1991.

_____. "Howard Adams (1921–2001): Profound Thinker, Fearless Activist, Cherished Friend." In *Connections: Non-Native Responses to Native Canadian Literature*, eds. Hartmut Lutz and Coomi S. Vevaina. New Dehli: Creative Books, 2003.

_____. "Natives within as Seen from Without: Ten Theses on German Perspectives on the Literature of Canada's First Nations." In *Native North America: Critical and Cultural Perspectives*, ed. Renee Hulan. Toronto: ECW Press, 1999.

Malloy, Jonathon. *Between Colliding Worlds: The Ambiguous Existence of Government Agencies for Aboriginal and Women's Policy*. Toronto: University of Toronto Press, 2003.

Manitoba. The Aboriginal Justice Implementation Committee. *The Death of John Joseph Harper. Vol. 3 of Report of the Aboriginal Justice Inquiry of Manitoba*. 3 Vols. November 1999. http://www.ajic.mb.ca/volumelll/toc.html (accessed 13 January 2006).

_____. *The Report of the Aboriginal Justice Inquiry of Manitoba*. By Paul L.A.H. Chartrand, Wendy Whitecloud, Eva McKay, and Doris Young. November 1999. http://www.ajic.mb.ca/volumel/chapter4.html#5 (accessed 29 June 2001).

Manossa, Geraldine. "The Beginning of Cree Performance Culture." In *(Ad)dressing Our Words: Aboriginal Perspectives on Aboriginal Literatures*, ed. Armand Garnet Ruffo. Penticton: Theytus, 2001.

Manuel, G., and M. Posluns. *The Fourth World: An Indian Reality*. Don Mills: Collier Macmillan Canada, 1974.

Manuel, Vera, with Peter Morin. "Letting go of Trauma On and Off Stage." *RedwireMag.Com* 7.1. http://redwiremag.com/lettinggooftrauma.htm (accessed 20 October 2005).

_____. "Strength of Indian Women." In *Two Plays About Residential School*. Vancouver: Living Traditions, 1998.

Maracle, Brian. *Crazywater: Native Voices on Addition and Recovery*. Toronto: Penguin, 1993.

Maracle, Lee. *Bobby Lee, Indian Rebel*. Toronto: Women's Press, 1990.

_____. *Sojourner's Truth and Other Stories*. Vancouver: Press Gang, 1990.

_____. *I Am Woman: A Native Perspective on Sociology and Feminism*. North Vancouver: Write-On, 1988.

Marken, Ron. "'There Is Nothing but White between the Lines': Parallel Colonial Experiences of the Irish and Aboriginal Canadians." In *Native North America: Critical and Cultural Perspectives*, ed. Renee Hulan. Toronto: ECW Press, 1999.

Marsden, Rasunah, ed. *Crisp Blue Edges: Indigenous Creative Non-fiction*. Penticton: Theytus, 2000.

Mazur Teillet, Kathleen. "Children Lost Through Welfare." *Saskatchewan Indian*, May 1980, 11. http://www.sicc.sk.ca/saskindian/a80may11.htm (accessed 25 February 2004).

McAdams, Dan P. *The Stories We Live By: Personal Myths and the Making of the Self*. New York: Guilford, 1993.

McIntosh, Peggy. "White Privilege: Unpacking the Invisible Napsack." *Independent School* (Winter 1990). http://www.case.edu/president/aaction/UnpackingThe Knapsack.pdf (accessed 11 May 2008).

McKegney, Sam. *Magic Weapons: Aboriginal Writers Remaking Community After Residential School*. Winnipeg: University of Manitoba Press, 2007.

_____. *Reclamations of the "dis-possessed": Narratives of Survivance by Indigenous Survivors of Canada's Residential Schools*. PhD diss., Queen's University, 2005.

McKenzie, Stephanie M. *Canada's Day of Atonement: The Contemporary Native Literary Renaissance, The Native Cultural Renaissance and Postcentenary Canadian Mythology*. PhD diss., University of Toronto, 2001. http://www.collectionscanada.ca/obj/s4/f2/dsk3/ftp04/NQ58966.pd (accessed 23 November 2004).

_____. *Before the Country: Native Renaissance, Canadian Mythology*. Toronto: University of Toronto Press, 2007.

McLean, Don. *Fifty Historical Vignettes: Views of the Common People*. Regina: Gabriel Dumont Institute and Publication Associates, 1987.

_____. *Home From the Hill· A History of the Metis in Western Canada*. Regina: Gabriel Dumont Institute, 1987.

McLeod, Neal. *Cree Narrative Memory: From Treaties to Contemporary Times*. Saskatoon: Purich, 2008.

_____. "Coming Home Through Stories." In *(Ad)dressing Our Words: Aboriginal Perspectives on Aboriginal Literatures*, ed. Armand Garnet Ruffo. Penticton: Theytus, 2001.

_____. *Songs to Kill a Wihtikow*. Regina: Hagios, 2007.

Mikulincer, Mario. *Human Learned Helplessness: A Coping Perspective*. New York: Plenum, 1994.

Miller, J.R. *Shingwauk's Vision: A History of Native Residential Schools*. Toronto: University of Toronto Press, 1996.

Milloy, John S. *A National Crime: The Canadian Government and the Residential School System— 1879 to 1986*. Winnipeg: University of Manitoba Press, 1999.

Mitchell, Terry L., and Dawn T. Maracle. "Post-Traumatic Stress and the Health Status of Aboriginal Populations in Canada." *Journal of Aboriginal Health* 2, 1 (2005): 14–25.

Mojica, Monique. "Postcolonial Traumatic Stress Syndrome: Ethno Stress." Address. Association of Canadian College and University Teachers of English Conference at the Congress of Humanities of Social Sciences, University of Ottawa, 30 May 1998.

_____. "Stories from the Body: Blood Memory and Organic Texts." Keynote address. Canadian Association of Commonwealth Literatures and Language Studies Conference at the Congress of Humanities and Social Sciences, University of Western Ontario, 30 May 2005.

_____. "Theatrical Diversity on Turtle Island: A tool towards the healing." *Canadian Theatre Review* 68 (1991): 3.

Mojica, Monique, and Ric Knowles. Introduction. *Staging Coyote's Dream: An Anthology of First Nations Drama in English*, eds. Monique Mojica and Rick Knowles. Toronto: Playwrights Canada Press, 2003.

Monture Angus, Patricia. "Native America and the Literary Tradition." In *Native North America: Critical and Cultural Perspectives*, ed. Renee Hulan. Toronto: ECW Press, 1999.

Moran, Bridget. *A Little Rebellion*. Vancouver: Arsenal Press, 1992.

Morris, David B. "Success Stories: Narrative, Pain, and the Limits of Storylessness." In *Narrative, Pain, and Suffering*, eds. Daniel B. Carr, John D. Loeser, and David B. Morris. Vol. 34 of *Progress in Pain Research and Management*. Seattle: IASP Press, 2005.

Moses, Daniel David. *Almighty Voice and His Wife*. Toronto: Playwrights Canada Press, 1991.

_____. "A Syphilitic Western: Making 'The…Medicine Shows.'" In *(Ad)dressing Our Words: Aboriginal Perspectives on Aboriginal Literatures*, ed. Armand Garnet Ruffo. Penticton: Theytus, 2001.

_____. "How My Ghosts Got Pale Faces." In *Speaking for the Generations: Native Writers on Writing*, ed. Simon J. Ortiz. Tucson: University of Arizona Press, 1998.

_____. *The Indian Medicine Shows: Two One-Act Plays*. Toronto: Exile Editions, 2002.

_____. "The Trickster's Laugh: My Meeting with Tomson and Lenore." *American Indian Quarterly* 28, 1/2 (2004): 110–1.

_____. "Write About Now: A Monologue in Changing Lights." *Canadian Theatre Review* 65 (1990): 46–48.

Moses, Daniel David, and Terry Goldie. Preface to First Edition: Two Voices. In *An Anthology of Canadian Native Literature in English*, eds. Daniel David Moses and Terry Goldie. 3rd ed. Toronto: Oxford University Press, 2005.

Mudrooroo. "White Forms, Aboriginal Content." In *The Post-Colonial Studies Reader*, eds. Bill Ashcroft, Garreth Griffiths, and Helen Tiffin. London and New York: Routledge, 1995.

Mukherjee, Arun P. "Ideology in the Classroom: A Case Study in the Teaching of English Literature in Canadian Universities." In *The Post-Colonial Studies Reader*, eds. Bill Ashcroft, Garreth Griffiths, and Helen Tiffin. London and New York: Routledge, 1995.

Mussell, W.J. (Bill). *Warrior-Caregivers: Understanding the Challenges and Healing of First Nations Men*. Ottawa: Aboriginal Healing Foundation, 2005.

National Aboriginal Achievement Awards. "National Aboriginal Achievement Awards Recipients." http://www.naaf.ca/html/past_recipients_e.html (accessed 19 June 2008).

National Indian Brotherhood/Assembly of First Nations. *Indian Control of Indian Education: A Policy Paper presented to the Minister of Indian Affairs and Northern Development*. 1972. http://www.afn.ca/Programs/Education/Indian%20Control%20of%20Indian%20Education.pdf>2001 (accessed 26 April 2004).

Nelson, Hilde Lindemann. *Damaged Identities: Narrative Repair*. Ithaca and London: Cornell University Press, 2001.

Neu, Dean, and Richard Therrien. *Accounting for Genocide: Canada's Bureaucratic Assault on Aboriginal People*. Black Point: Fernwood, 2003.

New, W.H., ed. *Native Writers and Canadian Writing*. Vancouver: University of British Columbia Press, 1990.

Newhouse, David. "A Tale Twice Told: Academic Freedom and Responsibility and Aboriginal Governments." First Nations Higher Education and The First Nations University of Canada: A Symposium. First Nations University of Canada, Regina, SK, 10 November 2005.

Nicks, Trudy, and Kenneth Morgan. "Grand Cache: The historic development of an indigenous Alberta métis population." In *The New Peoples: Being and Becoming Métis in North America*, eds. Jacqueline Peterson and Jennifer H. Brown. Lincoln: University of Nebraska Press, 1985.

Nock, David A. *A Victorian missionary and Canadian Indian Policy: Cultural Synthesis vs. Cultural Replacement*. Waterloo: Wilfred Laurier University Press, 1988.

Nolan, Yvette, ed. *Dramatic Writing from First Nations Writers and Writers of Colour*. Toronto: Playwrights Canada Press, 2004.

O'Brien, Susie. "'Please Eunice, Don't Be Ignorant': The White Reader as Trickster in Lee Maracle's Fiction." *Canadian Literature* 144 (1995): 78–92.

Ochankugahe. "A Yoke of Oppression." In *". . . And They Told Us Their Stories,"* eds. Jack Funk and Gordon Lobe. Saskatoon: Saskatoon District Tribal Council, 1991.

Ontario. The Honourable Sidney B. Linden's Report of The Ipperwash Inquiry. 30 May 2007. http://www.attorneygeneral.jus.gov.on.ca/inquiries/ipperwash/report/vol_1/pdf/E_Vol_1_Conclusion.pdf (accessed 17 June 2008).

Owen, W.J.B., ed. *Wordsworth's Preface to Lyrical Ballads*. Copenhagen: Rosenkilde and Bagger, 1957.

Owens, Louis. *Other Destinies: Understanding the American Indian Novel*. Norman: University of Oklahoma Press, 1992.

Pacholike, Barb. "Abductions: More awareness urged." *Regina Leader-Post*, 6 January 2006, B2.

Parker, Robert Dale. *The Invention of Native American Literature*. Ithaca: Cornell University Press, 2003.

Payment, Diane. "Batoche After 1885: A Society in Transition." In *1885 and After: Native Society in Transition*, eds. Laurie F. Barron and James Waldram. Proceedings of the Canadian Plains Conference, University of Saskatchewan, Saskatoon, SK, May 1985. Regina: Canadian Plains Research Center, 1986.

Payne, Brenda. "*A Really Good Brown Girl*: Marilyn Dumont's Poems of Grief and Celebration." In *(Ad)dressing Our Words: Aboriginal Perspectives on Aboriginal Literatures*, ed. Armand Garnet Ruffo. Penticton: Theytus, 2001.

Peequaquot, George. "We Missed the Bus." In *Voices Under One Sky: Reflections in Fiction and Non-fiction*, ed. Trish Fox Roman, Scarborough: Nelson, 1994.

Pennebaker, James W. *Opening Up: The Healing Power of Confiding in Others*. 2nd ed. New York: Guilford, 1997.

Perreault, Jeanne. "In Search of Cheryl Raintree, and Her Mother." In *In Search of April Raintree: Critical Edition*, by Beatrice Culleton Mosionier. Ed. Cheryl Suzack. Winnipeg: Peguis, 1999.

_____. "Memory Alive: An Inquiry into the Uses of Memory in Marilyn Dumont, Jeannette Armonstrong, Louise Halfe, and Joy Harjo." In *Native North America: Critical and Cultural Perspectives*, ed. Renee Hulan. Toronto: ECW Press, 1999.

Perreault, Jeanne, and Sylvia Vance, eds. *Writing the Circle: Native Women of Western Canada*. Edmonton: NeWest, 1990.

Peterson, Jacqueline. "Many Roads to Red River: Métis Genesis in the Great Lakes Region, 1680–1815." In *The New Peoples: Being and Becoming Métis in North America*, eds. Jacqueline Peterson and Jennifer H. Brown. Lincoln: University of Nebraska Press, 1985.

Petrone, Penny. *First People, First Voices*. Toronto: University of Toronto Press, 1983.

_____. *Native Literature in Canada from the Oral to the Present*. Toronto: Oxford University Press, 1990.

Porter, Joy, and Kenneth M. Roemer, eds. *The Cambridge Companion to Native American Literature*. Cambridge: Cambridge University Press, 2005.

Proulx, Sharon, and Aruna Srivastava. "A Moose in the Corridor: Teaching English, Aboriginal Pedagogies, and Institutional Resistance." In *Creating Community: A Roundtable on Aboriginal Literatures*, eds. Renate Eigenbrod and Jo-Ann Episkenew. Penticton: Theytus, 2001.

Pulitano, Elvira. *Toward a Native American Critical Theory*. Lincoln: University of Nebraska Press, 2003.

Purich, Donald. *The Metis*. Toronto: Lorimer, 1988.

Quiring, David M. *CCF Colonialism in Northern Saskatchewan: Battling Parish Priests, Bootleggers, and Fur Sharks*. Vancouver: University of British Columbia Press, 2004.

Ray, Arthur J. *I Have Lived Here Since The World Began*. Toronto: Lester, 1996.

Reber, Susanne, and Rob Renaud. *Starlight Tour: The Last, Lonely Night of Neil Stonechild*. Toronto: Random House, 2005.

Reder, Deanna. "Stories of Destruction and Renewal: Images of Fireweed." In *Creating Community: A Roundtable on Aboriginal Literatures*, eds. Renate Eigenbrod and Jo-Ann Episkenew. Penticton: Theytus, 2001.

Rice, Brian, and Anna Snyder. "Reconciliation in the Context of a Settler Society: Healing the Legacy of Colonialism in Canada." In *From Truth to Reconciliation: Transforming the Legacy of Residential Schools*, eds. Marlene Brant Castellano, Linda Archibald, and Mike DeGagné. Ottawa: Aboriginal Healing Foundation, 2008.

Richards, John. "Closing the Aboriginal—Non-Aboriginal Education Gap: A S.I.P.P. Armchair Discussion." Presentation to the Saskatchewan Institute of Public Policy, Regina, SK, 4 March 2008.

_____. "Neighbors Matter: Poor Neighborhoods and Urban Aboriginal Policy." *C.D. Howe Institute Commentary* 156 (2001): 1–38.

Richardson, Boyce. *People of Terra Nullius: Betrayal and Rebirth in Aboriginal Canada*. Vancouver: Douglas and McIntyre, 1993.

Ridington, Robin. "Happy Trails to You: Contexted Discourse and Indian Removals in Thomas King's *Truth and Bright Water*." *Canadian Literature* 167 (2000): 89–107.

Riel, Louis. *Selected Poetry of Louis Riel*. Ed. Glen Campbell. Trans. Paul Savoie. Toronto: Exile Editions, 1993.

Riley, Patricia. "'That Murderin' Halfbreed': The Abjectification of the Mixedblood in Mark Twain's *The Adventures of Tom Sawyer*." In *Native North America: Critical and Cultural Perspectives*, ed. Renee Hulan. Toronto: ECW Press, 1999.

Robertson, Leslie, and Dara Culhane, eds. *In Plain Sight: Reflections on Life in Downtown Eastside Vancouver*. Vancouver: Talonbooks, 2005.

Robinson, Eden. *Monkey Beach*. Toronto: Knopf, 2000.

_____. *Traplines*. Toronto: Knopf, 1996.

Ross, Ian. *fareWel*. Toronto: Scirocco Drama, 1998.

_____. Reading of *fareWel*. *I is for Identity: Looking Beyond the Mirror*. Postcolonial Spring School 2005 on New Literatures in English, Free University, Berlin, 7 April 2005.

_____. *The Gap*. Toronto: Scirocco Drama, 2001.

_____. *The Book of Joe*. Winnipeg: J. Gordon Shillingford, 1999.

Ruffo, Armand Garnet. *At Geronimo's Grave*. Regina: Coteau, 2001.

_____. "A Windigo Tale: Contemporizing and Mythologizing the Residential School Experience." In *Aboriginal Drama and Theatre: Critical Perspectives on Canadian Theatre in English, Volume One*, ed. Robert Appleford. Toronto: Playwrights Canada Press, 2005.

_____. *Grey Owl: The Mystery of Archie Belaney*. Regina: Coteau, 1996.

_____. "Healing Words: Expressing the Poison." Health Colloquium Public Roundtable, Association of Canadian College and University Teachers of English Conference, Congress of Humanities and Social Sciences, University of Ottawa, Ottawa, ON, 30 May 1998.

_____. Introduction. In *(Ad)dressing Our Words: Aboriginal Perspectives on Aboriginal Literatures*, ed. Armand Garnet Ruffo. Penticton: Theytus, 2001.

_____. "Why Native Literature?" In *Native North America: Critical and Cultural Perspectives*, ed. Renee Hulan. Toronto: ECW Press, 1999.

Said, Edward. "Orientalism." In *The Post-Colonial Studies Reader*, eds. Bill Ashcroft, Garreth Griffiths, and Helen Tiffin. London and New York: Routledge, 1995.

Salat, M.F. "Other Word, Other Worlds: Of Ruby Slipperjack." In *Intersexions: Issues of Race and Gender in Canadian Women's Writing*, eds. Coomi S. Vevaina and Barbard Godard. Creative New Literatures Series 7. New Delhi: Creative Books, 1996.

Sawchuk, Joe. *The Dynamic of Native Politics: The Alberta Metis Experience*. Saskatoon: Purich Publishing, 1998.

Sarbadhikary, Krishna. "Of Angels and Dead Indians: Daniel David Moses' *The Indian Medicine Shows*." In *Connections: Non-Native Responses to Native Canadian Literature*, eds. Hartmut Lutz and Coomi S. Vevaina. New Dehli: Creative Books, 2003.

Schaub, Danielle. "Getting In and Out of the Dark Room: Canadian Texts as Neutral Ground for Self-Expression and Empathy in Conflicts." In *Connections: Non-Native Responses to Native Canadian Literature*, eds. Hartmut Lutz and Coomi S. Vevaina. New Dehli: Creative Books, 2003.

Scheff, T.J. *Catharsis in Healing, Ritual, and Drama*. Berkley: University of California Press, 1979.

Schutzman, Mady. "Brechtian Shamanism: The Political Therapy of Augusto Boal." In *Playing Boal: Theatre, Therapy, Activism*, eds. Mady Schutzman and Jan Cohen-Cruz. London and New York: Routledge, 1994.

Schutzman, Mady, and Jan Cohen-Cruz, eds. Introduction. *Playing Boal: Theatre, Therapy, Activism*. London and New York: Routledge, 1994.

Sealy, D. Bruce. *Statutory Land Rights of the Manitoba Metis*. Winnipeg: Manitoba Métis Federation Press, 1975.

Seidlitz, Laurie Shannon. *Native Theatre for the Seventh Generation: On the Path to Cultural Healing*. MA thesis, Dalhousie University, 1994.

Sewell, Anna Marie. "Natives on Native Literature: What do We Rightly Write? Or: Shot Headfirst From the Canon." In *Creating Community: A Roundtable on Aboriginal Literatures*, eds. Renate Eigenbrod and Jo-Ann Episkenew. Penticton: Theytus, 2001.

Shackleton, Mark. "The Trickster Figure in Native North American Writing: From Traditional Storytelling to the Written Word." In *Connections: Non-Native Responses to Native Canadian Literature*, eds. Hartmut Lutz and Coomi S. Vevaina. New Dehli: Creative Books, 2003.

Shepard, R. Bruce. *Deemed Unsuitable: Blacks from Oklahoma move to the Canadian Prairies in Search of Equality in the Early 20th Century only to find Racism in their new Home*. Toronto: Umbrella Press, 1997.

Shipley, Nan. *Almighty Voice and the Red Coats*. 1967. Canada: Burns and MacEarchern, 1974.

Shore, Fred J., and Laurence J. Barkwell, eds. *Past Reflects the Present: The Metis Elders Conference*. Winnipeg: Manitoba Métis Federation, 1997.

Siggins, Maggie. *Bitter Embrace: White Society's Assault on the Woodland Cree*. Toronto: McClelland and Stewart, 2005.

Siggner, Andrew J. "Urban Aboriginal Populations: An Update Using 2001 Census Results." In *Not Strangers in These Parts: Urban Aboriginal Peoples*, eds. David Newhouse and Evelyn Peters. Proceedings of Aboriginal Policy Research Conference, November 2002, University of Western Ontario, London, ON. Ottawa: Government of Canada, 2004.

Slipperjack, Ruby. *Honour the Sun*. Winnipeg: Pemmican, 1987.

_____. *Silent Words*. Saskatoon: Fifth House, 1992.

_____. *Weesquachak and the Lost Ones*. Penticton: Theytus, 2000.

Smith, Linda Tuhiwai. *Decolonizing Methodologies: Research and Indigenous Peoples*. London and New York: Zed, 1999.

Spears, Shandra. "Strong Spirit, Fractured Identity: An Ojibway Adoptee's Journey to Wholeness." In *Strong Women Stories*, eds. Kim Anderson and Bonita Lawrence. Toronto: Sumach Press, 2003.

Spivak, Gayatri Chakravorty. "Can the Subaltern Speak?" In *Colonial Discourse and Post-Colonial Theory: A Reader*, eds. Patrick Williams and Laura Chrisman. New York: Columbia University Press, 1994.

Spry, Irene M. "The métis and mixed-bloods of Rupert's Land before 1870." In *The New Peoples: Being and Becoming Métis in North America*, eds. Jacqueline Peterson and Jennifer H. Brown. Lincoln: University of Nebraska Press, 1985.

Stackhouse, John. "Canada's Apartheid." *Globe and Mail*, 3 November 2001. http://www.theglobeandmail.com/series/apartheid/stories/introduction.html (accessed 7 December 2005).

Stanley Park Ecological Society. "Coyotes: *Canis Latrans*." http://stanleyparkecology.ca/programs/urbanWildlife/naturalHistory/coyote.php (accessed 3 November 2004).

Sterling, Shirley. *My Name is Seepeetza*. Toronto: Groundwood Books, 1992.

St-Onge, Nicole J.M. *Race, Class and Marginality: A Métis Settlement in the Manitoba Interlake, 1850-1914*. PhD diss., University of Manitoba, 1990.

Stokes, Janice, Ian Peach, and Raymond Blake. *Rethinking the Jurisdictional Divide: The Marginalization of Urban Aboriginal Communities and Federal Policy Responses.* Regina: Saskatchewan Institute of Public Policy, 2004.

Stout, Madeleine Dion, Armand Ruffo, Alanis Obomsawin, Richard Wagamese, Monique Mojica, Thomas King, and Katsi Cook. "Native Cultures and the Healing Arts." Health Colloquium Public Roundtable, Association of Canadian College and University Teachers of English Conference, Congress of Humanities and Social Sciences, University of Ottawa, Ottawa, ON, 30 May 1998.

Surtees, Robert J. *Canadian Indian Policy: A Critical Bibliography.* Bloomington: Indiana University Press, 1982.

Suzack, Cheryl. Introduction. In *In Search of April Raintree: Critical Edition*, by Beatrice Culleton Mosionier. Ed. Cheryl Suzack. Winnipeg: Peguis, 1999.

_____. "On the Practical 'Untidiness' of 'Always Indigenizing.'" *English Studies in Canada* 30, 2 (2004): 1–3.

Tafoya, Terry. "Teams, Networks and Clans: The Circle of Support." Epidemics in Our Communities 2005, Regina, SK, 3 February 2005.

_____. "A Little Less Talk and A Lot More Action: The Clan Approach to Cooperation." Epidemics in Our Communities 2005, Regina, SK, 3 February 2005.

Taylor, Drew Hayden. *AlterNatives.* Burnaby: Talonbooks, 2000.

_____. *Buz'Gem Blues.* Vancouver: Talonbooks, 2002.

_____. *Fearless Warriors.* Burnaby: Talonbooks, 1998.

_____. *Funny, You Don't Look Like One: Observations of a Blue-eyed Ojibway.* Penticton: Theytus, 1996.

_____. *Furious Observations of a Blue-eyed Ojibway: Funny You Don't Look Like One Two.* Penticton: Theytus, 2002.

_____. *Futile Observations of a Blue-eyed Ojibway: Funny You Don't Look Like One #4.* Penticton: Theytus, 2004.

_____. *Only Drunks and Children Tell the Truth.* Burnaby: Talonbooks, 1998.

_____. *The Baby Blues.* Burnaby: Talonbooks, 1999.

_____. *The Bootlegger Blues.* Saskatoon: Fifth House, 1991.

_____. *The Boy in the Treehouse and Girl Who Loved Her Horses.* Vancouver: Talonbooks, 2000.

_____. *Toronto at Dreamer's Rock and Education is Our Right: Two One-Act Plays.* Saskatoon: Fifth House, 1990.

Taylor, Philip. *Applied Theatre: Creating Transformative Encounters in the Community.* Portsmouth: Heinemann, 2003.

Thom, Jo-Ann. "The Effect of Readers' Responses on the Development of Aboriginal Literature in Canada: A Study of Maria Campbell's *Halfbreed*, Beatrice Culleton's *In Search of April Raintree*, and Richard Wagamese's *Keeper 'n Me*." In *In Search of April Raintree: Critical Edition*, by Beatrice Culleton Mosionier. Ed. Cheryl Suzack. Winnipeg: Peguis, 1999.

_____. *A Study of Narrative Voice, Discursive Authority and Ideology in the Works of Leslie Marmon Silko.* MA thesis, University of Regina, 1994.

_____. "When the Good Guys Don't Wear White: Narration, Characterization, and Ideology in Leslie Marmon Silko's *Almanac of the Dead*." In *Native North America: Critical and Cultural Perspectives*, ed. Renee Hulan. Toronto: ECW Press, 1999.

Thomlinson, Nellie Erickson, and Mabel Cook. "Family Violence: How Can We Tell What is Happening?" In *Aboriginal Health, Identity and Resources*, eds. Jill Oakes, Rick Riewe, Skip Koolage, Leanne Simpson, and Nancy Schuster. Winnipeg: Native Studies Press, University of Manitoba, 2000.

Thompson, Laurence, and Terry Thompson. *Dictionary of N'laka'pamux (Thompson) Language*. Billings: University of Montana Occasional Papers in Linguistics, 1996.

Tibbetts, Janice. "Supreme Court rules treaties may not be final." *Regina Leader Post*, 25 November 2005, F5.

Tierney, William G., and Yvonna S. Lincoln, eds. *Representation and the Text: Reframing the Narrative Voice*. Albany: State University of New York Press, 1997.

Timpson, Joyce Barbara. *Four Decades of Child Welfare Services to Native Indians in Ontario: A Contemporary Attempt to Understand the "Sixties Scoop" in Historical, Socioeconomic and Political Perspective*. PhD diss., Wilfrid Laurier University, 1993.

Trafzner, Clifford E. "Spirit and Law in Native American Narratives." In *Native North America: Critical and Cultural Perspectives*, ed. Renee Hulan. Toronto: ECW Press, 1999.

Treaty 7 Elders and Tribal Council, Walter Hildebrandt, Sarah Carter, and Dorothy First Rider. *The True Spirit and Original Intent of Treaty 7*. Montreal and Kingston: McGill-Queens University Press, 1996.

Trémaudan, A.-H. de. *Hold High Your Heads: History of the Métis Nation in Western Canada*. Trans. Elizabeth Maguet. Winnipeg: Pemmican, 1982.

Treuer, David. *Native American Fiction: A User's Manual*. Saint Paul, MN: Graywolf Press, 2006.

Turcotte, Gerry. "Re/marking on History, or, Playing Basketball With Godzilla: Thomas King's Monstrous Post-colonial Gesture." In *Connections: Non-Native Responses to Native Canadian Literature*, eds. Hartmut Lutz and Coomi S. Vevaina. New Dehli: Creative Books, 2003.

Tyman, James. *Inside Out: An Autobiography by a Native Canadian*. Saskatoon: Fifth House, 1989.

Two Worlds Colliding. Dir. Tasha Hubbard. Prod. Bonnie Thompson. National Film Board of Canada, 2004.

United Nations Office of the High Commissioner for Human Rights. *Convention on the Prevention and Punishment of the Crime of Genocide*. Approved and proposed for signature and ratification or accession by the General Assembly Resolution 260 A (III) 9 December 1948 *entry into force* 12 January 1951 in accordance with article XIII. http://www.unhchr.ch/html/menu3/b/p_genoci.htm (accessed 12 July 2004).

University of Winnipeg. "Shirley Anne Stirling [sic]: 1948–2005." *Canadian Children's Literature*, 21 June 2005. http://cybrary.uwinnipeg.ca/cclj/announcements/stirling.shtml (accessed 3 November 2005).

Upisasik Theatre of Rossignol School. "Gabrielle." In *The Land Called Morning*, ed. Caroline Heath. Saskatoon: Fifth House, 1986.

Van Camp, Richard. *Angel Wing Splash Patterns*. Cape Croker Reserve, ON: Kegedonce, 2002.

———. *The Lesser Blessed*. Vancouver: Douglas and MacIntyre, 1996.

Van Fossen, Rachel. "Writing for the Community Play Form." *Canadian Theatre Review* 90 (1997): 10–14.

Van Fossen, Rachel, and Darrel Wildcat. *Ka'ma'mo'pi cik / The Gathering. The West of All Possible Worlds: Six Contemporary Canadian Plays*. Ed. Moira Day. Toronto: Playwrights Canada Press, 2004.

Vasi, Vibha. "Laughter and Survival: Métis-Women Tricksters." In *Connections: Non-Native Responses to Native Canadian Literature*, eds. Hartmut Lutz and Coomi S. Vevaina. New Dehli: Creative Books, 2003.

Vevaina, Coomi S. "Articulating a Different Way of Being: The Resurgence of the Native Voice in Canada." In *Intersexions: Issues of Race and Gender in Canadian Women's Writing*, eds. Coomi S. Vevaina and Barbard Godard. Creative New Literatures Series 7. New Delhi: Creative Books, 1996.

_____. "Never Smile at a Crocodile: The Politics of Globalization in Jeannette Armstrong's 'whispering in shadows.'" In *Connections: Non-Native Responses to Native Canadian Literature*, eds. Hartmut Lutz and Coomi S. Vevaina. New Dehli: Creative Books, 2003.

_____. "Crossings." In *Intersexions: Issues of Race and Gender in Canadian Women's Writing*, eds. Coomi S. Vevaina and Barbard Godard. Creative New Literatures Series 7. New Delhi: Creative Books, 1996.

Visvis, Vikki. *Beyond the "talking cure": Narrative Alternatives for Telling Trauma in Canadian Fiction*. PhD diss., University of Toronto, 2004.

Vizenor, Gerald. "Native American Indian Literatures: Narratives of Survivance." In *Native North America: Critical and Cultural Perspectives*, ed. Renee Hulan. Toronto: ECW Press, 1999.

_____. *Fugitive Poses: Native American Indian Scenes of Absence and Presence*. Lincoln: University of Nebraska Press, 1998.

Wagamese, Richard. *Dream Wheels*. Toronto: Doubleday, 2006.

_____. *For Joshua: An Ojibway Father Teaches His Son*. Toronto: Doubleday, 2002.

_____. *Keeper 'n Me*. Toronto: Doubleday, 1994.

_____. *Quality of Light*. Toronto: Doubleday, 1997.

_____. *Terrible Summer*. Toronto: Warwick, 1996.

Waldram, James B. *Revenge of the Windigo: The Construction of Mind and Mental Health of North American Aboriginal Peoples*. Toronto: University of Toronto Press, 2004.

_____. "The 'Other Side': Ethnostatus Distinctions in Western Subarctic Native Communities." In *1885 and After: Native Society in Transition*, eds. Laurie F. Barron and James Waldram. Proceedings of the Canadian Plains Conference, University of Saskatchewan, Saskatoon, SK, May 1985. Regina: Canadian Plains Research Center, 1986.

Warick, Jason. "Admitting a Wrong: Churches Played an Integral Role in the Residential School System and now some Denominations are Trying to Right a Past Wrong." *Saskatoon Star Phoenix*, 2 August 2004. http://www.afn.ca/residentialschools/PDFarticles/MediaClips/Saskatoon%20Star%20Phoenix%20-%20July-Sept.%202004.pdf (accessed 16 August 2004).

_____. "Money Didn't Help: Two of William Starr's Victims Tell their Stories of How Repeated Sexual Assaults Ruined Their Live." *Saskatoon Star Phoenix*, 2 August 2004. http://www.afn.ca/residentialschools/PDFarticles/MediaClips/Saskatoon%20Star%20Phoenix%20-%20July-Sept.%202004.pdf (accessed 16 August 2004).

Warrior, Robert Allen. *The People and the Word: Reading Native Nonfiction*. Minneapolis: University of Minnesota Press, 2005.

_____. *Tribal Secrets: Recovering American Indian Intellectual Traditions*. Minneapolis: University of Minnesota Press, 1995.

Watson, Christine. "Autobiographical Writing as a Healing Process: Interview with Alice Masak French." *Canadian Literature* 167 (2000): 32–42.

Weaver, Jace. *Other Words: American Indian Literature, Law, and Culture*. Norman: University of Oklahoma Press, 2001.

_____. *That the People Might Live: Native American Literatures and Native American Community*. New York: Oxford University Press, 1997.

Weaver, Jace, Craig Womack, and Robert Warrior. *American Indian Literary Nationalism*. Albuquerque: University of New Mexico Press, 2005.

"Weesageechak Begins to Dance XVIII." *Native Earth Performing Arts Page*. http://www.nativeearth.ca/wee0506.html (accessed 24 January 2006).

Wesley-Esquimaux, Cynthia C., and Magdalena Smolewski. *Historic Trauma and Aboriginal Healing*. Ottawa: Aboriginal Healing Foundation, 2004.

Wiebe, Rudy, and Yvonne Johnson. *A Stolen Life: The Journey of a Cree Woman.* Toronto: Knopf, 1998.

Wheeler, Jordan. "A Revolution in Aboriginal Theatre: Our Own Stories." *Canadian Theatre Review* 66 (1991): 8–12.

_____. *Brothers in Arms: Three Novellas.* Winnipeg: Pemmican, 1989.

_____. Speaker. Fifth Annual Aboriginal Roundtable, Canadian Association of Commonwealth Literatures and Language Studies at the Congress of Social Sciences and Humanities, University of Manitoba, 30 May 2005.

White, Michael, and David Epston. *Narrative Means to Therapeutic Ends.* New York: Norton, 1990.

WhitePrivilege.com. Ed. Kendall Clark. 5 September 2005. WordPress Entries (RSS). http://white-privilege.com (accessed 7 October 2005).

William, Gerry. *The Black Ship.* Penticton: Theytus, 1994.

_____. *The Woman in the Trees.* Vancouver: New Star, 2004.

Williamson, Janice. *Sounding Differences: Conversations with Seventeen Canadian Women Writers.* Toronto: University of Toronto Press, 1993.

Wilke, Gundula. "Look Twice: Thomas King's *Coyote Columbus Stories.*" In *Connections: Non-Native Responses to Native Canadian Literature*, eds. Hartmut Lutz and Coomi S. Vevaina. New Dehli: Creative Books, 2003.

Woods, Allan. "Abuse victims to get $4B." *Regina Leader Post*, 23 November 2005, A1.

_____. "Aboriginal health is 'unconscionable:' Martin." *Regina Leader Post*, 25 November 2005, A3.

Womack, Craig S. *Red on Red: Native American Literary Separatism.* Minneapolis: University of Minneapolis Press, 1999.

Wotherspoon, Terry, and Vic Satzewich. *First Nations: Race, Class, and Gender Relations.* Regina: Canadian Plains Research Center, 2000.

Wright, Ronald. *A Short History of Progress.* Toronto: House of Anasi Press, 2004.

_____. *Stolen Continents: The "New World" Through Indian Eyes.* 1992. Toronto: Penguin, 1993.

Yellow Horse Brave Heart, M. "Oyate Ptayela: Rebuilding the Lakota nation through addressing historical trauma among Lakota parents." *Journal of Human Behavior and Social Environment* 2, 1/2 (1999): 109–126.

Young-Ing, Greg. "Aboriginal Text in Context." In *(Ad)dressing Our Words: Aboriginal Perspectives on Aboriginal Literatures*, ed. Armand Garnet Ruffo. Penticton: Theytus, 2001.

Young, Robert J.C. *Postcolonialism: A Very Short Introduction.* Oxford: Oxford University Press, 2003.

Zwicker, Heather. "The Limits of Sisterhood." In *In Search of April Raintree: Critical Edition*, by Beatrice Culleton Mosionier. Ed. Cheryl Suzack. Winnipeg: Peguis, 1999.

Index

629086